Egyptian Mummies

Egyptian

Mummies

Unraveling the Secrets of

an Ancient Art

Bob Brier

Brockhampton Press

First published in Great Britain in 1996 by
Michael O'Mara Books Limited
9 Lion Yard
Tremadoc Road
London SW4 7NQ

A CIP catalogue record for this book is available from the British Library

This edition published 1999 by Brockhampton Press,
a member of Hodder Headline PLC Group

ISBN 1 86019 920 8

1 3 5 7 9 10 8 6 4 2

Printed and bound in Great Britain by
Creative Print and Design (Wales), Ebbw Vale.

BOOK DESIGN BY ARLENE SCHLEIFER GOLDBERG

For Pat, who shared the adventure

Acknowledgments

Because of the degree of specialization in Egyptology today, I have repeatedly called upon my friends and colleagues for advice in their areas of expertise. For example, the paleopathology chapter was read and corrected by my colleagues in the Paleopathology Association, Dr. Benson W. Harrer, Jr., Dr. Theodore A. Reyman, and Dr. Jeanne Riddle. In addition, Eve Cockburn, who for twenty years has edited the *Paleopathology Association Newsletter*, not only read the chapter for content, but also corrected my grammar and made significant suggestions. Any error that may remain is solely my doing.

The chapter on the mummy in literature and film has benefited considerably from the thoughtful suggestions of Dr. Frank Dello Stritto, one of the great authorities on horror films. Richard Fazzini, chairman of the Department of Egyptian, Classical, and Near Eastern Art at the Brooklyn Museum, and also an expert on Egyptomania, read and corrected this chapter.

The illustrations for this book have come from a variety of sources. In Cairo, Dr. Muhammed Salah, director of the Egyptian Museum, was extremely helpful in supplying photographs of the royal mummies. Closer to home, in Boston, Dr. Rita Freed, Dr. Peter Lacovara, and Sue D'Auria were most generous in tracking down photographs in the collection of the Museum of Fine Arts. Still closer to home, Dr. Dorothea Arnold and Dr. Catharine Roehrig of the Metropolitan Museum of Art in New York supplied photos of the objects in their museum as well as photos from their archive of Harry Burton's Tutankhamen photographs. Dennis Forbes, editor of *KMT*, kindly supplied illustrations from his collection. With characteristic generosity, David Moyer supplied many slides from his vast personal archives and also read the entire manuscript, making many suggestions. Thanks are also due to the "two Ians"—Brier and Remler—who inked the line drawings.

Dr. Hoyt Hobbs served as my unofficial editor, making hundreds of detailed editorial changes and greatly improving the organization of the entire work. My official editor, Bob Shuman, asked all those questions editors should and made the book far more readable than the manuscript that was handed to him.

·Thank you all!

Contents

Preface

LONG ISLAND UNIVERSITY/C.W. POST CAMPUS

MEMORANDUM

TO: Walter Jones (Vice-President), Rita Langdon (Public Relations), Maithili Schmidt (Dean), David Steinberg (President) Jeff Zeisler (Biology)

FROM: Bob Brier (Philosophy)

SUBJECT: Possible National Geographic TV Special

As some of you know, as part of my studies on ancient Egyptian mummies, I intend to mummify a human cadaver this summer. National Geographic is currently filming their special on mummies and DNA and called me for some advice and video taped an interview with me at my house. When Amy Wray, my contact with National Geographic in Washington, told the producers about my plans they decided they wanted to include the mummification in the documentary.

They would like to film on campus for four days this summer. The mummification will take 70 days and the film days would not be consecutive—so they could show the process from beginning to end. I intend to follow as closely as possible ancient techniques. Because the purpose of the study is to empirically determine if how we think the Egyptians mummified is really possible, (Can you remove the kidneys through a 5-inch abdominal incision?) we must adhere to the ancient practice. As a consequence, some legal problems may arise. The purpose of this memo is to describe the project.

Because I will be using a medical cadaver the question may be asked, does mummification constitute "reasonable use"? I believe it does, but we should be sure. Also, if at all possible, I want to use a cadaver which has not been embalmed. This raises a health issue which must be cleared. We will of course use double gloves and other standard precautions used in high-risk situations, but may not be permitted to obtain an unembalmed body. Also related is my intention not to refrigerate the body for 70 days.

The god of embalming, Anubis, was called He-who-is-in-his-tent and also He-who-is-upon-his-hill. This suggests that mummification took place out of doors on a hill, under a tent. This may have been necessary because of the odors associated with mummification. I thus would like to work under a tent. A remote area of the campus would be best—perhaps behind Hutton House, or perhaps behind Bush-Brown Hall at the University Center. Security is a concern. The body must be attended 24 hours a day for 70 days. My colleagues, students, etc., can spell each other, camping out for the period. Perhaps Public Safety can also help. For one 35-day stretch the body will merely be immersed in natron and nothing has to be done with it. After this period, I might be able to move it indoors since it should be dehydrated by then.

After mummification, the body will be wrapped in the Egyptian style and for all practical purposes will look like an ancient Egyptian mummy. One question is what to do with the mummy after the study. Right now I favor burial.

There will undoubtedly be problems which I have not foreseen, but this is a sketch of what is intended. National Geographic wants to take me to Egypt with them in February. I must go to the Wadi Natrun to get the natron used in dehydration and also the Cairo spice bazaar for the frankincense and myrrh needed for the mummification. The Geographic people feel this would be good background footage.

Since time is short, please let me know, as soon as possible, what you think of the project.

Bob

LONG ISLAND UNIVERSITY

MEMORANDUM

TO: Professor Bob Brier

FROM: Dr. Walter S. Jones

SUBJECT: Mummification Project

DATE: November 15, 1993

During a meeting last Friday, the University Officers reviewed your memorandum regarding your proposal to mummify an unembalmed human cadaver on University property during the summer of 1994. Consideration was given to all the issues you raised in your recent memorandum as well as to others such as public relations, health and security, external approval processes, etc.

The unanimous judgment of the group was that the project ought not to take place on University property. Perhaps a site in Egypt would be more appropriate. In your continuing conversations with the National Geographic Society, please exclude the possibility of using a University site.

Thank you very much.

For fifteen years I had been working toward the goal of mummifying a human. I had repeatedly traveled to Egypt, studying the royal mummies in the Egyptian Museum in Cairo, collecting samples in the deserted Wadi Natrun, where ancient embalmers obtained the salts used in mummification, descending into long tunnels housing millions of mummified animals, and translating fragile papyri that I hoped might contain lost details of the mummification process. During this time I experienced many setbacks, major and minor—but rejection by my own university's officers came as a shock. I had never thought that they might not support my work.

The idea of reversing the usual study—creating rather than unwrapping a mummy—had occurred to me years before, when I watched Jeff Zeisler, a colleague of mine in the biology department, dissect a cadaver in his anatomy class. It had been nearly thirty years since I had worked on a medical cadaver, and I envied his crisp technique. As I watched I began to think about the dissecting skills of the ancient Egyptian embalmers. Zeisler cut a large abdominal incision in his cadaver so he could exhibit its internal organs, but the Egyptians used only a seven-inch slit when they removed the viscera. I knew it wouldn't be easy to remove the kidneys through such a narrow opening and wondered if Zeisler could do it, even with his fine technique and modern surgical tools.

The more I thought about how the Egyptians mummified their dead, the more it struck me that we really don't know much about how they did it. The few good books on mummification tell the same story—that the practice is not very mysterious—but their authors had never seriously considered trying it themselves. When I conducted a thought experiment, a kind of mental mummification, I realized that there were plenty of problems I would encounter if I ever got my chance to mummify a human. As I imagined myself before the body, I wondered what would I do with the blood. The goal of mummification was to dehydrate the body, so it makes sense to drain the blood, but no text, ancient or modern, even talks about this. As I continued my mental mummification, I repeatedly was presented with practical questions that had never been asked before. It was then that I realized that mummifying a human cadaver was the only way to fully understand the practice. Experimental Egyptology was the way to go.

No human has actually been mummified in the Egyptian way in modern times, so before a successful mummification could take place, I knew that I had to gather all the information I could from every available source. Ancient hieroglyphic papyri, autopsies on mummies, tomb paintings, and even nineteenth-century newspaper accounts of mummy unwrappings would have to be studied for overlooked clues.

The first question that had to be answered was not about the specifics of mummification; it was much more broad. The ancient Near East harbored many civilizations, so why was it only the Egyptians who practiced mummification? The search for that answer had to begin in Egypt.

1

Introduction
Egypt, Land of the Mummies

It is not an accident that mummification began in a dry, arid country. Egypt covers nearly 400,000 square miles, the vast majority of it uninhabited and inhospitable desert. Life clustered on the banks of the Nile, the only major river in the world that flows from south to north. It is an indication of how huge Africa is that up until the middle 1800s the river's source was unknown. Actually, it has two—the White Nile, which flows out of Lake Victoria in East Central Africa, and the Blue Nile, which originates in Ethiopia and joins the White Nile at Khartoum, several hundred miles south of the Egyptian border.

We know very little about the earliest inhabitants of the Nile Valley because no human remains have been found from this period. We do know that the area was first inhabited around 500,000 B.C. by settlers whose only tool, judging from the artifacts they left, was the hand ax. This marked the beginning of the Paleolithic era, or Stone Age. By modern standards the rate of change was slow. When we consider the advances of the last hundred years, it is almost inconceivable to think that in the first 450,000 years of Egyptian culture the only improvement was a better ax. When the Egyptians developed different tools during the Middle Paleolithic period, Egypt must have been moister than it is now; tools are found in regions that are now desert, so there had to have been more water available then. Hominids of this era were Neanderthal, a term that today connotes a savage, but Neanderthal societies practiced simple surgery, cared for their injured and old, and buried their dead with

FIG 1. *A predynastic burial.* ORIENTAL INSTITUTE, UNIVERSITY OF CHICAGO

rituals. Mummification was, however, introduced by modern man, *Homo sapiens sapiens*.

By around 30,000 B.C. the Late Paleolithic period, *Homo sapiens sapiens* had supplanted Neanderthal man. The level of the Nile was declining, and these people were forced to live in or near swamps. Subsisting on mollusks and fish, they cooked on clay hearths and fashioned grindstones on which they prepared wild cereal grains and pigments. Sometime around 15,000 B.C. they began using the bow and arrow. When the Nile reached its lowest level between 10,000 and 5,000 B.C. and most of the land had turned to desert, survival became a difficult matter. At this point the *Homo sapiens* population probably numbered no more than a few thousand.

During this period the Egyptians buried their dead in shallow pits in the desert, riverine land being too precious to waste on cemeteries. This was fortunate because the moisture and high mineral content of that soil would have rotted cadavers. On the other hand, simple desert burials, with no coffins enclosing the deceased, allowed hot, dry sand to quickly dehydrate bodies. Bacteria do not act on soft tissue in the absence of moisture, so the bodies were naturally preserved.

Because these graves were shallow, on occasion the sand would blow away to reveal the shocking sight of a dead body that had retained its flesh and hair—a still-recognizable individual. Whether such events gave rise to the idea of eternal life or whether they merely reinforced a preexisting religious belief in life after death cannot be determined. What is clear is that the evidence of their own eyes told the ancient Egyptians that a dead person did not vanish from existence altogether.

Fayoum Lake, Egypt's only major body of standing fresh water, had dried up millennia earlier but began reappearing around 5,000 B.C., facilitating survival and population growth. Around this time pottery was also developed, and the Egyptians began farming and raising cattle. After the birth of farming, the history of Egypt becomes so closely associated with the Nile that to understand the civilization one must also understand the river.

It was the Blue Nile, swollen by spring monsoons and the runoff of melting snow and ice in Ethiopia, that caused the river to overflow its banks each year. The annual rising of the river determined the fate of Egypt for the year. Each time the Nile overflowed its banks, the fine topsoil it carried from the south was deposited on the land. First the river turned red because of the soil suspended in it, then green because of the vegetation floating on top; finally it rose twenty feet, spilling over the land for miles. If the river was high, it would be a good year with abundant crops. If the river was low it wouldn't cover as much land when it flooded, and crop acreage would be reduced. In times of extremely low water, famine became a reality. So valuable was the topsoil that the Egyptians did not build their houses on arable land, the "black land," but lived at its edge, on the "red land" of the desert. It was the desert that would ultimately give rise to mummification.

Soon after recorded history began, which was around 3,100 B.C., Egyptian burials grew more elaborate and threatened the natural preservative process. Shallow pits became brick-lined tombs; bodies were covered with animal skins and placed upon woven mats. The size of these brick structures expanded as time passed and varied with the importance of the deceased; the woven mats were extended to encompass the whole body like a sort of crude coffin. All these changes removed the bodies farther and farther from the natural drying produced by contact with hot sand. The longer bodily fluids are retained, the more a corpse undergoes a slow combustion that destroys its soft tissues. Burials in tombs forced the Egyptians to devise means of preserving of the dead.

While the natural preservative action of the desert may have spawned the idea of mummification, Egyptian religion required it. Contrary to what many modern occultists claim, the ancient Egyptians did not believe in reincarnation, the idea that a soul returns to earth after the body's death to inhabit a different body, and that this cycle of birth, death, rebirth is repeated many times. Mummification would not have been necessary had the Egyptians been reincarnationists, because the soul of the deceased could inhabit anyone's body, not just its own. The ancient Egyptians believed in *resurrection*—that people exist just once, but that their earthly bodies reanimate in the afterworld.

The Osiris Myth

Central to the religious beliefs of the ancient Egyptians was the story of Isis and Osiris, from which all the crucial elements of Egyptian funerary practices derived. Like any myth, this one was seen as presenting important truths about nature and the universe, including life after death. No complete Egyptian copy of the myth exists: our best ancient version comes from Plutarch, a Greek priest at Delphi, who wrote around 100 A.D.

Osiris and Isis were both brother and sister and husband and wife. Their brother, Seth, and another sister, Nephthys, were also husband and wife. Osiris brought civilization to Egypt, introducing farming and cattle-raising, thus freeing the early inhabitants of the Nile Valley from misery. Then he left Egypt to bring civilization to the rest of the world, leaving Isis, the powerful goddess of magic, to keep their evil brother Seth in check.

Upon Osiris's return, Seth obtained his exact bodily measurements by trickery, and constructed a highly ornamented wooden chest to fit him precisely. During a banquet Seth offered the magnificent chest as a gift to whoever could fit into it, but guest after guest attempted and failed. Then Osiris tried, and succeeded. However, as soon as he settled inside the chest, Seth threw the bolts, sealing the chest, and poured molten lead over it. He then threw the chest into one of the branches of the Nile Delta. A violent storm subsequently carried it to Byblos, in Lebanon, where it washed up in the branches of a tree. In time the tree grew to extraordinary size, its trunk enveloping both the chest and Osiris inside it. In the course of building his palace, the king of Byblos cut down the tree for one of the pillars.

As soon as Isis learned what had happened to her husband she set out to recover his body. Enlisting the aid of the queen of Byblos, Isis had the pillar cut open so she could recover the body of Osiris and bring it back to Egypt for proper burial. When the body was returned to Egypt, Seth discovered it, hacked it into fourteen pieces, and scattered them throughout Egypt. Isis then recovered every piece, except one, the phallus, which had been thrown into the Nile and eaten by fish. She reassembled her deceased husband and fashioned an artificial phallus for him. Transforming herself into a bird, Isis hovered over Osiris's body and brought him back to life by reciting magical words.

Almost all the beliefs of the ancient Egyptian funerary cult can be parsed from this myth. The chest that exactly fit Osiris was the precursor of the anthropoid coffin, which is shaped like the deceased and is intended to protect his body. The importance of a proper burial on Egyptian ground is emphasized by the efforts that Isis made to recover the body. The importance of an intact corpse is demonstrated by Isis's search for all the pieces of her deceased husband's body and the fact that she fashioned an artificial phallus to replace the missing one. Isis

FIG. 2.
*Osiris, god of the dead,
is always shown
mummiform. Tomb of
Queen Nefertari,
Thebes.* PHOTOGRAPH
BY I. SOLIMAN

hovers over a *complete* body. Finally, and most important, she speaks the proper words and he resurrects. He retains after death the same body he inhabited while alive. Mummification thus becomes essential to immortality; the body must be preserved for the afterlife.

The discovery by both tomb robbers and official inspectors that the bodies of the deceased still remained in the tomb after centuries of repose and that they had not "gone west" and resurrected must have led to a questioning of the basic principle of resurrection. Eventually the belief in resurrection became less literal and material and became more abstract and spiritual. Preservation of the body was essential, not because it would resurrect, but because the spiritual double of the deceased needed a place to dwell till this nonmaterial entity united with the personality of the deceased in the netherworld.

Budge's Theory of Cannibalism

While it is reasonable to conclude that the ancient Egyptian belief in resurrection stems from observation of naturally mummified bodies, E. A. Wallis Budge, Keeper of Egyptian and Assyrian Antiquities at the British Museum during the early part of this century, had a different theory as to why the cult of Osiris was introduced into Egypt—to stop cannibalism. In his two-volume work, *Osiris and the Egyptian Resurrection*, Budge claims that in predynastic times the Egyptians were, in fact, maneaters.[1] He based his theory both on some human bones found in Egyptian graves that he claimed showed human tooth marks and on a religious text on a wall of King Unas' pyramid at Saqqara.

The physical evidence Budge cites comes from an excavation by Sir William Flinders Petrie, a colorful (as we will see) character first who came to Egypt as a surveyor but stayed to establish many of the scientific techniques for excavating. He was the first to realize that non-glamorous objects, such as pottery shards, were important for dating sites, and also published his excavation reports promptly so that the whole scientific community could share them. However, there were situations that Petrie could not control. His site at Naqada—the one that Budge used as his evidence—is one such case.

Naqada, thirty miles north of Luxor on the west bank of the Nile, was excavated by Petrie in 1895. At the time little was known about predynastic Egypt, so that when Petrie found this trove of thousands of predynastic graves, he believed they consisted of non-Egyptian conquerors who either expelled or killed the native population. Further, he thought these people belonged to a "New Race." We know now that these conclusions were wrong, but it is less clear what to make of his theory that these burials indicated cannibalism.

Many of the graves contained skeletons in disarray, which is not surprising for a plundered cemetery. As tomb robbers went through a grave looking for valuables, they frequently disturbed the human remains. Thus for bones to be scattered about a tomb, or even missing, is not unusual. However, in some tombs the bones were disarticulated but repiled in an orderly fashion. For example, in one tomb labeled T42 by Petrie, the ribs lay in a heap, with the vertebrae laid out in a clear circle around them. The arms were collected in the middle of the tomb, and the legs neatly placed in the northern corners. Such reorganizing of bones is not to be expected from tomb robbers. Of course, it is possible that the bones were rearranged by Egyptian priests after they found the tombs plundered.

One problem with this theory is that Petrie found some tombs that seemed undisturbed—pots were unbroken, jewelry still present—but the cadavers were disarticulated and often missing their skulls. Budge's evidence comes from Petrie's grave T5, a seemingly undisturbed tomb that contained six skulls and many disarticulated bones. Almost all of the bones had their ends broken, as if to remove the marrow. Petrie says, "Not only were the ends broken off, but in some bones the cellular structure had been scraped and forcibly, what remained of it being very firm and strong; and besides this there were grooves left by gnawing on the bones. . . . After these instances we must conclude *that bodies were sometimes—with all respect—cut up and partly eaten.*"[2]

These tombs remain a puzzle to this day. But Petrie's conclusion is not the only one consistent with the evidence. One might even question the accuracy of his report, especially considering the rapidity of his excavations—by his own admission, he excavated more than 3,000 tombs in five months! He says, " . . . that allows but twenty or thirty minutes for a grave, so that only the most important parts can be done by the recorder."[3] While twenty or thirty minutes for the excavation of a tomb seems incredible today, there was a reason for the rush. Petrie knew that when he left the site, illegal antiquities dealers would arrive to take whatever he left, and the data would be lost forever. While his haste was a necessary evil, one must be cautious of any conclusions based on such excavation practices, which is upon what Budge founded his theory. It is important to note that in none of the predynastic burials was there any evidence of mummification. That was an advance introduced hundreds of years later, in dynastic times.

As evidence of cannibalism Budge also used a religious text in which King Unas is described as devouring the gods:

Unas is the bull of heaven
Who rages in his heart
Who lives on the being of every god,
Who eats their entrails. . . .

Unas is he who eats men, feeds on gods.

It is far from clear that the text was meant to be taken literally, but Budge, an extreme racist who claimed that Africans had an innate desire for human flesh, was quite willing to do just that. For Budge, the Osirian religion was introduced to make dismemberment of the human body taboo, and thus end cannibalism.

Budge's theory of cannibalism also led him to a unique explanation for an often discussed remark made by Plutarch, who claimed that there was a custom in ancient Egypt called "the Mummy at the Feast," in which the deceased's mummy was borne around banquet halls among the guests at the funeral dinner. Plutarch thought that the reason for the practice was to remind the diners of the transitory nature of life; Budge's ex-

FIG. 3.   The Mummy at the Banquet, *a nineteenth-century engraving.*

planation is that the practice recalled the days when human bodies were brought to the banquet table to be eaten. There is, however, a more simple resolution to the "Mummy at the Feast" problem: the practice never existed!—or at least there are no Egyptian records that it did. Plutarch was probably conflating it with a similar ritual whose point was entirely different. At the time of burial, members of the deceased's family and close friends did in fact gather at the tomb for a meal in front of the mummy. It is probably this custom that Plutarch misinterpreted as "the Mummy at the Feast."

The Osiris Myth, Continued

The Osiris myth does not end with Osiris' resurrection. Isis and Osiris have a son, Horus, who takes the form of a falcon.

To avenge his father's death at the hands of Seth, Horus fights his evil uncle and defeats him. During the battle Seth gouges out Horus' eye, but it is later magically restored by Thoth, the god of magic. The eye of Horus remained a magical talisman for health throughout Egyptian history.

Horus' four sons also played a role in the funerary ritual. The internal organs removed from the body during mummification were placed in four receptacles, called "canopic jars." (The name comes from that of Canopis, whom Homer tells us was the pilot of Menelaus; other ancient writers mention that he was deified and worshipped in the form of a jar, so when early Egyptologists discovered jars with lids shaped like human heads, they quickly named them "canopic.") Each jar was protected by one of the sons of Horus, and its lid was carved into the shape of the appropriate head. Imsety had a human head, Duamutef a jackal's, Hapi a baboon's, and Qebhsenuf a falcon's. The large and small intestines, lungs, stomach, liver, etc., were placed in these jars. At times, the four sons of Horus also appear as protective amulets sewn onto the outer wrappings of the mummy.

The cult of Osiris thus required mummification and an extensive ritual and paraphernalia. Mummification was practiced for thousands of years and, as one might expect, techniques changed. Even politics affected the art of embalming. When centralized government weakened and guarding the tombs of the pharaohs became impossible, the pharaohs' mummies were plundered. When stability returned to the country, embalmers repaired the damaged mummies and for the first time saw how the craftsmanship of earlier embalmers had held up over the centuries. This led to a renaissance of embalming techniques. Later, when foreign rulers conquered Egypt, changes in burial customs resulted. Thus the history and development of mummification becomes entwined with ancient Egyptian history and politics.

Two factors enabled Egypt to become the dominant country of the Near East. One was geography. While the Nile was bountiful and provided ample food supplies, the desert on either side protected Egypt from invasion. Any foreign army attempting to enter Egypt from the east or west would first face a haz-

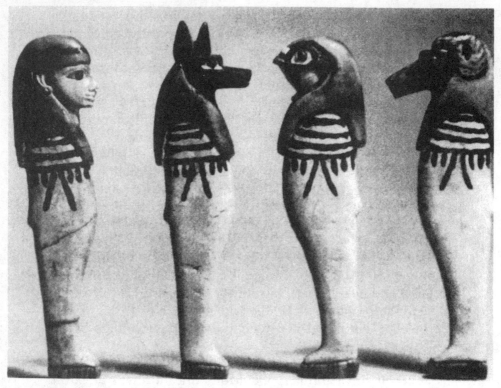

FIG. 4. *Set of the four sons-of-Horus amulets intended to protect the mummy's internal organs.* BRITISH MUSEUM; PHOTOGRAPH BY JOHN FREED

ardous journey. The second factor was a strong central government. In any country, it is more productive if a single leader focuses national resources on collective projects than if municipalities work separately.

The conversion of Egypt from divided political segments to a centralized government may have been the work of one man, the famous Narmer. We have few records of this king, but by far the most important is the Narmer Palette in the Egyptian Museum in Cairo.

The Narmer Palette is carved on both sides. One side shows Narmer wearing the traditional white crown of Upper Egypt and striking an enemy he is holding by the hair. The other side shows him walking in a procession and wearing the red crown

FIG. 5. *The Narmer Palette. One of the world's oldest historical documents, it commemorates the unification of Egypt by King Narmer.* EGYPTIAN MUSEUM, CAIRO

of Lower Egypt, which suggests that at this point he was king of both the north and south. The Egyptians used similar small slate palettes to grind various ingredients for eye paints. To commemorate important events, they frequently carved scenes in relief on palettes about twice the normal size.

The event commemorated on the Narmer palette may be no less than the unification of the two politically distinct sections of Egypt and the beginning of centralized government. Narmer is thus considered by many to be the first king of the First Dynasty. Unification probably took place around 3100 B.C., approximately the time that hieroglyphic writing began in Egypt. Narmer's name is given on the palette in the form of two pictures, a fish and a chisel—*nar* and *mer*.

Because their survival was assured by a combination of geography and centralized government, the Egyptians could devote energy to major agricultural projects. The creation of an extensive system of irrigation canals to channel and control the overflow of the Nile resulted in increased farm production and of surplus crops to trade for foreign goods. (So important was the system of irrigation that, in some versions of the *Book of the Dead*, the deceased was instructed to tell the gods judging him that he had never illicitly diverted water from it.) In addition, the government was able to marshal an efficient standing army. Not only could invasions be repulsed easily, but also new lands could be conquered and taxed.

Surplus crops and increased taxes made possible the first large leisure class in the history of the world—the priests of ancient Egypt. These were the men who could read and write hieroglyphs, and who created the religious liturgy and rituals that surrounded the mummification procedure.

2
How To, Part I:
What the Ancients Say

In looking for the details of mummification, the natural place to start is in the ancient Egyptian texts that describe it. Here, knowledge of the ancient Egyptian language becomes crucial—a mistranslated word or idiom could result in the loss of an important detail. Hieroglyphs are the key.

Tacitus, the historian, tells us that when the Roman general Germanicus visited the ruins of Thebes he was puzzled by the meaning of the hieroglyphic inscriptions on the walls of the temples. He found an old man wandering through the crumbling buildings and asked him what the carvings said. The old man claimed that he was the last man alive who could read the writings of the Egyptians, and he told Germanicus what they said. The old man was probably lying. In the early first century A.D., when Germanicus visited Egypt, few could read the hieroglyphs, and this probably included Germanicus' elderly guide. Only a small vestige of the priestly cast remained who could read ancient Egyptian, and even they would soon be gone.

For the next 1,500 years, scholars could only wonder what the carvings of birds, feet, animals, and other symbols meant. Many of their speculations were based on the belief that the inscriptions were mystical in nature, a guess that was not far from correct. When the Greeks first came into Egypt they called the writings "hieroglyphs," or "sacred carvings," since only priests could read them. When the knowledge of the hieroglyphs died, this association lived on.

Early attempts to decipher hieroglyphs failed primarily because they were based on the assumption that hieroglyphs were picture writing: a carving of a foot represented the concept of a foot; a carving of a duck meant the text was discussing a duck. Horapollo of Nilopolis, a writer of the third century A.D., did much to foster this erroneous belief. Working on the theory of pictorial-symbolic meanings, he says that the nightowl symbolizes death: "For it suddenly descends upon the young of the crow in the night, as death comes suddenly." (The owl actually denoted the *m* sound in the Egyptian alphabet, and had nothing to do with the concept of death.) Even when Horapollo gets the meaning of a word correct, it is for the wrong reason. As he says, the vulture hieroglyph did mean "mother"—but that was, he continues, " . . . because in this race of creatures there is no male." The philology is as poor as the biology: the vulture hieroglyph represented the sound *mut,* which was the ancient Egyptian word for "mother." The sign does not represent a concept, but a sound that in turn denotes a concept.

In the fifteenth century Horapollo's text was translated from the Coptic into Greek, and with the greater availability of his writings scholars strayed farther and farther from the truth. In the seventeenth century the Jesuit scholar Athanasius Kircher came across a volume of engravings of the obelisks that had been erected in Rome. Convinced that the inscriptions contained answers to mysteries of the universe, he studied the engravings and wrote a book about them entitled *Sphinx Mystagogia,* which contained Kircher's imagined translations of the hieroglyphs based on the principles set down by Horapollo.

Not until the eighteenth century did linguists begin to suspect that ancient Egyptian writing was less pictogram-based than it was composed of signs with specific phonetic values. But while some suggested that the signs represented sounds, no one knew which signs represented which sounds, or what concepts those vocalizations stood for. It wasn't until the nineteenth century that, through a combination of brilliant scholarship and good fortune, the hieroglyphs could once again be read.

The good fortune was the discovery of the Rosetta stone. When Napoleon went to Egypt, he took with him a large corps of savants to study its architecture, measure its monuments, and copy its inscriptions and artwork. The most significant discovery of the expedition was accidental, one that none of the expedition members could have expected.

In August 1799, the French, who were fortifying a strongpoint a few miles from the town of Rosetta, near Alexandria, discovered a large black stone covered with writing in three different scripts. The linguists present immediately realized that the top script was hieroglyphs and the bottom Greek (the middle script was subsequently identified as demotic, a late form of Egyptian writing that we will discuss below). The same message was conveyed by all three scripts. Basically it was a thank-you note from the priests of Memphis to Ptolemy V for gifts and concessions the pharaoh had given to the temple.

The stone was taken to Cairo, where Napoleon had established an institute to study ancient Egyptian civilization; copies were sent to France. Later the stone was sent to the house of the French commanding general in Alexandria for safekeeping. In 1801, when the French surrendered to the British, all Egyptian antiquities collected by Bonaparte's expedition were confiscated. By 1802 the Rosetta Stone was in the British Museum, where it remains today.

Ancient Egyptian was written in three different scripts, of which only the first two appear are on the Rosetta Stone: hieroglyphic, demotic, and hieratic. Hieroglyphic and hieratic scripts developed at approximately the same time. Hieroglyphic corresponds to our printed letters, hieratic to our handwriting. The hieroglyphic script was used for important documents, on temples and tombs, and wherever artistic value was important. It is the script most people picture when they think of Egyptian writing. The signs used are representations of clearly identifiable objects familiar to the Egyptians. In a hieroglyphic text, an owl is clearly identifiable as an owl.

Because it took a scribe or artist considerable time to form each sign in a hieroglyphic script, hieratic, a more cursive form of writing, was used for such mundane things as letters, receipts, inventories, and other business matters. While derived from the hieroglyphs, the relation of the sign to the hieroglyph is not clearly identifiable. For example, the hieroglyphic 🦉

became the hieratic ~. In the latest form of ancient Egyptian

Fig. 6.   *The Rosetta Stone. A proclamation written in three scripts: hieroglyphic at the top, demotic in the middle, and Greek at the bottom. It was the key to deciphering the ancient Egyptian language.*

writing, demotic, the hieratic was transformed into an even more cursive form, with the objects still less recognizable.

One of the most important early decipherers of the Rosetta Stone was a brilliant English physicist, Thomas Young. A physician and scientist by training, Young had made ancient languages his hobby, and the Rosetta Stone was just the kind of challenge he loved. By decoding it, he hoped to open the door to discovering the sciences of the ancient Egyptians. He decided to work on the demotic text first.

Young quickly realized that groupings of signs in the demotic inscription corresponded to names of the pharaoh and queen in the Greek text. Soon he deduced that the demotic signs were basically phonetic—but, more important, he began to see similarities between the demotic-sign groups and groups of signs in the hieroglyphic text. This proved that the hieroglyphs also were phonetic. By 1818 he had determined with some accuracy the hieroglyphic alphabet, but then lost interest in the project. That task was left for a Frenchman, Jean-François Champollion, to complete.

As a youth Champollion had demonstrated a unique talent for languages. Because his father was a librarian, Champollion was accustomed to playing among books written in various languages. He eventually mastered Latin, Greek, Arabic, Syriac, Chaldean, Hebrew, and Coptic, the language that would be of most use to him in translating the Rosetta Stone.

Named for the Copts, the Egyptian Christians who spoke the language in Egypt during the first centuries A.D., Coptic is written in the Greek alphabet with seven special extra characters. It provides a link between written hieroglyphs and how the words were pronounced. For example, the hieroglyph ♀ meant "life." The later Coptic word for life was *onch*. Thus when we see the sign ♀ , we can be reasonably sure that it was pronounced "*onch*."

While still a teenager, Champollion obtained a copy of the Rosetta Stone and began his relentless pursuit of its meaning. He first realized that there were in fact three Egyptian scripts— hieroglyphic, demotic, and hieratic (the one not on the stone). He deduced this by comparing hieratic papyri with hieroglyphic and demotic inscriptions. Champollion then began comparing the hieroglyphic inscription on the Rosetta Stone with its Greek counterpart. The key was the name "Ptolemy." It had been known that the pharaohs wrote their names in ovals called "cartouches." The oval represented a rope that symbolized the pharaoh's dominion over everything. Since the Greek inscription mentioned Ptolemy, the name in a corresponding cartouche in the hieroglyphic text had to be Ptolemy. The cartouche read: ⬭. Here the □ = p, ⌒ = t, ⌐\ = o, ⌂ = l, ⌐ = m, ⟨ ⟨ = i, and ⌐ = s. ("Ptolmis" was the Greco-Egyptian way of writing "Ptolemy.") With these letters established, Champollion went on to other names.

From an inscription on an obelisk found on the island of Philae he had the name "Cleopatra." (He knew it was Cleopatra's name because the base of the obelisk had an inscription in

Greek mentioning her.) Her cartouche read: ⬭ .

Given letters in Ptolemy's name, Champollion knew that the lion (⌂) was "l," the reed (⟨) something close to "i," the loop (⌐\ ) an "o," and the reed mat (□) a "p." That gave: —L—OP————. The first blank had to be the hard "c," or "k," sound, and the second blank an "e." The bird that appeared twice was obviously "a," while the hand was "t." (In earlier times, the hand represented something closer to a "d" sound.) The mouth sign was an "r." Thus Champollion was left with "Cleopatra." Champollion had noticed the same two extra signs at the end of the name after names of other queens. The loaf,

⌒, is the ending "t," which is appended to Egyptian names and to words that are feminine. The egg indicates a woman's name in particular.

Champollion's work on the hieroglyphic alphabet is the basis of what we know today. The Egyptians omitted vowels but did have what are called semivowels. On the facing page is the Classical Egyptian alphabet, the alphabet used in Egypt for approximately 3,000 years.

Classical Egyptian Alphabet

Hieroglyph	*Object Depicted*	*Sound*
𓄿	vulture	a
𓃀	foot	b
𓐍	placenta	ch
𓂧	hand	d
𓂝	arm	e
𓆑	horned viper	f
𓎼	jar stand	g
𓎛	twisted flax	h
𓇋	reed leaf	i
𓆓	snake	j (dj)
𓎡	basket	k
𓅓	owl	m
𓈖	water	n
𓊪	mat	p
𓈎	hill	q
𓂋	mouth	r
𓋴	folded cloth	s
𓈙	pool of water	sh
𓏏	loaf of bread	t
𓍿	tethering ring	tch
𓅱	quail chick	u or w
𓇌	two reed leaves	y
𓊃	door bolt	z

There were quite a few signs on the Rosetta Stone other than those of the alphabet. Another of Champollion's discoveries was that some of these were "determinatives"—that is, signs at the end of the word that indicated what sort of object the word denoted. For example, in the word 𓂧𓊪𓏏𓊛, the hieroglyphs 𓂧, 𓊪, and 𓏏 tell how the word was pronounced (*dpt*—we don't know the vowels). The last sign showed that the word meant "boat."

Funerary Papyri

It is obvious that hieroglyphs will play an important part in the search for details about mummification, but the task is complicated by the fact that the Egyptian embalmers left us no manual on how they performed their art. This is surprising, since mummification was a major industry in Egypt for three thousand years. Just as we have funeral parlors and undertakers today, the Egyptians employed professionals to handle every aspect of burial—coffin makers, scribes who wrote out copies of the *Book of the Dead*, and embalmers. Yet no Egyptian papyrus has ever been found that teaches how to mummify a body.

While at first this may seem surprising, it is less so when one realizes that the Egyptians did not commit everything to writing. No architectural papyri have been found, either, although the major temples must have surely required extensive plans. Why instructional papyri do not exist for such major industries as building and mummification is debated by Egyptologists, some of whom believe that such papyri once existed and have yet to be discovered. There is a problem, however, with this theory. Quite a few literary papyri, several medical papyri, mathematical papyri discussing solutions to problems, and many religious papyri have been found, but no papyri at all that deal with any manual trade. There are no formulae for pottery glazes, none for kiln construction, none providing directions for mixing paint, etc. It is more likely that information for such trades was handed down from father to son as a part of an oral tradition—thus we shouldn't expect to find any embalmer's manuals.

However, a group of papyri known as the "Embalmers' Archive" shows that this trade was, indeed, a family affair. These papyri came from the northern town of Hawara, in the Fayoum district, about fifty miles from Cairo. Written in demotic at the end of the Ptolemaic period, they contain deeds to tombs, contracts, and even an oath administered by an embalmers' guild. In these papyri the term "Men of Anubis" (the jackal-headed

god of embalming), which was applied to the undertaking profession in general, referred at the same time to "sealer-embalmers," who were responsible for tomb maintenance and inspection, as well as to those who performed the actual mummification and to those who merely carried out funerary rituals.

The tomb industry was a vast and complicated business. The need for contracts arose because generations were buried in one tomb that remained in the family for hundreds of years. When the family finally moved or died out, disputes over ownership of the tomb would arise. Contracts were needed to specify who was or was not to be an occupant of a particular tomb and how much space he was allotted. When a father wished to arrange space for his children, a portion of the tomb was deeded to them. As time passed the tomb was repeatedly divided, so successive inhabitants received smaller spaces. A deed written by an embalmer from Memphis illustrates this situation:

> *Thou hast caused me to agree in full heart to the purchase money for the half share of my half share which makes the 1/4 share of the stone-built shrine which is called the "Shrine of Ptah-maa-kherow" which measures 18+1/3 divine cubits from south to north by 21 divine cubits from west to east, and also for the half share of my half share which makes the 1/4 share of the four storage rooms which are in it; their inventory being: two storage rooms at the southern wall, two storage rooms at the northern wall, and also for the half share of my half share which makes the 1/4 share of the burial chamber which forms its western side . . .* [1]

Overseeing a particular tomb was the responsibility of an embalmer deeded hereditary rights in the tomb's contract, which he passed on to his son. The embalmer was responsible for the maintenance and inspection of the tomb and its occupants, as well as for embalming any future bodies placed inside it.

The Hawara archives contain an oath administered to ten embalmers from two families to delineate the territory they controlled. They agreed to keep to their area so as not to encroach on embalmers of neighboring towns.

*They are stating unitedly: we bind (?) ourselves by oath unto
ourselves not to proceed to El-Lahun, (or) the Enclosure of the
Syrians, (or) Pnuger of Suchos, (or) the division of Polemon, it
being three localities which are in the outer districts [of the division of Heracleides of] the Arsinoite [nome], to perform embalmer's function(s), to anoint with unguent, not to allow
another member to perform the prescribed ceremoni(es) of any
kind on earth in our name, (and) the function aforesaid. And
we shall not take responsibility for [the burial places
therein]. . . .*[2]

Although the Hawara archives tell us something about the
organization of the embalming profession, they do not describe
actual embalming practices.

Some papyri, however, do describe mummification rituals,
and these indirectly reveal something about the practice of
mummification. Two of these papyri are known as the "Rhind
Papyri," after their discoverer, Alexander Rhind, a Scottish law-
yer who visited Egypt in 1856, became enthralled with its antiquities, and eventually obtained permission to excavate. He
made several important discoveries, but the most significant
was an intact tomb dating from the Roman period.

While excavating in 1860 at Gourna, a village near the Valley
of the Kings, honeycombed with tombs, Rhind uncovered a
doorway cut into the rock. Plastered over in antiquity, the doorway still retained a seal of Amenhotep III, indicating a tomb of
the Eighteenth Dynasty. Inside, Rhind found a large, plundered
tomb with the remains of mummies scattered about, on the
floor, fourteen wooden mummy tags written in hieratic script.
These tags were placed on the mummies at embalmers' shops
to ensure that bodies didn't get switched—much like the wrist
bracelets for newborns in hospitals today.

Although disappointed at finding only a plundered tomb,
Rhind cleared more debris from beside the doorway. Then,
twenty feet to the left, he found another entrance, which led to
a room eight-and-a-half feet wide and fifty-five feet long that
contained a few stone vessels as well as a beautiful, brightly
painted funerary canopy of the kind used to enshrine a coffin.
In the rear of the tomb stood a massive wooden door sealed

FIG. 7.
*Tag placed on the mummy of Lady
Takhenmet for identification at the
embalmer's shop. It states that she
died on the tenth day of the third
month of spring in the ninth year of
Caesar's reign. She died at the age of
seventy-five, having been a temple
servant for forty-five years.* MUSEUM
OF FINE ARTS, BOSTON

and barricaded by large stones. The door itself was an object of
wonder, strong and beautifully constructed. (Rhind's local assistants coveted it for their homes, but he allegedly gave it to
an unidentified church in Cairo, where it may still hang today.

If so, the church has a door that is older than Christianity itself.) The door opened onto a tunnel more than fifty feet long that led to a pit still bridged by the beams used to lower the deceased into the tomb twenty centuries before. At the bottom of this pit Rhind found an intact Roman grave containing the papyri subsequently named after him.

One chamber contained an unfinished sarcophagus carved of pink Aswan granite with its lid still cemented to it. When the lid was removed a mummy was revealed, stuck to the inside of an inner coffin by bitumen poured around it. After considerable effort, the bitumen—which had coagulated into a hard adhesive—was chipped away and the mummy brought up from the pit into the open air.

The mummy's face was encased in a gilded mask; encircling the head was a bronze wreath of gold-painted leaves. Within the wrappings Rhind found figures of gods cut from sheet gold. This is not unusual, but even the skin of the mummy's torso had been gilded. Because it does not tarnish, embalmers used gold whenever a client could afford it. The burial chamber was referred to as "the Gold Room."

The arms of the mummy rested along its sides; on the left side was a papyrus identifying its owner as Montu-Sebef, who lived in Hermonthis and died, at the age of fifty-nine, in 9 B.C., during the twenty-first year of the reign of Emperor Augustus. The papyrus is extraordinary for two reasons: First, it gives details on how a mummy was wrapped; second, it is written in both hieratic and demotic scripts. For the latter reason, the papyrus is often called the "Rhind Bilingual Papyrus." Technically it is not bilingual,[3] the only language on the papyrus being Egyptian. Although the use of two scripts seems redundant, the papyrus proved helpful to Egyptologists trying to perfect their understanding of the very difficult demotic script.

The papyrus specifies the exact dates on which various stages of the funerary rite took place. The process of the funeral stretched from the tenth to the fifteenth of the month of Epiphi, beginning with "Purification on the Entire Earth." The mummy was bathed in the "Pool of Khonsu"; the legs, arms, torso, and back were "at rest for thirty days in the 'Place of Cleansing.' " Two hundred six jars of fat were boiled down to produce the

FIG. 8. *Set of jars for the seven sacred oils used in mummification.* METROPOLITAN MUSEUM OF ART

base for some of the oils spread on the body. Frankincense, cedar oil, and other balms were used on all the limbs, which were then enclosed in the best linen—"the fabrics of the gods and goddesses." Linen was a status symbol for the ancient Egyptians, the best being "linen of Sais." The text states, "Thou hast had a salted embalment, and linen cloth for thy limbs of the best linen."

Toward the end of the papyrus the deceased, now mummified, is told: "The gods of the openings adore thee, saying thou art the best prepared of spirits. They rejoice to see thy form, rising in its shapes, dressed in linen . . . Thy fore and hind parts are mummified like the gods in their shapes." The term "gods of the openings" refers to the seven openings in the head: two eyes, two ears, two nostrils, and the mouth. Numbers were important to the Egyptians, and seven was sacred—seven oils were used for the various rites.

Seventeen and seventy were also important numbers repeated throughout the Rhind papyrus. For example, mention is made of the seventeen members of the god (every deceased Egyptian became, like Osiris, a god):

7 openings of the head
4 sons of Horus (internal organs)
2 legs
2 arms
1 front torso
1 back
_____
17

The papyrus states that during the first thirty-six days of mummification eight ceremonies were performed, followed by an additional nine through the seventieth day of the ritual, when the mummy was placed in the tomb. Thus the number of ceremonies totalled seventeen, one for each part of the body.

This description of ceremonies and wrappings is confirmed in the second papyrus found in the tomb, once again on the left side of a mummy. This one had been prepared for Taani, the wife of the owner of the first papyrus. Written in the same hand as the other papyrus, it too is a "bilingual" text with vignettes. Taani, who died only forty-eight days after her husband, had but a short period to mourn her spouse. The word used in the papyrus to indicate her mourning is interesting: ⚍⚎ 𓈎 𓂋 𓊹 .The first four signs show how the word was pronounced, probably something like "*mehew*." The last two signs are determinatives; the second of the two indicates that the word denotes "woman," while the first, a lock of hair, symbolizes grief. (Many Egyptian words concerning grief are determined by a lock of hair, which stems from a time when mourning was accompanied by tearing one's hair.) Thus the determinatives refer to a woman in mourning.

The vignettes at the top of the two papyri also reveal facets of the mummification process. On most of the papyri pages, the deceased is shown on a funerary couch. Actual examples of these couches were found in Tutankhamen's tomb, couches so high that the embalmers would not have to bend down over the body. A priest wearing a jackal mask participated throughout the ritual. (Jackals were associated with Anubis, and thus the dead, because they were frequently seen in cemeteries. Their digestive systems are such that they prefer rotten meat to fresh, and cemeteries attracted them because not every corpse was protected by a tomb.)

Aside from the two Rhind Papyri, the only other papyri that tell us anything about mummification are those called "The Ritual of Embalming." One version is in the Egyptian Museum in Cairo; the other is in the Louvre in Paris.[4] The Cairo text, with eight of its nine pages well preserved, was discovered in 1857, in a tomb at Thebes belonging to a man named Heter, who bore the titles of "Divine Father," "Prophet of Amun," and "Chief of the Priests of Sekhmet." Exactly what purpose the papyrus served is difficult to understand. While it describes the details of bandaging a mummy, it was certainly not intended as an embalmer's reference, since it was written to be sold to the family of the deceased and placed in his coffin. In fact, it is an early form letter. The papyrus was written in a fine, professional hieratic hand dating from the Roman period, but the places where the deceased's name would occur were left blank; the blanks were later filled in by the family in a crude hand. Perhaps the purpose of such papyri was to magically guarantee that the embalmers performed the ritual correctly. The papyrus in the Louvre also dates from the Roman period, perhaps indicating that embalming procedures had become so slipshod by this time that such papyri were considered essential backups.

The Louvre papyrus stipulates that the embalming was to begin four days after the death, to let the deceased remain at home for a period of mourning and to allow his friends and relatives to organize the procession to ferry the body across to the west bank of the Nile, where it would be buried. The bandaging itself took place forty-six days after death, which leaves forty-two days for the embalming process itself.

Both the Cairo and Louvre papyri stipulate that the head be anointed with frankincense and the rest of the body with an unguent ("sacred oil") poured by a priest called "Treasurer of the God." The back of the mummy is to be anointed with fat and the skull packed with aromatic spices. Details are given for bandaging the head, each bandage having a magical name. After the entire head was wrapped, a linen strip two fingers wide was affixed with "thick oil," that is, resin, obtained primarily from the Aleppo pine tree in Syria. Separate instructions are

FIG. 9. *Vignette from the Rhind Bilingual Papyrus showing Taani, wife of Montu-Sebef, on a funerary couch.*

Fig. 10.   *One of Tutankhamen's funerary couches* in situ.   METROPOLITAN
MUSEUM OF ART

Fig. 11.   *Tomb painting of Anubis embalming.*   PHOTOGRAPH BY I. SOLIMAN

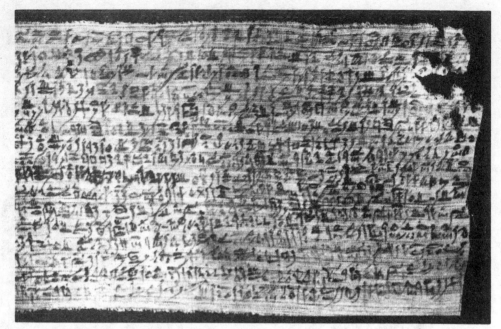

FIG. 12. *Mummy bandage with Chapter Seventeen of the* Book of the Dead. *It declares Djed-Her, son of Septu, to be pure.* COURTESY VICTOR PAFUNDI, JR.

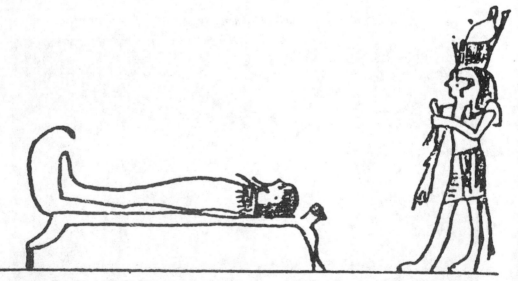

FIG. 13. *The god Horus bringing a bandage to the mummy. Note the ragged edges of the bandage.* AFTER A DRAWING BY S. SAUNERON

provided for wrapping the hands and legs.

A vignette at the top of the Cairo papyrus shows the gods bringing bandages to the mummy. Indeed, bandages were sacred and frequently had magical spells written on them. The word for bandage was 𓎛𓂝𓏤, which was pronounced *"wet,"* with an oval bandage symbol at the end as a determinative.

The same word with a different determinative— 𓎛𓂝𓊖 — meant a place of embalming; with a man sign as a determinative— 𓎛𓂝𓊖𓀀 —the word meant "embalmer." The 𓊖 hieroglyph was used after words that referred to smelly things, indicating that embalming houses and embalmers smelled from the chemicals used. In fact, because of this unpleasant aspect of embalming, the procedure was performed out of doors, on hills where breezes could dissipate odors. As I mentioned in the memo to my university's officers, two of the names of Anubis were "He-who-is-in-his-tent," and "He-who-is-on-his-hill."

In the Louvre papyrus, seven gods bring the various materials used for the wrapping. One vignette shows Horus carrying the bandages (an interesting touch of detail is that the bandages, normally torn from old sheets and clothes, are shown with ragged edges). According to this papyrus, the final words of the bandaging ritual were, "You live again, you live again, forever. You are young again, forever."

Tomb Inscriptions

An additional source of information about the process of mummification is tombs, especially those of the ancient Egyptian nobility, whose walls tend to depict their daily activities. These even include scenes of preparing funerary furniture, of the funeral, and, in rare instances, of preparing the body itself.

One example, the tomb of Pepi-Ankh, a Sixth Dynasty vizier buried at Meir in central Egypt, provides some fascinating details of his mummification. His tomb was not yet finished when he died, so, drawn in black ink on one wall, are scenes of what

FIG. 14a. *Scene from the tomb of Pepi-Ankh. The rectangular coffin, under a canopy, is being taken to the west bank of the Nile for mummification by a group including kneeling female mourners, embalmers, and the ship's crew.*

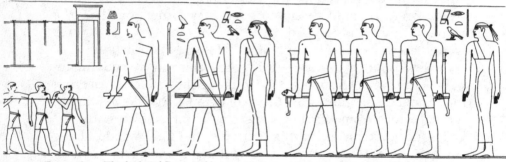

FIG. 14b. *The body of Pepi-Ankh is carried on a funerary bed to the Tent of Purification.*

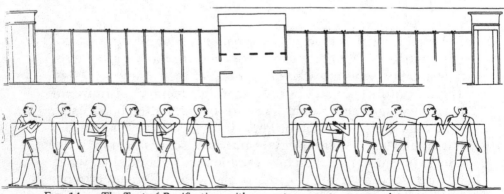

FIG. 14c. *The Tent of Purification, with separate rooms to accommodate many bodies. Workers are shown in front.*

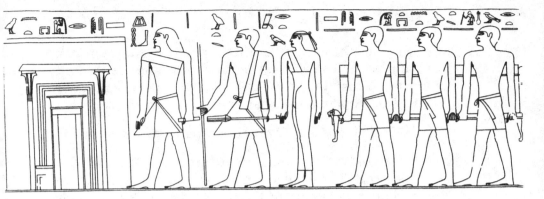

FIG. 14d. *Taking the body to the embalmer's workshop. The hieroglyphs proclaim that Pepi-Ankh reached a venerable age.*

FIG. 14e. *Food offerings at the embalmer's shop.*

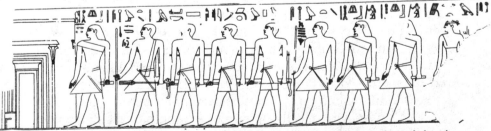

FIG. 14f. *Retrieving the now-mummified body of Pepi-Ankh from the embalmer's shop. The crudely drawn hieroglyphs above the shoulder of the man in the middle identify him as the scribe Zushen, a friend of Pepi-Ankh.* FIGURES 14A–F COURTESY THE COMMITTEE OF THE EGYPT EXPLORATION SOCIETY

happened to his body after he died.[5] The body, in its rectangular coffin, is shown being carried in a procession to the Nile, then ferried across to the west bank, where the embalmers worked. The people on the boat are labeled. In the stern was the 𓀀𓂝𓏤𓏤𓏤𓂝, the "Overseer of the Crew." Kneeling females are labeled 𓃀𓂝𓂋𓀀, a word frequently translated as "kite," meaning the hawklike bird. It was also a term for professional mourners in ancient Egypt, harking back to the time when Isis and Nepthys, in the form of birds, lamented the death of Osiris. Also in the boat are two men, one standing, one kneeling, labeled 𓀀𓂝𓏲, "embalmer." They were probably needed to handle the body and to lead the family to the embalmers' shop on the west bank. The boat in which the coffin rests has neither sails nor oars; instead it is towed by two others, both rowed. The caption above the funeral boat reads: "A successful trip! The way is completed. Behold, the ships have arrived."

We next see the procession—led by a priest holding a papyrus roll, an embalmer, and a female mourner—on its way to the "Tent of Purification." The body in its coffin is carried on a funerary bed. Because religious rituals were performed inside, the Tent of Purification is laid out like a temple. After the body was purified, the procession moved on to the embalmer's workshop. Hieroglyphs above the men carrying the coffin read: "Escorting to the embalmer's workshop. A great, old age."

The workshop contained many small rooms in which bodies could be individually prepared, and a larger room with food where a priest could call upon the deceased to join spiritually in a feast with his friends and family. The body now deposited with the embalmers, the empty coffin was ferried back to the house of the deceased while the family waited through the forty days of mummification. They then would be ferried across again with the coffin, claim the body at the embalmer's shop, and then proceed to the Tent of Purification for the "Opening of the Mouth" ceremony. This last ceremony before burial involved a priest symbolically opening the mouth of the deceased so he could breathe and speak in the next world.

The painting in the tomb of Pepi-Ankh does not show what

FIG. 15.   *Tomb of Thoy at Thebes. Embalmers brush resin on the wrapped mummy.*   AFTER A DRAWING BY N. DE GARIS DAVIES; COURTESY THE COMMITTEE OF THE EGYPT EXPLORATION SOCIETY

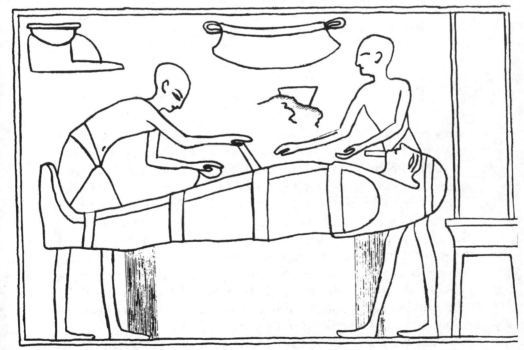

FIG. 16.   *Tomb of Amenemope at Thebes. Embalmers wrapping a mummy supported by blocks.*   AFTER A DRAWING BY N. ROSELLINI

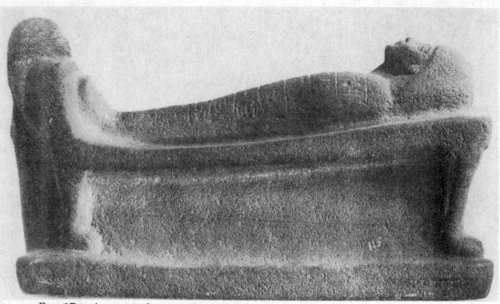

FIG. 17.   *An unusual statue of a mummy on a funerary couch with a woman peering over the foot of the couch.*   RIJKSMUSEUM, LEIDEN

goes on inside the embalmer's workshop, but two New Kingdom tombs at Thebes do provide such a glimpse. Several scenes in a Nineteenth Dynasty tomb at Thebes show the body of a person named Thoy being prepared by the embalmers. In one scene they hold cups from which they brush a coating of resin on the wrapped mummy. Beneath the mummy stands a two-handled pan for refilling the small cups. It is interesting to note that at this stage of preparation the body rests not on a funerary couch but on two supports, so that the bandages could be passed all around the body. (An unusual statue in the Rijksmuseum in Leiden shows the deceased on a funerary couch, a woman forlornly looking over from its foot.)

What we learn about embalming from the Egyptians themselves is that the prescribed time for the entire process was seventy days, for at least thirty-six days of which the body was immersed in natron, a naturally occurring mixture of baking soda and salt. (Composed mostly of sodium carbonate and sodium bicarbonate, it frequently contains a considerable amount of sodium chloride—salt—and lesser amounts of other impurities. The two chief sources of natron in ancient Egypt were El Kab, a city in Upper Egypt, and the Wadi Natrun, an area just outside of Cairo. "Wadi," in Arabic, means a dry river bed, and this is where natron occurs naturally.) The Bible confirms this time frame. When Joseph was in Egypt, he was joined by his father, Jacob (who was called Israel), who eventually died there. In Genesis 50: 1–3 we are told: "And Joseph commanded his servants the physicians to embalm his father. So the physicians embalmed Israel; forty days were required for it, for so many are required for embalming. And the Egyptians wept for him seventy days." Thus the immersion in natron, etc., took approximately forty days, leaving thirty days for rituals.

The Burial of Queen Mersyankh III

There were exceptions to this schedule, the best-known being the burial of Queen Mersyankh III, a granddaughter of the pharaoh Cheops, builder of the great pyramid. Mersyankh was buried in the eastern cemetery at Giza, near her grandfather's pyramid. Her tomb is one of the best-preserved of the Fourth Dynasty. An inscription on one side of the doorway to her chapel tells of her body being brought to the embalmer's. Although the Egyptian dating system will be outlined below, it can be translated as: "King's daughter Mersyankh, year 1, month 1 of Shomu, day 21. The resting of her ka and her proceeding to the house of purification (embalming)."[6] The other side of the doorway tells when the queen's body was placed in the tomb: "King's wife Mersyankh. Year after 1 [year 2], month 2 of Proyet, day 18. Her proceeding to her beautiful tomb."[7]

The ancient Egyptians did not number their years consecutively from a fixed starting point; instead, whenever a new king came to the throne, counting started at year one. His next year was year two, and so on till the end of his reign. When the next

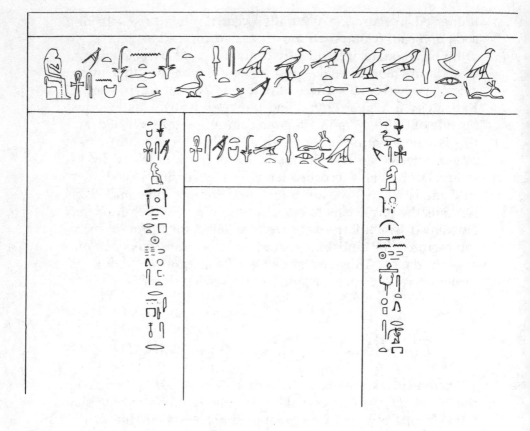

FIG. 18. *Inscriptions over the doorway of the funerary chapel of Queen Mersyankh stating that 273 days elapsed between the time her body was brought to the embalmer's shop and the day the mummy was placed in the tomb.* EGYPTIAN DEPARTMENT, MUSEUM OF FINE ARTS, BOSTON

king took over, counting began anew from year one of *his* new reign. Our inscriptions say that in year one of some king's reign (probably Mycerinus) the queen's body was taken to the embalmer's shop, but the body was placed in the tomb during the second year of his reign. To determine just how much time elapsed, knowledge of the months are crucial.

The Egyptian calendar differed from ours in having only

three seasons: (1) "Inundation" (, pronounced *"akhet"*) was the season when the Nile overflowed its banks to cover the farmland; (2) "Emergence" (⊡ ⊖, pronounced "*proyet*") indicated the time of the water's receding; (3) "Summer" (▭ ≋ ⊙, pronounced "*shomu*") was the following hot, dry season. Each season consisted of four months of thirty days, giving 360 days to the standard year. To these the Egyptians added "five yearly days" to make a calendar of 365 days.

Thus, the tomb inscriptions say that 273 days elapsed from the time Mersyankh's body was brought to the embalmer's shop to the day it was placed in its tomb. Because the period of seventy days for embalming is so well documented, some have suggested that the inscriptions must contain a scribal error. Others have argued for an elaborate, time-consuming embalming procedure, but this seems unlikely. The body in question was found in its sarcophagus when George Reisner discovered the tomb in 1927, and there was no evidence of any special treatment. The more likely explanation for the long delay in burying Mersyankh is that her tomb was not ready when her mummy was. Perhaps construction of her novel chapel in some way delayed the burial of the queen for more than half a year. Mastabas, the benchlike Old Kingdom tombs, normally included funerary chapels at ground level in which the family and priests could make offerings for the deceased, but Mersyankh's lies beneath her mastaba, reached by a flight of steps. Therefore, she could have been embalmed for the normal seventy days, then stored while her tomb was being completed. The unique architectural feature of the queen's tomb may have had something to do with this.

Herodotus of Halicarnassus

The earliest description of the mummification process itself comes not from the Egyptians, but from Herodotus of Halicarnassus, a Greek tourist who visited Egypt around 450 B.C. He traveled widely, recording what he saw and what he was told, and called his writings *Historia*, the Greek word for "researches,"[8] from which comes our own word "history." The travels of Herodotus are divided into nine books; the second, which is devoted to Egypt, provides a description of mummification. But the question is, how much of it can we believe?

Even in ancient times Herodotus was called a liar, and some modern scholars have gone so far as to question whether he ever actually set foot in Egypt. While the latter view is certainly extreme, there are reasons for doubting some of the claims made by the father of history. He says, for example, that much of the gold in India was mined by ants, larger than foxes, who excavated gold-rich dirt when they dug their ant hills. He adds that the king of Persia had a zoo where he caged some of these animals (*Histories*, Book III, 102–5). Herodotus also claims that the semen of Ethiopians is not white like other people's, but rather black like their skin (*Histories*, Book III, 101). If Herodotus tells such tales, can we accept his account of mummification?

It must be recognized that Herodotus does not say he saw these more fantastic things; he merely reported what he was told. Sometimes his informants gave him accurate information, sometimes not. If the reader keeps in mind that Herodotus' account of mummification is almost certainly what he was *told* by Egyptians, we can view it in its proper light. As a mere tourist, he would not have witnessed actual mummifications being performed, but he mentions that he did interview priests. Since his account of mummification contains no fantastic tales, it may well be a fairly accurate description of the procedure circa 450 B.C. Because the Egyptians themselves left no full descriptions, the secondhand report of Herodotus becomes all the more important.

Herodotus tells us there were three different prices for three different levels of mummification, and he describes each in some detail. From their examinations of mummies, modern Egyptologists have confirmed some of these details. Because Herodotus' account is so important for an understanding of mummification, it might be best to look at his own words before we discuss them.

*As to mourning and funerals, when a nobleman dies, all the
women of the house put mud on their heads and faces. Then,
leaving the body inside, they walk around the town with the
deceased's female relatives, their dresses fastened with a girdle,
and they beat their breasts. The men also, for their part, do the
same thing, wearing a girdle and beating themselves, as do the
women. When the ceremony is ended, they take the body to be
mummified.*

*Mummification is a distinct profession. The embalmers,
when a body is brought to them, bring out sample statues in
wood, painted to resemble nature, and ordered as to quality.
The best and most expensive [sample] is said to resemble a being whose name I cannot mention in this connection. The second best is somewhat inferior and less expensive, and the third
is the least costly of all. After pointing to these differences in
quality, they ask which of the three is desired, and the relatives
of the dead man, having agreed on a price, depart and leave
the embalmers to their work.*

*The most perfect procedure is as follows: As much of the
brain as it is possible is extracted through the nostrils with an
iron hook, and what the hook cannot reach is dissolved with
drugs. Next, the flank is slit open with a sharp Ethiopian
stone and the entire contents of the abdomen removed. The
cavity is then thoroughly cleansed and washed out, first with
palm wine and again with a solution of pounded spices. Then
it is filled with pure crushed myrrh, cassia, and all other aromatic substances, except frankincense. [The incision] is sewn
up, and then the body is placed in natron, covered entirely for
70 days, never longer. When this period, which may not be
longer, is ended, the body is washed and then wrapped from
the head to the feet in linen which has been cut into strips and
smeared on the underside with gum which is commonly used
by the Egyptians in the place of glue. In this condition the
body is given back to the family, who have a case of wood
made, which is shaped like the human figure, into which it is
placed. The case is then sealed and stored in a sepulchral
chamber, upright, against the wall.*

*When for reasons of expense, the second quality is required,
the procedure is different. No cut is made and the intestines*

are not removed, but oil of cedar is injected with a syringe into the body via the anus, which is then stopped up to prevent the liquid from running out. The body is then immersed in natron for the proscribed number of days, on the last of which the oil is drained out. The effect is so strong that as it leaves the body it takes with it the stomach and intestines in a liquid form. And because the flesh too is dissolved by the natron, nothing is left of the body but the bones and the skin. After this, it is returned to the family with no further treatment.

*The third method used for embalming the bodies of the poor, is merely to evacuate the intestines with a purge, and keep the body in natron for 70 days. It is then given back to the family to be taken away.*⁹

This account has a ring of truth to it. It is reasonable to expect that there would be different prices for different qualities of mummification, just as there are today in modern funeral parlors. The account of mourning also fits with what we know of the ancient Egyptians, and is confirmed by tomb paintings showing women acting the way Herodotus describes.

The mention of mummification as a distinct profession is an important detail. To some degree, it supports our earlier speculation that one reason for the absence of mummification papyri is that the profession safeguarded its skills by passing them along orally. The statement about sample statues is interesting, although none has ever been found. One wonders what they would have looked like. Would the least expensive sample have depicted a ghastly mummy? Undoubtedly the most expensive model resembled the mummiform god of the dead, Osiris, the name Herodotus didn't want to mention for some obscure religious reason.

The first written detail of the actual process of mummification is Herodotus' statement that the brain was removed through the nostrils with a hook. This technique is the most difficult way to remove the brain, but has been repeatedly confirmed by modern autopsies on mummies. The ethmoid bone, located at the front part of the skull base, is broken by probing through the nasal passage with the "hook" described by Herodotus.

FIG. 19.   *Mourners at the funeral of the vizier Ramose.*   PHOTOGRAPH BY
I. SOLIMAN

This bone, honeycombed with air cells, is delicate and easily
broken, allowing the probe to pass into the skull for extracting
a small portion of the brain. The probing would be repeated
many times to remove most of the mass of the brain, and modern experiments in extracting the brain through the nostrils
have shown that this method works. Indeed, a "hooked" rod
is not necessary.[10] Because the brain is viscous, it adheres even
to a straight probe, which would do less damage to the nasal
passages.

The fate of the brain in mummification is curious. There is
no doubt that the brain was usually removed, but we don't
know what was done with it. Of the few Egyptian references
to internal organs in connection with mummification, none
mentions the brain. Many internal organs that were removed
surgically and preserved in their entirety in canopic jars have

been found, but no brain preserved in this manner has been discovered.

Indeed, it's probable that the brain was simply thrown away. Because it was removed piecemeal with a hooked instrument, it would be shreds when the embalmers finished their task. Yet if the Egyptians were aware of the important function of the brain in life, they shouldn't have just thrown it away, not with their belief that the body would come to life again after death.

Did the Egyptians understand the function of the brain? In the "Edwin Smith Surgical Papyrus," three specific, traumatic head injuries, so serious that the brain is exposed, are discussed. It is clear that the author of this papyrus was aware of the meningeal membranes surrounding the brain, and of the brain's convolutions. The word for the meninges is *ntnt*, in hieroglyphs

⌒ ⌒ ꝶ. The final sign, the determinative, is an animal skin, which makes sense since the meninges is a kind of skin. Even more interesting is the way in which the convolutions are described. They are likened to "those ripples which form on molten copper."

The possibility of the limbs being affected by a severe injury to the head is also discussed, and it is mentioned that one symptom might be a limp. James Henry Breasted, who translated the papyrus, comments: "Here then is discovery of the fact that the brain is the source of control of the movements of the body."[11] Note, however, that the text merely acknowledges that severe trauma to the skull may affect the functioning of the limbs. No direct connection is drawn between the brain and dysfunction of the limbs. Indeed, the papyrus suggests that the limb on the side of the trauma is the one affected. Normally it is the opposite limb that would be affected, since the left side of the body is controlled by the right side of the brain. Egyptian medicine was highly specialized, with experts in eye ailments, gynecological ailments, etc., but there seem to have been no brain specialists, which would be surprising if Egyptians understood that the brain was the most important organ.

To the contrary, the ancient Egyptian believed that the heart managed the body. This is reasonable since your heart beats

quickly when you are excited, while the brain registers no

change at all. The word for heart, ⟋⌒ \\ ⱱ, pronounced *"haty"*, also meant "foremost one," and Biblical phrases such as "Pharaoh's heart was hardened" attest to the crucial role attributed to the organ by the ancients. If the Egyptians had recognized the brain to be very important, as Breasted claims they did, it is unlikely that they would have permitted it to be mutilated during mummification, let alone thrown away.

The next detail supplied by Herodotus is that an incision was made in the abdomen with a "sharp Ethiopian stone." Numerous mummies have been found with this incision, frequently covered by an oval of sheet gold. The fact that Herodotus mentions a sharp Ethiopian stone as the tool used for making the incision indicates that every aspect of the procedure was ritualized. At the time of Herodotus, the Egyptians had razor-sharp bronze knives, so there was no practical need to use a stone knife. That was demanded only because of tradition.

Later in his description, Herodotus again indicates just how ritualized the procedure was. He explains that the process took seventy days, but this is not an accidental number. He says "... never longer. When this period, which *may not be longer....*" It is clear that this was a number established by tradition.

While Herodotus' account seems reasonably accurate, it is far from complete. He correctly mentions that after the incision was made, the internal organs were removed, but does not discuss the fact that they were preserved and placed in canopic jars so that the deceased could be complete in the next world. One detail that Herodotus alone mentions is the filling of the abdominal cavity with aromatic spices before immersion in natron. Smith and Dawson, two of the great authorities on mummification, questioned this, claiming that Herodotus has it backward. They say, "It is curious to note that the body cavity was packed with aromatic substances before its immersions in the salt (natron) bath. Herodotus is evidently at fault here...."[12] If the mummy was immersed in a *bath* of natron, then it would indeed make no sense to pack the abdominal cavity before weeks of soaking the body. The packing would become soggy

and wash out. Later we will discuss the question of whether the body was bathed in natron or merely placed in dry natron, but here one point about packing the abdominal cavity should be added, a point in favor of Herodotus' account.

Two Egyptian scientists recently analyzed embalmers' refuse found in several tombs.[13] They discovered that numerous packets of natron wrapped in linen as well as packets of sand contained globules of fat that almost certainly came from contact with a body. The sodium carbonate in the natron would emulsify any body fats with which it came in contact, so these packets probably came from inside the abdominal or thoracic cavities, serving to assist the dehydration of the body. With such packets inside, dehydration would take place internally as well as externally. After the dehydration process, these temporary packets would be removed before the body was wrapped. Thus Herodotus may be right when he said the body was first packed with "spices" and then placed in natron.

The purpose of natron is clear—to dehydrate the body. The question is whether it was used in dry form or in solution. Either way, it could dehydrate the body.

The idea that natron was used in solution originally stemmed from an improper translation of Herodotus' account. When Herodotus describes the three methods of mummification, he uses the word ταρχεύονπι to describe how the natron was applied. The word has often been translated as "bathed" or "washed," but in the time of Herodotus its basic meaning was to preserve fish with salt. Herodotus thus is explaining that mummification was similar to the salting of fish. To make clear that salt was not used, in one place he attaches the word λιτρω, "with natron."

It is more plausible that natron would be used dry rather than in a solution. If one wants to dehydrate something, one does not begin by immersing it in a liquid. Also, from earliest times the Egyptians salted fish to preserve it, and this could be the origin of using natron to preserve human bodies. However, Warren R. Dawson, a great authority on mummification, suggested in 1927[14] not only that natron was used in solution, but more specifically that the immersion took place in large pottery jars with the deceased in contracted position. As evidence he

mentions two examples of pottery figures of a man in contracted position in a jar.[15] Yet if the bodies of the deceased were desiccated in contracted position, it would be difficult to straighten them for wrapping. Also, if they were soaked in a solution, flat trays rather than rounded jars would seem a more likely receptacle. If Dawson were correct, there would have been thousands of such vats from the millennia during which mummification was practiced, yet none has ever been found. However, there is one case where a solution of natron was known to be used in mummification, but not for the body of the deceased. This example comes from the tomb of Queen Hetepheres, the mother of Cheops (or Khufu), who built the great pyramid at Giza.

In 1925, a photographer from the Harvard–Boston Museum expedition to Giza noticed white plaster on the bottom of one of the legs of his tripod. He had thought the tripod was resting on bedrock, but discovered that the plaster covered a shaft descending one hundred feet into the rock. When the shaft was cleared, the sealed burial chamber of Queen Hetepheres was discovered at the bottom. Inside the chamber was her alabaster sarcophagus, still sealed, as well as funerary furniture and a canopic chest containing her internal organs. Chemical analyses proved that the organs had stood in a solution of 3 percent natron—an example of a solution being used for the internal organs, but not for the body.

One additional example is known of natron used in solution. Excavating a royal tomb of the Twelfth Dynasty at El Lahun, Guy Brunton found an alabaster canopic jar whose contents, analyzed by Arthur Lucas, chief chemist for the Egyptian Antiquities Service, were immersed in a solution of natron.[16] It is important to note that the two known instances of natron in solution involve canopic containers, where it was possible to keep the organ permanently immersed in the liquid, the way we might store something in formaldehyde. Such containers were not used for mummies, and thus dry natron almost certainly was the substance used to preserve bodies.

Lucas attempted to settle the question experimentally in the 1930s by mummifying chickens and pigeons in natron, some in solution and others in dry natron.[17] The chickens, soaked in a

FIG. 20.   *Canopic chest of Queen Hetepheres at the bottom of the shaft where it was found. It contained the earliest example of internal organs removed and preserved in natron.*   MUSEUM OF FINE ARTS, BOSTON

solution of natron for forty days and then dried, were well pre-served—so much so that thirteen years later they showed no signs of deterioration—but those mummified in dry natron were preserved even better, and are still intact in the Egyptian Museum today. Since the dry method produced a better chicken mummy, and since natron in solution required the extra step of drying, Lucas concluded that dry natron was used.

A little over half a century later, a study of DNA in mummies added support to Lucas' conclusion. When DNA was examined in various tissue samples from mummies, it was found to be better preserved in tissue closer to the surface of the body. Skin samples, for example, showed better-preserved DNA than deeper muscle or organ samples.[18] This would make sense if dry natron was used to preserve the body because the skin would come in contact with the natron and be desiccated first, while it would take longer for the deeper tissues to be dehydrated, allowing them more time to decay.

In addition to its practical use in embalming, natron also played a ritual role in purification ceremonies. The hieroglyphs for natron underscore its sacred nature: 𓃀𓂋𓎛𓏥. The first two hieroglyphs indicate that the word was pronounced *"bed."* The next hieroglyph is really a combination of two, 𓋔 and 𓎛.

The 𓋔 hieroglyph, which represents a banner on a pole, means "god." The 𓎛 hieroglyph is a piece of linen tied up to form a pouch. The banner signifies the divine nature of natron; the pouch shows how it was stored.

One area in ancient Thebes that seems to have served as a place of embalming is Deir el Bahri, on the west bank of the Nile. Herbert Winlock excavated there for the Metropolitan Museum of Art in the 1920s and found embalmers' refuse at several spots. After a person was embalmed, the used paraphernalia were gathered and buried in a pit outside his tomb. These items included rags, jars, packets of natron, straw, etc. Because these materials had been involved in a religious ritual, they were sacred and had to receive a proper burial.

In 1921 Winlock found an undisturbed pit containing materials used in embalming a nobleman of the Eleventh Dynasty named Ipy.[19] The sixty-seven sealed jars contained soiled rags, packets of natron, broken jars, sawdust, and oils. Also in the pit lay an embalmer's wooden platform approximately seven feet long and five feet wide. Across the platform were four blocks of wood, about a foot high, so that the body would be elevated to permit its fluids to drain. A wooden ankh (☥) amulet was placed at each of the four corners, magically transforming the embalming platform into a table of life.

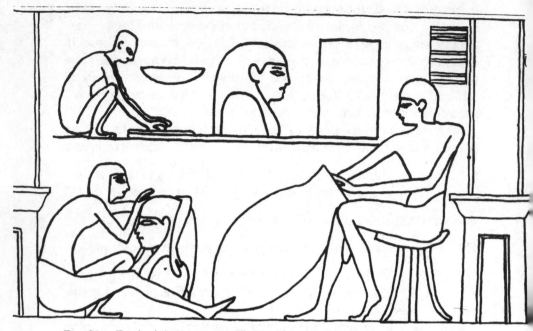

FIG. 21. *Tomb of Amenemope at Thebes. The striped rectangle in the upper right corner is probably an embalmer's board.* AFTER A DRAWING BY N. ROSELLINI

A depiction of an embalming board like the one Winlock found probably appears in a series of tomb paintings copied over a century and a half ago by Niccolò Rosellini, the founder of Egyptology in Italy. After a series of scenes depicting the bandaging of the mummy, a man is shown putting the finishing touches on the cartonage mask that would cover the head of the deceased. Another workman is pictured with his hand in a large storage jar, much like the ones in which Winlock found the embalmers' refuse. In the upper right corner of the scene is something that looks like the embalmers' board, with the planks going across its width.[20]

Two years after the discovery of Ipy's tomb and the embalming equipment, Winlock found an embalmer's cache of the Twenty-first Dynasty belonging to the Lady Henettowey.[21] Although a thousand years later than Ipy's, the cache was remarkably similar, indicating that little had changed in the embalmers' shops. The only difference was that the wood platform had been replaced by a wicker bed and mat.

Embalmers' caches such as these are not uncommon; one from the embalming of King Tutankhamen was discovered in January 1908 by Theodore Davis in a small pit dug into the bedrock about a hundred yards from where the tomb of Tutankhamen would be discovered in 1922. The pit was about six feet long, four feet wide, and four feet deep. In it were about a dozen large storage jars sealed with mud. The jars contained the usual embalmer's equipment—packets of natron, linen, etc., some with the name of Tutankhamen written on them. Along with the embalming equipment were the remains of the meal eaten by Tutankhamen's family and close friends on the day he was buried, including jars and dishes ritually broken after the meal, meat and fowl bones, and even the floral collars the participants had worn.

These findings were given to the then-young Metropolitan Museum of Art in New York, where they were studied by Winlock, who was a curator in the Egyptian Department. He realized that the museum had been given the embalmers' cache of a king. His analysis of the finds gives us more insight into how embalmers worked—in this case, on the body of a pharaoh.[22] The jars contained large quantities of linen, mostly torn into long strips from sheets and rolled so they could be used the way we do our modern bandages. But fifty of these rolls were finished on both edges, indicating that they had been woven specifically for the wrapping of Tutankhamen. The packets of natron were made by placing natron in the middle of a square of linen, gathering the four corners, then tying them with a piece of cloth. But some of these packets were miniature versions so small that they could not have had any practical use. These may have been amulets created to invoke the magical attributes of natron.

When natron is found in pits outside tombs, it is the remains of the act of mummification. Because it was also considered divine and purifying, it was also placed *inside* tombs in prescribed locations. It was, for example, found in four dif-

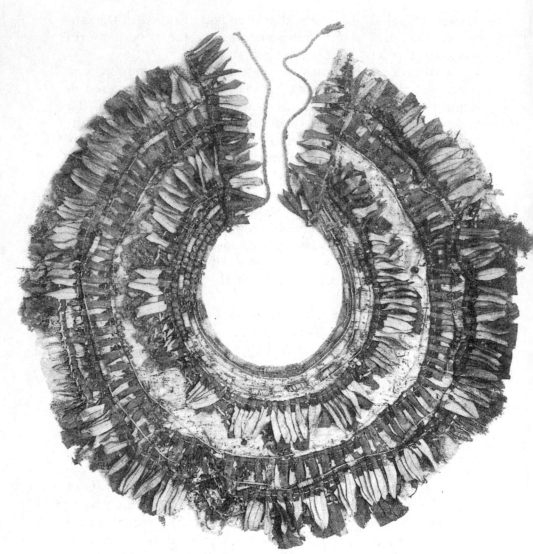

FIG. 22. *Floral collar worn by one of the participants in the ritual meal at Tutankhamen's funeral.* METROPOLITAN MUSEUM OF ART, GIFT OF THEODORE DAVIS, 1909

ferent places in Tutankhamen's tomb, all relating to immortality, among them inside hollow dishes on two alabaster stands in front of the canopy that contained the king's alabaster canopic chest. Given the religious and practical importance of natron for mummification, it is not surprising that Herodotus reports its use even in the least expensive kind of mummification.

As to the aromatic spices Herodotus mentions—myrrh, cassia, etc.—they all are well attested. Indeed, our word "embalm" comes from the Latin *in balsamum,* meaning to preserve in balm. The detail Herodotus offers about frankincense being excluded from the abdominal cavity is interesting and confirmed by the papyrus in the Egyptian Museum in Cairo that deals with the ritual of embalming. The papyrus specifies that unguents for embalming are to be used on the entire body except for the head, which is to be anointed with frankincense. Thus frankincense did have a special use among the embalming spices.

Herodotus' statement that the linen used to wrap the body from head to foot was "cut into strips" is also true, as we have already seen, but somewhat surprising. Because mummification was such a large and important industry, it might be expected that one auxiliary business would have been the weaving of bandages specifically for mummification, at least for the nobility. But this is not the case; for both commoner and prince, old sheets were used as bandages. Perhaps there was a custom of using the bed sheets that one slept on in life for the sleep till resurrection.

And so Herodotus seems to have left us a plausible account of mummification in his time that adds considerably to the scant, indirect evidence left by the Egyptians themselves. After Herodotus, the historical record is silent for four centuries until another Greek wrote about Egyptian mummification. That Greek was Diodorus, called "Diodorus Siculus" because he was born in Sicily. Like Herodotus, he too intended to write a history of the known world.

Diodorus Siculus

Diodorus' work, which he called the *Library of History,* ran to forty books, of which only fifteen have survived.[23] Fortunately, we have his first book, which deals with Egypt and embalming.

Diodorus visited Egypt in 59 B.C., when the country was under Roman control, so the mummification process he describes would be from the final period of its practice. Diodorus' account is similar to that of Herodotus, so similar in fact that it cannot be viewed as independent corroboration. We know that Diodorus read Herodotus, for he frequently quotes him, and thus may be parroting a secondary source rather than reporting what he himself learned in Egypt. While he often attempts to correct some of the wild tales of Herodotus, Diodorus has his own share of unlikely information. For example, when discussing the method of embalming in Ethiopia, he says:

> *In the burial of their dead the inhabitants of Ethiopia follow customs peculiar to themselves; for after they have embalmed the body and have poured a heavy coat of glass over it they stand it on a pillar, so that the body of the dead man is visible through the glass to those who pass by. This is the statement of Herodotus. But Ctesias of Cnidus, declaring that Herodotus is inventing a tale, gives for his part this account. The body is indeed embalmed, but glass is not poured about the naked bodies, for they would be burned and so completely disfigured that they could no longer preserve their likeness. For this reason they fashion a hollow statue of gold and when the corpse has been put into this they pour the glass over the statue, and the figure, prepared in this way, is then placed at the tomb, and the gold, fashioned as it is to resemble the deceased, is seen through the glass. Now the rich among them are buried in this wise, he says, but those who leave a smaller estate receive a silver statue, and the poor one made of earthenware....* [24]

A gold-plated, glass-encased mummy on a pillar would be a rather dramatic sight, but unfortunately neither Diodorus nor anyone else saw such a thing. It should be noted that Diodorus never claims that he did. In fact, he may never have been in Ethiopia at all; he is merely reporting what he heard about it.

On the other hand, Diodorus too mentions the three classes of embalming. Since he did visit Egypt, his account of mummification, while resembling that of Herodotus, adds some details that should be looked at seriously:

But not least will a man marvel at the peculiarity of the customs of the Egyptians when he learns of their usages with respect to the dead. For whenever anyone dies among them, all his
relatives and friends, plastering their heads with mud, roam
about the city lamenting, until the body receives burial. Nay
more, during that time they indulge in neither baths, nor wine,
nor in any other food worth mentioning, nor do they put on
bright clothing. There are three classes of burial, the most expensive, the medium, and the most humble. And if the first is
used, the cost, they say, is a talent of silver, if the second,
twenty minae, and if the last, the expense, they say, is very little indeed. Now the men who treat the bodies are skilled artisans who have received this professional knowledge as a family
tradition; and these lay before the relatives of the deceased a
price-list of every item connected with the burial and ask then
in what manner they wish the body to be treated. When an
agreement has been reached on every detail and they have taken
the body, they turn it over to men who have been assigned to
the service and have become inured to it. The first is the scribe,
as he is called, who, when the body has been laid on the ground,
circumscribes on the left flank the extent of the incision; then
the one called the slitter cuts the flesh, as the law commands,
with an Ethiopian stone and at once takes to flight on the run,
while those present set out after him, pelting him with stones,
heaping curses on him, and trying, as it were, to turn the profa-
nation on his head; for in their eyes everyone is an object of
general hatred who applies violence to the body of the same tribe
or wounds him or, in general does him any harm.

The men called embalmers, however, are considered worthy
of every honor and consideration, associating with the priests
and even coming and going in the temples without hindrance,
as being undefiled. When they have gathered to treat the body
after it has been slit open, one of them thrusts his hand
through the opening in the corpse into the trunk and extracts
everything but the kidneys and heart, and another one cleanses
each of the viscera, washing them in palm wine and spices.
And in general, they carefully dress the whole body for over
thirty days, first with cedar oil and certain other preparations,

*and then with myrrh, cinnamon, and such spices as have the
faculty not only of preserving it for a long time but also of
giving it a fragrant odour. And after treating the body they
return it to the relatives. . . .* [25]

Like Herodotus, Diodorus mentions that embalming was a
family profession. But while Herodotus only says that an overall price was reached, Diodorus gives exact figures and mentions that an itemized price list was provided for customers.
Such lists have been found dating from the Greek occupation
of Egypt; one, translated by H. I. Bell in the 1920s, is quite in-
structive.

Embalmer's Price List

Item	*Price*	
....	12 drachmae	2 obols
Earthenware pot		2 ob.
Red paint	4 dr.	19 ob.
Wax	12 dr.	
Myrrh	4 dr.	4 ob.
Song		4 ob.
Tallow		8 ob.
Linen clothes	136 dr.	16 ob.
Mask	64 dr.	
Cedar oil	41 dr.	
Medicament for the linen	4 dr.	
Good oil	4 dr.	
Turbon's wages	8 dr.	
Lamp-wicks	24 dr.	
Old tunic		24 ob.
Sweet wine		20 ob.
Barley	16 dr.	
Leaven	4 dr.	
Dog	8 dr.	
Little mask (?)	14 dr.	

2 artabae of loaves	21 dr.	
Pine cone (?)		8 ob.
Mourners	32 dr.	
Carriage by donkey	8 dr.	
Chaff (?)		12 ob.
Total	440 dr.	16 ob.

The most expensive item on the list is the linen, which is not surprising, given the large quantity used. The next most expensive item, a mask, undoubtedly was the jackal-head mask worn by the embalmer/priest in his role as Anubis, the god of embalming. What is interesting is that the charge for the mask indicates that a separate mask was prepared for each embalming. One wonders where all these masks are, or what was done with them—only one has survived. It is possible that the masks were ritually "killed," or destroyed after the ceremony.

One item that may be related to the mask is the item further down the list labeled "dog." Anubis was a jackal, but was frequently called a dog, and this item may refer to a small Anubis statue commissioned for the embalming. Many of the other items on the list confirm the accounts of Herodotus and Diodorus. The charge for mourners attests to the fact that they were professionals hired to bemoan the death.

Among details Herodotus did not include, Diodorus mentions that one priest marks where the incision is to be made on the left abdomen and that someone else makes the actual incision. This was similar to the production stages for paintings and carvings on tomb walls. After a grid was laid out to establish proportions, one person drew the outlines of the scenes in black paint, a master corrected these in red, then the sculptor came to carve the relief, and finally a painter added the color. This division of labor is not unlike the embalmers' division of labor with wrappers, cutters, etc.

Diodorus' claim that the incision was made on the left side is accurate and shows that he had real knowledge of the process. As Herodotus had also, Diodorus mentions that a stone was used for the incision and adds that this was "as the law commands," which explains why a bronze knife was not used.

FIG. 23.
Anubis mask worn by a priest at a mummification. HILDESHEIM;
PHOTOGRAPH BY DAVID MOYER

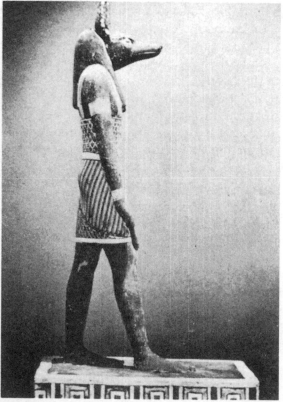

FIG. 24.
Statue of Anubis, god of embalming. BRITISH MUSEUM;
PHOTOGRAPH BY JOHN FREED

Another indication of the ritualized nature of embalming is his statement that the "slitter" was pelted and fled after completing his job. Clearly this was a ritual, not a serious attempt to injure the man.

Diodorus offers the first account of the internal organs, and while he does not say what was done with them after they were removed, it is evident that he knew they were not merely discarded, for he says they were washed. His statement that the heart was left inside the body is correct. This was because the heart, viewed as the controlling organ of the body, would be needed to get things going in the next world. Diodorus' statement that the kidneys were normally left inside the body, however, is only partly correct. Because they are located in back of the thorax, the kidneys were difficult organs to remove through a small incision in the abdomen, and sometimes were left inside.

As to the final fate of the removed internal organs, two classical sources disagree. Porphyry tells us:

> *There is one point which must not be passed over, namely that when they embalm the dead of the wealthy class, among other observances paid to the corpse, they privately remove the intestines and place them in a chest, which they make fast and present before the Sun, while one of those occupied in embalming the body recites a prayer. And this prayer, which Ekphantos translated from his native language, is to the following effect: 'O Lord Sun and all you gods who give life to men, receive me favourably and commit me to abide with the everlasting gods. For as long as I continued in that life, I have steadfastly reverenced the gods whom my parents instructed me to worship, and I have ever honored those who brought my body into the world; while, as concerns my fellow men, I have done no murder, nor betrayed a trust, nor committed any other deadly sin. But if, during my life, I have sinned in eating or drinking what was unlawful, the fault was not mine, but this' (showing the chest in which was the stomach.)*[26]

Porphyry is the only ancient source to mention the canopic chest used to store the internal organs. There is no Egyptian text that cites the prayer he quotes, but several features of it seem truly Egyptian. First, it is a hymn to the sun, similar to many known examples from ancient Egypt. Second, its content is not unlike Chapter 125 of the *Book of the Dead*, the "Negative Confession," where the deceased appears before the gods of judgment and enumerates the evil things he has *not* done.

The other classical text that discusses the final disposition of the internal organs is by Plutarch. He says that the internal organs were removed, held up to the sun, then thrown into the Nile! (*Convivium Septem Sapientium,* XVI) Numerous surviving canopic chests for the deceased's organs support Porphyry's account.

With the introduction of Christianity into Egypt in the first century A.D., the practice of mummification declined since it violated the tenets of that religion. Church fathers spoke out against mummification. Athanasius (whose name means "without death" in Greek) quotes the dying St. Anthony as asking his followers to assure that he will not be mummified:

> *And if your minds are set upon me, and ye remember me as a father, permit no man to take my body and carry it into Egypt, lest according to the custom which they have, they embalm me and lay me up in their houses, for it was [to avoid] this that I came into this desert. And ye know that I have continually made exhortation concerning this thing and begged that it should not be done, and ye well know how much I have blamed those who observed this custom.*[27]

From scanty Egyptian sources and often incorrect classical writers, we can construct an outline of the process of mummification. For the details, we must examine the mummies themselves.

3
How To, Part II:
The Mummies Speak

The few ancient Egyptian texts that discuss mummification and the classical writers' descriptions are just a beginning. Thousands of mummies have survived, and they will enable us to reconstruct a more complete picture of the ancient Egyptian embalmer's art. What emerges from a study of these mummies is not one but several different techniques, which change with the historical period. Mummification in Egypt was practiced for nearly 3,000 years and, as one would expect, there were improvements as well as regressions in the methods employed. These changes are so clear that awareness of the technique often makes it possible to determine when a mummy was embalmed, even in the absence of other dating clues. It is the mummies themselves who may supply those details of mummification that the classical authors omitted, and thus enable us trace the entire development of mummification.

The Earliest Mummies

Sand burials in the prehistoric period (prior to 3100 B.C.) led to natural mummification, and thus embalming techniques were neither needed nor used. The oldest attempt at mummification as yet discovered is of a king of the First Dynasty, whose recovery is a tribute to Flinders Petrie and his treatment of his workmen.

Because Petrie often simultaneously excavated several tombs, he could not personally supervise work on them all. Concerned that important finds made in his absence might be kept and sold by the workmen who discovered them, Petrie instituted the practice of paying his workmen a market price for objects they found. The workmen trusted Petrie to be fair, and this led to the discovery of the oldest mummy.

At the close of the nineteenth century, Petrie was excavating at Abydos, 150 kilometers north of Thebes. Abydos was known as "the Sacred City," since it boasted a special connection to the Egyptian funerary cult. From the earliest times, it was believed that after Osiris' bodily parts were reassembled by Isis, she buried him at Abydos. Although some ancient authors have said that it was the head that was buried there, and others the backbone, the important fact is that they all agreed that Abydos was the burial place of the god of immortality. A unique megalithic structure in Abydos, the Osirion, was said to be the god's actual tomb. Therefore, every Egyptian wished to be buried there. Of course, this was not always practical, but Egyptians buried elsewhere often sent small funerary offerings to Abydos for symbolic burial.

Even the earliest kings had tombs there; if the kings were buried in the north, they sometimes had cenotaphs (false tombs) at Abydos. They wanted to resurrect as Osiris did and be associated with the "Lord of Abydos." Of these earliest kings, little was known in the nineteenth century other than their names. Because the French archaeologists Auguste Mariette and Emile Amelineau had both worked at Abydos, most later excavators believed that little would be learned from further work at that site. Petrie, however, realized how important Abydos was to the knowledge of the First Dynasty and began excavations in 1899. His disdain for those who had preceded him is clear in his introduction to *The Royal Tombs of the First Dynasty, Part I*: "It might have seemed a fruitless and thankless task to work at Abydos after it had been ransacked by Mariette, and had been for the last four years in the hands of the Mission Amelineau."[1] (Amelineau threw away or broke what he didn't want to keep!) Petrie knew that much remained to be recovered at Abydos after Amelineau's shoddy work. He called his excavation a "recovery."

Arthur Mace, who later would join Carter in the excavation of Tutankhamen's tomb, assisted Petrie at Abydos while the tomb of King Zer of the First Dynasty was being excavated. Four of the workmen on the tomb found part of an arm wrapped in linen, and under the cloth they could see a large gold bead. Well trained by Petrie, the men left the arm where they found it and called Mace to the spot. Mace brought it to Petrie, who called one of the workmen to his dig house that night to watch as Petrie cut open the bandages, revealing four bracelets of gold and faience on the arm. For the next two hours, Lady Petrie and Mace rethreaded the beads; when they were finished, Petrie took the gold, placed it on a scale, weighed it against English gold sovereigns, and gave the delighted workman the sovereigns. Thus Petrie recovered the bracelets of King Zer, the oldest known royal jewelry.[2]

It is generally acknowledged that the particular interests of an excavator will influence what he finds and, even more so, what he records. If an excavator is a philologist, his publications tend to stress inscriptions, not objects. In his excavations at Abydos, Petrie was attempting to reconstruct the chronology of the kings of the First and Second dynasties, and this he did. He had no interest in trying to discover the earliest techniques used in mummification, so he recorded few details about the arm or its wrappings. He does, however, mention its fate in his memoirs, *Seventy Years in Archaeology*:

> When [James] Quibell came over on behalf of the Museum, I sent up the bracelets by him. The arm—the oldest mummified piece known—and its marvelously fine tissue of linen were also delivered at the Museum. Brugsch only cared for display; so from one bracelet he cut away the half that was of plaited gold wire, and he also threw away the arm and linen. A museum is dangerous place.[3]

A careful recording of the condition of this mummified body part could have told us a great deal, but we are left to infer from other early mummies what technique might have been used on King Zer. Actually, few mummies from the archaic period (the first two dynasties) remain, probably because they

Fig. 25.   *The arm of King Zer, the earliest remains of a pharaoh, was thrown
away at the turn of the century by a curator at the Boulaq museum.
Only this photograph remains.*   COURTESY PETRIE MUSEUM OF
EGYPTIAN ARCHAEOLOGY, UNIVERSITY COLLEGE, LONDON

were badly preserved, but also because the population of Egypt was relatively small at this time. We do know that bodies were buried in a flexed (fetal) position and that efforts at preservation were limited to merely covering the body.

Old Kingdom Mummies

From the time of the unification of the north and south, Egypt grew steadily and rapidly until, by the end of the Third Dynasty, its technology was sufficient to undertake what was then the greatest building project in the history of the world—the construction of the step pyramid at Saqqara, which was soon eclipsed by the great pyramids at Giza. Egypt's prosperity continued throughout most of the Old Kingdom, resulting in the development of two large and important classes of people— priests and artisans—who developed the artistic styles and religious conventions that were soon formalized and remained virtually unchanged for two thousand years.

The prosperity of the Old Kingdom continued until the Sixth Dynasty, or 2181 B.C. Its abrupt decline is still not fully understood. One intriguing possibility is that the pharaoh Pepi II, whose ninety-four-year reign is the longest in history, outlived his effectiveness as a ruler. In ancient times the pharaoh was not only the political leader of the country but, in times of war, its commanding general as well. It may be that Pepi became too old and feeble to lead his army or even to oversee its upkeep, with the result that the strong centralized government weakened. Pepi II's longevity cannot be the only cause of the fall of the Old Kingdom, but it was probably one of the factors that plunged Egypt into an anarchic period from which we have no records, not even lists of the pharaohs. This period, known as the "First Intermediate Period"—intermediate because it comes between the Old Kingdom and the Middle Kingdom— lasted for about fifty years. There was such turmoil that the priest-historian Manetho says that at one point there were seventy kings in seventy days. Egypt ceased to be the dominant power in the Middle East as the nomearchs, the governors of the states into which Egypt was divided, battled for power. Eventually one emerged to unite the country and Egypt once more was a nation with centralized government.

James Quibell found the body of a young woman of the Old Kingdom (Third through Sixth dynasties) at Saqqara, wrapped in more than a dozen layers of linen. Each limb had been wrapped separately, with the more coarse linen placed inside, nearer the body, and more than ten layers of fine linen on the outside. This suggests that the purpose of wrapping was more cosmetic than preservative.

The goal in Old Kingdom burials was more to make the deceased look like a living person than to preserve the body. In a tomb at Meidum Petrie found a mummy whose outer wrappings had been soaked in resin and modeled, like papier maché, to record every detail of the face, even its mustache. The penis was also indicated, and the body cavity had been stuffed with resin-soaked linen to preserve its shape. This body is not in the flexed position, so it probably dates from the Fourth Dynasty, the period during which mummies were first laid out in a prone position.

There was little attempt to dehydrate body fluids during the Old Kingdom, which resulted in the decay of corpses. Petrie, who found the body of a Fourth Dynasty nobleman, Nefermaat, in a mastaba at Meidum, concluded that the flesh had been removed before the body was wrapped because pieces of linen were found adhering to the bare bone.[4] He did not realize that a total disintegration of the soft tissue is possible in such a way that the linen does indeed move next to the bone. Dr. Douglas Derry demonstrated this in his subsequent work on Old Kingdom mummies.[5]

During the Fourth Dynasty the internal organs were removed from the body for preservation in canopic jars. The practice of placing the organs in jars continued through the Twenty-first Dynasty without interruption. There were, however, changes in the shapes of these jars.

As we have seen, the lids actually represented the four sons of Horus who were supposed to protect the internal organs of the deceased. It is often claimed that each one was assigned to watch over a particular organ, with Imsety guarding the stomach and large intestines, Hapi the small intestines, Duamutef the lungs, and Qebhsenuf the liver and gall bladder,[6] or some similar arrangement.[7] In practice there was little correlation between god and organ.

Usually made of limestone, or in the case of the wealthy, alabaster, the jars have inscriptions carved or painted on the outside. Each mentions one of the sons of Horus and his attributes. A typical spell is:

> *Words spoken by Hapi: "I am Hapi, thy son, Oh Osiris. I have come to be under thy protection. I bind for thee thy head and limbs, killing for thee thy enemies under thee. I give to thee thy head, for ever."*

The internal organs of Queen Hetepheres, discussed in the previous chapter, were placed in an alabaster canopic chest with four compartments; three of the compartments still held liquid when Reisner found them (the fourth probably was cracked which permitted the liquid to run out). In each compartment lay a packet that almost certainly contained the queen's internal organs. This is the earliest known instance of preserving these organs in a canopic chest.

Throughout the Middle Kingdom and into the Eighteenth Dynasty, canopic jar lids were shaped like human heads. Toward the end of the Eighteenth Dynasty they were replaced by animal heads. As mentioned in the first chapter, Duamutef became a jackal, Imsety a human, Hapi a baboon, and Qebhsenuf a falcon. Sometime during the Twenty-first Dynasty, the use of canopic jars ceased altogether because embalmers began the practice of removing the internal organs, preserving and wrapping them, and then replacing the preserved and wrapped organs inside the body cavity. In some burials after the Twenty-first Dynasty, false canopic jars—jars with the lid and body all one piece—were carved and placed in tombs purely for ritual purposes, perhaps so that the sons of Horus would still protect the organs.

As early as the Fourth Dynasty, the internal organs were being removed and preserved; a shift from a cosmetic approach to a deeper concern with the preservation of the actual body

FIG. 26.
Set of alabaster canopic jars for Princess Sit-Hathor-Yunet of the Twelfth Dynasty. The jars should have contained the princess's internal organs, but actually contained lumps of mud and cedar pitch, the work of irresponsible embalmers.   METROPOLITAN MUSEUM OF ART

FIG. 27.
False canopic jar. During the Twenty-first Dynasty, embalmers began replacing internal organs inside the body, so canopic jars were not needed. For ritual purposes, false jars with top and bottom carved in one piece were placed in tombs.   METROPOLITAN MUSEUM OF ART

must have occurred. While we can learn little about Old
Kingdom embalming techniques because there are so few mummies to study, our knowledge of embalming during the Middle
Kingdom is considerably greater, primarily because of several
Eleventh Dynasty queens' tombs discovered at Deir el Bahri.

Middle Kingdom Mummies

The second period of stability and consolidation, the Middle
Kingdom, is an important period of Egyptian history often
overlooked because the pharaohs are not memorable as individuals and the surviving monuments are not so significant as
those of the Old Kingdom. This period does reflect, however,
the country's ability to recover from almost total chaos and to
reestablish itself as the dominant power in the Near East. By
Egyptian standards the period of prosperity was short, lasting
only three hundred years before a second collapse.

The cause of turmoil during the Second Intermediate Period
(1786–1575 B.C.) is also not fully understood. Frequently it is
attributed to a single event, the invasion of the people known
as the Hyksos, or "foreign kings." There is no doubt that the
Egyptians were ruled by these foreigners, but the country must
have been in an already weakened state to have been conquered. The fact that, at the time of the invasion, the horse had
not yet been introduced into Egypt leads to the theory that the
Hyksos' use of chariots gave them a great advantage over the
Egyptian foot soldiers, but there is not much evidence to support this.

The Hyksos left few written records of their occupation, so
we still are uncertain who they are, but the best guess is that
they were Palestinians. Content to remain in the Delta in the
north, they let the Egyptians in the south rule themselves from
Thebes. We do have some documentation of the events that
supposedly led to the Hyksos' expulsion; it appears in the Sallier Papyrus, which is discussed in detail in the chapter "An
Inventory of Kings."

"Deir el Bahri" is Arabic for "place of the northern monastery"; the site is so named because there once was a Coptic monastery there. For most tourists to Egypt, it is synonymous with the mortuary temple of Queen Hatshepsut of the Eighteenth Dynasty. That famous queen was not, however, the first to build at the site. Five hundred years earlier, the kings of the Eleventh Dynasty began using the area as their cemetery. In fact, Hatshepsut's architect, Senenmut, was greatly influenced by an Eleventh Dynasty structure still standing when he designed his queen's funerary complex.

The Eleventh Dynasty, the start of the Middle Kingdom, is a confusing period because we are uncertain about both the sequence and the names of its kings. One reason for the confusion is that four kings of the dynasty shared the name Montuhotep. If an inscription with that name is damaged or incomplete, it may not be clear to which Montuhotep it refers. At the beginning of the Eleventh Dynasty there were only princes battling for power, but by its end we find true pharaohs. The pharaoh who built the temple at Deir el Bahri was Neb-Hepet-Re Montuhotep. Six pit tombs at the foot of the towering cliffs were dug for his wives: Mayet, Ashayet, Sadeh, Kauit, Kemsit, and Henenit. Above these pits stood six shrines; in front of these the king laid out his own huge funerary temple, with a small pyramid on top. At the end of the nineteenth century, Edouard Naville, a Swiss archeologist, began excavating in this area, and when he relinquished his concession—the Egyptian government's exclusive permission to dig a site—Herbert Winlock began excavating there for the Metropolitan Museum of Art in 1911. Naville and Winlock each discovered three of the queens' tombs, some with the mummies intact.

Naville found the site in such a ruined state that little of its original plan was obvious. He cleared away great quantities of rubble and made the first accurate map of the complex, noting where the six shrines once stood. He uncovered the tombs of Henenit, Kemsit, and Kauit, but when he discovered three anonymous pits in the neighborhood of the shrines he thought he had found the three missing tombs corresponding to the other three shrines. He was wrong, confused by the fact that the actual tombs for these queens had been dug before the king's courtyard was constructed, so they lay beneath the pavement. However, one of the tombs that he did discover contained the nearly intact body of Queen Henenit, and the other two tombs contained fragments of the other two queens. While he did publish a photo of the body of Henenit,[8] he said nothing about its condition or embalming techniques. Naville was interested in inscriptions, not bodies.

Realizing Naville's error, in 1920 Winlock removed the paving stones from the courtyard and discovered the remaining three tombs. The bodies of Mayet and Ashayet were intact, but Winlock had no interest in mummies either, and provided no details about the condition of the bodies. Later, however, these bodies were studied by Derry, whose findings are most interesting. None of these mummies had abdominal incisions—their internal organs had been left inside the abdominal cavities. This seems a surprising step backward from the Fourth Dynasty, when the viscera were placed in canopic chests. Nonetheless, an attempt was made to preserve the bodies, since they were found with bags of natron and stained bandages. But the bodies were in poor condition. Most of their dehydration took place after burial in the tomb, as evidenced by the many insect eggs found in the mummies. Also, the indentation marks of jewelry can be seen on one mummy's skin, indicating that the tissues were still soft and had not been completely dried by the mummification process before the body was wrapped.

The brain was not removed during the Middle Kingdom; it is only later that this refinement was added. But occasionally, during the Middle Kingdom, the internal organs were removed through an incision in the left side of the abdomen and placed in canopic jars. In such cases, the body cavity was packed with straw, sawdust, or linen to give it a lifelike appearance, and perhaps to promote dehydration. The final position of the mummified body in the Middle Kingdom is prone, with the hands stretched out alongside or covering the pubic region.

The New Kingdom

With the expulsion of the Hyksos, Egypt began an era of expansion and glory. The New Kingdom, which lasted for five hundred years, was ruled by only three dynasties, the Eighteenth, Nineteenth, and Twentieth. That the kingship remained in only a few families for hundreds of years is a sign of stability and prosperity. The pharaohs most associated with the greatness of Egypt—Tuthmose III, Amenhotep III, Tutankhamen, and Ramses II—ruled during this period. It was a time of expansion and building. One of the ways a pharaoh could demonstrate his greatness was to attack other countries and expand the borders of Egypt. With increased revenues from conquered countries, the pharaohs were able to initiate building projects to an extent not seen since the days of the pyramids. The Temple of Karnak, Luxor Temple, Ramses II's huge temples at Abu Simbel, and Hatshepsut's mortuary chapel at Deir el Bahri were built or begun during the New Kingdom. It was during this period of great prosperity that the pharaohs began carving their tombs in the Valley of the Kings at Thebes.

It was also the time when the priesthood of the god Amun rose to great power. Each pharaoh successively gave more and more land to the Amun priesthood until its holdings were almost as great as those of the pharaoh. At this point Amenhotep IV broke with the priesthood, changed his name to Akhenaten, and attempted to change the religion of Egypt from polytheism, with the major god being Amun, to monotheism and the worship of the solar disk, the Aten. Few mummies of this period have been found. It would be fascinating to know what the process was like for the followers of the cult of the Aten, the solar disk, but their cemetery at Tel al Amarna has not been found. Because this religion was monotheistic, believing in only a single solar god, it may not have recognized the Osirian doctrine of resurrection; it is possible that mummification was only minimally practiced, if at all. The new religion was never fully established, and upon Akhenaten's death, Tutankhamen and his successors returned to the old religion and reinstated the powerful god Amun.

The New Kingdom provides a significant number of well-preserved mummies, both of commoners and royalty. The large number of mummies is partly due to the extremely low humidity in the Valley of the Kings and adjacent areas that had become favored sites for burial.

During the Eighteenth Dynasty the brain was removed through the nose with a special instrument. The vacant brain cavity was often stuffed with narrow strips of linen forced in through the perforated ethmoid bone. It is also during this period that the use of resin on wrappings became so liberal, making the mummy more firm after it dried.

In an attempt to give the face a more lifelike appearance, the eye sockets were sometimes packed and the lids pulled over the stuffing. Mummies of this period are lain stretched out with hands at the sides; in the case of royalty, the hands are crossed over the breast. Mummification techniques are consistent through the Eighteenth to the Twentieth dynasties, probably, again, because the government was stable.

At the end of the Twentieth Dynasty, significant political decline led to new techniques of mummification. As this dynasty wound to a close, the power of the pharaohs was faltering. After the reign of Ramses III, the last strong king of the dynasty, weaker kings, each named Ramses, successively ruled for only brief periods, while again the power of the priests of Amun was growing greater and greater at Thebes. By the end of the Twentieth Dynasty, while Ramses XI was still pharaoh, the high priest of Amun, Hri-Hor, placed his own name in a cartouche, the oval signifying a pharaoh. The Twenty-first Dynasty consists of a series of priest-kings ruling the south of Egypt, though not Lower Egypt.

The eroding authority of the pharaoh lessened his ability to ensure the security of the Valley of the Kings and its surrounding necropolis. Consequently a series of tomb robberies occurred, which are recorded in several papyri that deal with the trials and punishments of the offenders. These fascinating documents give insights into the minds and motives of the plunderers. What emerges clearly is that robbers felt little respect for the bodies so painstakingly preserved by the embalmers of previous dynasties.

Mummies were ransacked in a search for gold amulets and jewelry in the wrappings. A tomb robber's confession in the Amherst papyrus offers a glimpse into the violation of two royal mummies.

> *The noble mummy of this king was all covered with gold, and his inner coffins were bedizened with gold and silver inside and outside with inlays of all kinds of precious stones. We appropriated the gold which we found on this noble mummy of this god and on his eye amulets and his ornaments which were at his neck and on the inner coffins in which he lay. [We] found the royal wife just (?) likewise and we appropriated all that we found on her too. We set fire to their inner coffins. We stole their outfit which we found with them, consisting of objects of gold, silver, and bronze, and divided them up among ourselves. We made this gold which we found on these two gods and on their mummies, their eye amulets and ornaments and their inner coffins into eight [parts].*[9]

An even more graphic description of the fate of a mummy comes from a papyrus in the British Museum.

> *We found the outer coffin of stone of Khenu [in] its burial chamber (?) We opened it and smashed up its mummy, and we left it there in the tomb. But we took his inner coffin and his shell and stripped off his gold.*[10]

However, one effect of such pillage in the necropolis at Thebes was that for the first time the results of the earlier embalmers could be observed first-hand. If no such robberies had occurred, if the bodies of the deceased had been permitted to remain undisturbed in their wrappings, the work of the embalmers would have gone untested. Inspecting the violated tombs and examining the damaged mummies gave the embalmers an impetus to better their fellow craftsmen from earlier dynasties, which in

FIG. 28.
*Internal organ (liver) with the wax
figure of a protective son of Horus.*
METROPOLITAN MUSEUM OF ART

turn precipitated the great changes in embalming that took
place in the Twenty-first Dynasty.

From this time on, after the internal organs had been removed, treated with natron, and wrapped, they were replaced
inside the body cavity. This was probably a direct result of noting that canopic jars were often smashed in the frantic search
for gold during robberies. Storage inside the body cavity lessened the chance of organs being separated from the body.

More than forty mummies of priests, kings, and queens from
the Twenty-first Dynasty have been found, giving us a vivid
picture of the embalmer's art in its highest form. The mummy
of the high priest Hri-Hor's wife, Nozme, demonstrates an extreme attempt to prevent the emaciated appearance observed
in mummies of the preceding dynasties. Not only was packing
material placed in her cheeks, but eyebrows were fashioned by

gluing human hair to her brow. Her mummy is the first with artificial eyes made of black and white stones, imitating the pupil. Queen Ka-Maat-Re's mummy shows an even more elaborate attempt at realism. Beneath her skin, the embalmers inserted a fat-and-soda mixture to give the mummy a fleshy appearance. This was done by inserting one's hand through the embalmer's incision in the left side of the abdomen, separating the skin from the muscles beneath it, and forcing the fat-and-soda mixture under the skin all the way up to the neck and down into the legs. When the embalmer's arm couldn't reach far enough, for example to the shoulder of the mummy, separate incisions were made to flesh out that part of the body. The mummy of Queen Henettowey, the wife of Pinedjem I, was also packed in this manner; she was literally overstuffed, and the skin around her chin, cheeks, and neck burst.

During the Twenty-first Dynasty the faces of male mummies were often painted red and those of females painted yellow, emulating the colors used for men and women in tomb paintings. Such cosmetic attentions show an intention to make the body resemble a statue. The painted faces, stone eyes, etc., were techniques that had been used for centuries on statues, and were now applied to mummified bodies.

The Late Period

Mummification in the Twenty-first Dynasty was the high point of the art. While cosmetic skills were lavished on the outside of the body in an attempt to achieve a lifelike result, the mummy's internal condition was not overlooked. This concern and craftsmanship continued through the Twenty-second Dynasty, but then declined, during the Late Period, to the point of embalmers creating what have been called "false mummies."

It was rare that anyone other than the embalmers saw what a body looked like just before the final stage of wrapping. Indeed, how would the relatives even know that they were given the correct body? In every era there are conscientious workmen and those who aren't. We can imagine what working in an em-

FIG. 29.   *Mummy of Queen Henettowey, wife of Pinedjem I. To create a lifelike appearance, embalmers packed the area under her skin, but overstuffing caused it to split.*   EGYPTIAN MUSEUM, CAIRO

balming house in ancient Egypt was like. Several bodies would be processed at any time, and mistakes would occur. Body parts would be broken off, then reattached, sometimes carefully, sometimes not, and occasionally lost. Yards and yards of bandages were used to cover such errors.

Such carelessness has been exposed in modern times by X-rays. Roy Moodie's pioneering studies in 1926 at Chicago's Field Museum of Natural History was one of the first to reveal shoddy work. X-rays showed that in order to fit the mummy of a seven-year-old boy named Pedi-Amun into a coffin that was much too small, the embalmers had removed his arms, broken his legs at mid-thigh, and thrown away the lower halves of the legs.[11]

One of the most curious examples of embalmers' skullduggery is that of the Lady Teshat in the Minneapolis Institute of Arts. Although the title "lady" may suggest that she was an adult, Teshat died as a teenager. A CAT scan of her mummy shows that her cadaver was roughly handled, resulting in several broken bones. It also revealed that between her legs lay a second adult skull! No one is sure why it is there, but it is quite possible that the head of another mummy became detached in the embalming house and was temporarily lost. Then, after that mummy was bandaged without its head and returned to the relatives, the head was found; not knowing what to do with an excess head, the embalmers bound it up with Lady Teshat. While a mummy with two heads is unusual, mummies missing body parts are common during the Late Period.

Sir Armand Ruffer, a former president of the Sanitary Council of Egypt, was a physician intrigued by mummies. Flinders Petrie gave him two mummies dating from the Persian period that Ruffer unwrapped in 1911. After describing the wrappings (one bandage was more than eighteen feet long), he discusses the sorry state of the mummies.[12] When a body is mummified it becomes brittle and with rough handling can break. In the case of one of Ruffer's mummies, the embalmers had broken the back and had run a stick through the body to restore its lost rigidity. When this was insufficient, heated gum was poured inside and outside the mummy. When cooled, the resin hardened to obscure the defects in the mummy.

FIG. 30. *X-rays revealed that the mummy of this seven-year-old boy had been crammed into a coffin far too small. Embalmers had discarded the arms and parts of the legs.* FIELD MUSEUM OF NATURAL HISTORY, CHICAGO; NEG. # A-59136

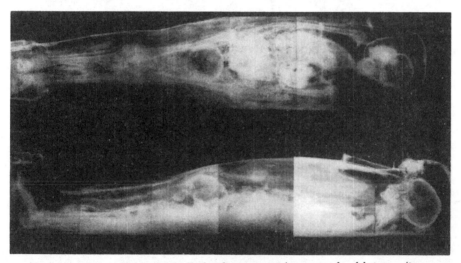

FIG. 31. *The mummy of Lady Teshat has a mysterious extra head between its legs. It may be the work of careless embalmers disposing of a detached head from a different mummy.* MINNEAPOLIS INSTITUTE OF ARTS

The second mummy looked like the first, but the foot bones were found in the abdominal region and the arm bones were where the thighs should have been. The atlas vertebra (so named because it tops the spinal column and supports the head) had been pierced by a stick that went through the foramen magnum and into the skull. So while the wrappings indicated a whole body, inside lay a disarticulated pile of bones. This is not an unusual situation.[13]

FIG. 32.
This mummy of the Saite period (664–525 B.C.), while badly decayed, shows an early attempt at the intricate crisscross bandaging technique that would be perfected during the Greco-Roman period. MUSEUM OF FINE ARTS, BOSTON

Another mummy of the Persian Period, this one discovered by Dr. Zaky Saad at Saqqara, betrayed a unique embalming procedure.[14] The nobleman, Amentefnakht, was mummified inside his sarcophagus. When the tomb was discovered in 1941, it contained a huge granite sarcophagus housing a smaller one inside. The lid of the inner sarcophagus was still sealed with plaster. When the lid was opened, an unwrapped mummy was found lying on its back in an inch of a brown liquid covering the bottom of the sarcophagus. The mummy's bottom half was in far better condition than its uppermost side, and when the brown liquid was analyzed the reason became apparent: Amentefnakht had been embalmed in his sarcophagus.

Apparently a bed of natron had been made in the bottom of the sarcophagus, Amentefnakht placed upon it, and then the sarcophagus sealed. As bodily fluids seeped out of Amentefnakht, the bottom of the mummy came in contact with the natron, now in solution, which penetrated the wrappings. The top of the mummy would be the last to come in contact with the natron; thus it was exposed to bacteria longest. Because the sarcophagus had been sealed with plaster, the brown liquid, a combination of natron and body fluids, could not evaporate.

This burial may suggest that by the time of the Persian period the basic principles and understanding of mummification had been lost. To wrap the body first and *then* place it on a bed of natron is more ritualistic than practical. Or, perhaps, no one really cared what happened to Amentefnakht. While the conditions of bodies within their wrappings deteriorated during the Late Period, the technique of bandaging improved. During the Greco-Roman period it rose to became an art form.

Greek Mummies

The Greeks had long revered the Egyptians, claiming that they learned how to build from them, derived their gods from them, and learned mathematics and law from them. Thus, when Alexander conquered Egypt in 332 B.C., he had no intention of imposing his culture on "barbarians." Instead, he went directly to the oracle of Amun at Siwa where he was declared the son of the sun, so he could be proclaimed pharaoh. When Alexander died in 323 B.C., his general, Ptolemy, seized control of Egypt and founded the Greek Ptolemaic Dynasty that ruled Egypt for nearly three centuries.

The Greek fascination with mummification was curious, since they practiced cremation and forbade any cutting of the human body. Indeed, so strict was the prohibition against dissection that Greek physicians frequently mentioned that they wished they could have studied at the Alexandria medical school, where dissection was permitted. Only Egyptian physicians had an intimate knowledge of anatomy.

Under the Greeks, bandages were for the first time woven in quantity specifically for use in mummification. Instead of being ripped from old bed linens, bandages were now woven with both edges finished and of uniform width. This enabled wrappers to create intricate geometric patterns as they wrapped the mummies, producing almost an illusion of depth with small squares within squares.

During the Ptolemaic period the Greeks ran Egypt much like a business, placing troops throughout the country to keep order and instituting oppressive taxes. There was no longer the possibility of a large leisure class of priests. With the reduced number of priests and the introduction of the Greek language, the number of Egyptians who could read hieroglyphs dwindled. By the time of the Roman occupation, there were few priests alive who could read the inscriptions on the temple walls that told of the glory of Egypt.

When the Romans took control of Egypt after the defeat of Cleopatra VII and Marc Antony at Actium, they continued the practice of mummification until it was banned by Theodosius II in A.D. 392. The contribution the Romans made to mummification was a realistic portrait of the deceased bound over the face of the mummy. These portraits evolved from the Egyptian practice of encasing the head in a lifelike cartonage mummy mask. Often made from discarded papyri glued together and molded, much like children today make papier maché puppets, these cartonage masks were plastered white and then painted. The papyrus sheets from which they were made are often more valuable for the information on them than for the masks them-selves, and Egyptologists frequently take them apart to read the contents of the papyri. Such highly stylized masks were not true portraits, so the realistic ones added by the Romans are a true innovation; they are in fact considered by many to be the world's first portraits.

Most of these portraits have been found in the area of Egypt known as the Fayoum and thus are called 'Fayoum portraits.' Most date from the first two centuries A.D. The first careful ex-cavations of sites containing these portraits were conducted in 1888 at Hawara by the indefatigable Flinders Petrie. He found almost all of the portraits painted on rectangular cedar or cy-press boards over a layer of white gesso. The best of the por-traits were done in an encaustic technique, mixing pigments with beeswax and applying them with brush and spatula.

While these portraits were intended for binding over the head of a mummy, most were probably commissioned during the life of the subject, so that the artist could produce a good likeness. Then they were framed and displayed in the household, to be enjoyed until the inevitable day when they would be used on the mummy. Most of the portraits show evidence of having been trimmed at the top corners, indicating that they were orig-inally painted on rectangles and later cropped to fit into the bandages. This is proved by one case where the portrait, still in its frame, was buried next to the mummy rather than over its face.

Several bandaging techniques were employed during the Ro-man period, but the most elaborate style is one in which band-ages were crisscrossed diagonally to form numerous squares. At times the procedure began by placing small gold squares on the mummy so that one would see gold at the center of each square, giving the impression that the mummy was entirely covered with gold. Sometimes there were as many as thirteen layers of bandages, giving each square considerable depth.[15] Of-ten to reduce expenses, a stucco yellow button replaced the gold square in the center.

Although these elaborate wrappings of the Roman period are spectacular, they too often concealed the carelessness of em-balmers. A possible mummy error in the National Cultural His-

FIG. 33.   *Photograph by Sir Flinders Petrie of an early find of a Roman-period mummy with its portrait. Petrie's tent is in the background.*   COURTESY PETRIE MUSEUM OF EGYPTIAN ARCHAEOLOGY, UNIVERSITY COLLEGE, LONDON

FIG. 34.   *Elaborately wrapped mummy of the Greco-Roman period.*   METROPOLITAN MUSEUM OF ART

tory Museum in Pretoria, South Africa, was reported by David Thompson.[16] The portrait shows a young man with a beard and mustache, but Thompson says that X-rays of the mummy revealed it to be a female! One wonders how and where the switch took place. Perhaps two mummies were being wrapped at the same time, and the portraits for the two were switched when attached to the bodies. Somewhere, in some museum collection, there may be a male mummy with a female portrait.[17]

Not every embalmer lacked a conscience, or performed his work poorly. Cases are known where embalmers carefully fashioned artificial limbs to replace ones lost either during life or at the embalmer's shop. A mummy from the Late Period in the Gulbenkian Museum of Oriental Art in Durham, England, of a fifty-five-year-old man whose left hand was severed above the wrist during his lifetime, is fitted with an artificial linen hand modeled to simulate fingers and thumb.[18]

The mummies we have discussed so far—nobles, princesses, high priests, etc.—were, for the most part, the upper class of ancient Egypt. For the lower classes embalming was rudimentary, if practiced at all. The poor farmer, who comprised most of the population of Egypt, often was wrapped in a sheet and placed with a few belongings in a sand-pit grave. Such burials provide little help in reconstructing ancient mummification techniques.

While the mummies of the upper class provided many details, I intended my modern mummification of a human to imitate the embalmers' art at its highest point. What I really needed was the bodies of the kings of Egypt, where no expense whatsoever would have been spared.

4
The Royal Mummies

The Deir el Bahri Cache

Not a single pharaoh's mummy had been discovered through most of the nineteenth century despite one hundred years of assiduous searching. All the pyramids had been robbed long before, all the royal tombs had been thoroughly looted—at least as far as anyone knew, or was saying. Yet someone was not saying, because in the 1870s spectacular objects once belonging to pharaohs began to appear on the antiquities market, harbingers of a great royal find.

Auguste Mariette, the director of the Egyptian Antiquities Service, had purchased a copy of the *Book of the Dead* belonging to Henettowey, a queen of the Twenty-first Dynasty. The book Mariette purchased was in remarkable condition; the colors of the vignettes accompanying the spells to assure resurrection remained vibrant and bright, suggesting that the book had been found recently. During the next few years other royal copies of the *Book of the Dead* appeared on the market, all from kings, queens, princes, and princesses of the family of Queen Henettowey. In addition to these papyri, beautiful jewelry also surfaced, and it became clear to Mariette that an intact royal tomb of the Twenty-first Dynasty had been discovered and its contents were being sold piecemeal. Mariette was determined to find the tomb before everything was sold or destroyed, but he died in 1881 before he could complete this search. His successor, Gaston Maspero, made this his top priority.

Maspero arrived in Luxor on April 3, 1881, determined to find the tomb. He enlisted the help of his former student, Charles Edwin Wilbour. Wilbour was an American businessman and politician who had become an expatriate, discovered Egyptology, and devoted his life to it. He studied in Paris under Maspero and became one of the most dedicated recorders of texts, although he never published. He was in Luxor for his first winter in Egypt when Maspero came to find the tomb.

Wilbour's passion was collecting antiquities, and many of his purchases now reside in the Brooklyn Museum. Maspero asked him to keep his ears open, and Wilbour soon heard rumors that the Abd er Rassoul family was plundering some new tomb. This family lived in Gourna, the village adjoining the Valley of the Kings. For generations its inhabitants had followed the vocation of robbing tombs, and now it appeared as if they had made their greatest find. Wilbour had been offered the outer leather straps that encircled the mummy of King Pinedjem I. In a letter to his wife dated March 8, 1881, he says:

> *Did I tell you about the curious pair of red Morocco suspenders shown me in Goornah with cartouches of Pi-nodjem I of the Twenty-first Dynasty. They are so fresh that the mummy must have been opened lately and I am going to try to find the tomb, now unknown, except for the fellahs who found it.*[1]

One month later he believed he had learned the location of Pinedjem's tomb.

> *Tuesday I found out that our quiet Mr. Campbell of Islay, who has published four volumes of Scotch Folk Stories in Gaelic and English and who went away ten days ago, on a previous visit to Luxor, bought of Moustapha the Book of the Dead papyrus of Pharaoh Pi-nezem I and that Abd-er Rasool's new white house is said to be built over the King's Tomb to hide it.*[2]

Wilbour was quite wrong.

With Maspero in Luxor, the Abd er Rassoul family was undoubtedly nervous. They knew that the "Grand Moudir of Antikas" had come to find their tomb and take away a fortune in antiquities that the entire village of Gourna viewed as its heritage. Maspero sent for Ahmed Abd er Rassoul, who denied everything. When his white house was searched, only a few worthless antiquities were found.

Maspero sent two of the Rassoul brothers, Ahmed and Hussein, to Qena for questioning by Daud Pasha, who was feared by all the fellaheen (peasant farmers). He was a thorough interrogator—one of the Rassouls limped for the rest of his life—but neither brother confessed. By this time Maspero had to leave for France, but the Rassouls knew this would not be the end of the questioning, and Muhammed, the oldest brother, went to Daud Pasha and told him that he knew where the tomb was and that it contained forty mummies. Daud sent word to the museum in Boulaq (the Egyptian Museum in Cairo had not yet been built) and Émile Brugsch, Maspero's assistant, came immediately to Qena.

Daud Pasha presented Brugsch with three beautiful copies of the *Book of the Dead*. Daud had reasoned that the Abd er Rassouls would make one last trip to the tomb before revealing its location and found the papyri when he searched the white house for a second time. Two days later, Brugsch was being led by the Rassouls along an elevated, winding path overlooking the Valley of the Kings.

The path wound through the area known as Deir el Bahri. As Brugsch, his two assistants, and the Abd er Rassouls walked, they must have had quite different thoughts. The Rassouls must have mourned what they were about to lose and Brugsch and his party could only imagine what they would discover. Chimney-like outcroppings of rock lined the way, and the Rassouls stopped at the base of one of these. There a shaft eight feet by ten feet descended forty feet. Muhammed placed a palm log across the opening and let himself down by a rope so he could clear away the sand blocking the small entrance at the bottom. Then Brugsch was lowered down. When he squeezed through the entrance, the first thing he saw was the huge coffin of Nebseny, a priest of the Twenty-first Dynasty. Behind were three more coffins, and past these, on the right, ran a corridor more than seventy feet long. Littering the floor were bright blue faience *ushabtis*—servant statues for the next world. Along with these were faience cups, canopic jars and chests, and other equipment an Egyptian needed for the next world.

At the corridor's end stood a room seventeen feet square. Almost every foot of space was covered with splendid coffins containing kings of the New Kingdom. Here lay Amenhotep I, Tuthmose I, Tuthmose II, and Tuthmose III of the Eighteenth Dynasty, along with the Nineteenth Dynasty pharaohs Ramses I, his son, Seti I, and *his* son, Ramses II. It was more than Brugsch could have ever expected.

Farther back in the tomb was another room, much higher than the others and twenty feet long. It was here that the search came to an end; Brugsch had found the Twenty-first Dynasty royal family whose *Book of the Dead* copies had initiated the quest. Here were the mummies of Pinedjem I and Pinedjem II, Queen Henettowey, and others of this family of priest-kings. Still, there remained the puzzle of how kings of different dynasties came to be together in one tomb.

As mentioned in the previous chapter, toward the end of the Twentieth Dynasty the power of the pharaoh weakened while a series of kings named Ramses lost their grasp on the throne. Finally, at the end of the dynasty, the high priest of Amun, Hri-Hor, wrote his name in a cartouche and declared himself king. The descendants of Hri-Hor, also priests, were the rulers of Thebes and now formed the Twenty-first dynasty. Ruling from Tanis in the Delta was another concurrent Twenty-first Dynasty, which controlled the north. With the loss of power of the kingship, guarding the Valley of the Kings became more difficult. Even before the Twenty-first Dynasty, some of the royal tombs had been broken into and robbed. An inspection of the Valley of the Kings during the Twenty-first Dynasty revealed that nearly all the tombs of the kings had been violated. Now, rather than attempting to protect isolated tombs, the bodies of the pharaohs were rewrapped, labeled with dockets, placed in new coffins when necessary, and removed to other tombs in the Valley deemed safe. Graffiti written in black ink on the walls of the original tombs and records on the pharaohs' coffins and bandages detailed the dates and places of transit. Combining these records made it possible to reconstruct the steps these pious priests of the Twenty-first Dynasty took to preserve their ancestors. The inscriptions recording the last movements are at the bottom of the shaft leading to the entrance to the Deir el Bahri tomb.

One inscription records that on the twentieth day of the fourth month of winter, during the tenth year of the king's reign, the deceased high priest of Amun-Re, Pinedjem I, was buried. The names of the committee that interred Pinedjem are listed and include Nespekeshuty, the mayor of Thebes, Pedia-mun, son of Enkhefenkhons (who had the titles of Divine Father of Amun and Overseer of Secrets), and other officials. Additional records showed that attempts to protect the bodies of the pharaohs began even before the start of the dynasty. On the coffin of Seti I (underneath Seti's cartouche, which was added later), is an inscription of the high priest Hri-Hor stating that he restored the mummy. The same inscription appears on the coffin of Ramses II, and was probably once on the damaged coffin of Ramses I. But it was not Hri-Hor who placed these mummies in the Deir el Bahri cache. We know, for example, that the mummies of Ramses I and Ramses II—Seti's father and son—were placed first in Seti's tomb for safekeeping long before being carried to Deir el Bahri.

As the years passed, the damaged mummies of the greatest kings of Egypt were gathered by the priests and placed in the high tomb at Deir el Bahri. The cache was considered secure enough that the priest-king Pinedjem II chose it for his own resting place. On his burial day, the bodies of Seti I and Ramses II were interred with him, and there they remained, undisturbed, for 3,000 years.

Ironically, as important and unique as the discovery was, the findings were poorly documented. After two hours in the tomb, Brugsch realized that their candles might set fire to the dry wood coffins, and quickly left the tomb. He then decided that the mummies and other equipment had to be moved to Cairo as quickly as possible. The inhabitants of Gourna had for years made their living by robbing tombs, and when the magnitude of what was to be lost to them became public, there was no telling what they would do. In six days all the coffins, canopic chests, and funerary equipment were hoisted to the surface, and it took 300 men to carry the finds to the west bank of the Nile. There was no time to record where each coffin was found in the tomb, and not a single photograph was taken or drawing made of items *in situ*.

The coffins were wrapped and ferried to the east bank, where they were loaded on the museum's steamer for their journey to Cairo. The boat left Luxor on June 15, and when word of its royal cargo became public, fellaheen women lined the banks of the Nile and wailed mourning cries, just as their remote ancestors must have marked the passing of the pharaohs.

The mummies and coffins arrived safely at the Egyptian Museum in Boulaq. Brugsch unwrapped only one of the mummies, that of Tuthmose III, the greatest of the warrior pharaohs. The mummy had been buried in the Valley of the Kings, plundered, rewrapped by Twenty-first Dynasty embalmers, and reburied in the Deir el Bahri tomb, where it suffered one final indignity at the hands of the Rassouls. They had hacked a hole in the wrappings in the area of the heart, looking for a heart scarab, a highly saleable antiquity. These large, beetle-shaped amulets were placed over the heart to assure that it would not desert the deceased. The Rassouls must have thought such a finely wrapped mummy would have a heart scarab of precious silver or gold. What they did not realize is that the mummy had already been robbed three thousand years earlier, and if there ever had been such an amulet it would have been taken then.

When Brugsch unwrapped this Egyptian king, he and his colleagues became the first in modern times to see the mummy of one of the greatest pharaohs of ancient Egypt. What they saw was shocking. The king's body was in a horrible state. The head was separated from the body, the legs and arms disarticulated, and the feet broken off at the ankles. Brugsch performed a crude, quick autopsy that yielded little information and did not continue with the other mummies, perhaps fearful that he would find them in a similar sad condition.

In an attempt to sort out who was who, for the next five years Maspero concerned himself not with the bodies of the pharaohs, but with the labels attached to them and the writings on their wrappings and coffins. During their hasty reburial many of the pharaohs had been transferred to coffins that were not origi-

FIG. 35.
*1882 sketch of the
removal of the Deir el
Bahri cache.*

FIG. 36.
Gaston Maspero
(reclining) *with the
Rassouls* (standing, left)
*at the site of the Deir el
Bahri cache. When the
cache was discovered,
Maspero was in Paris; he
visited the site only after
the mummies had been
removed.* PHOTOGRAPH
COURTESY DAVID MOYER

FIG. 37.   *Mummy of Tuthmose III as unwrapped by Émile Brugsch at the Boulaq museum.*   PHOTOGRAPH COURTESY DENNIS FORBES

nally made for them, so it was not always obvious which pharaoh lay in which coffin. Even today the identity of some mummies in the Deir el Bahri cache is debated. For example, recent research suggests that the mummy normally considered to be Seti II of the Nineteenth Dynasty may in fact be Tuthmose II of the Eighteenth.

The Deir el Bahri cache supplied the museum with its first royal mummies; it seemed like a once-in-a-lifetime find, but it was not. Seventeen years later another cache of royal mummies was discovered, this time in the Valley of the Kings itself.

The Amenhotep II Cache

Maspero resigned as director of the Antiquities Service in 1896 and was succeeded by a series of his former students. In

1898 Victor Loret, the new director, undertook the first comprehensive survey of the Valley of the Kings. Among his many discoveries was the tomb of Tuthmose III and that of his son, Amenhotep II.

When the entrance to the tomb of Amenhotep II was cleared of the rubble blocking it, it became obvious that this was a plundered tomb. Broken bits of blue faience and wooden funerary objects with Amenhotep II's name littered the entrance passage. Loret was still excited about what he might find, however, because the body of Amenhotep II had not been among those at Deir el Bahri. After crawling through the passageway, Loret came to a square shaft, or "well," designed to catch water so that the burial chamber would remain dry during the rare cloudbursts that occurred in the Valley of the Kings. This feature is typical of New Kingdom tombs and supported Loret's theory that the tomb was that of Amenhotep II.

Loret placed a ladder across the well and crossed into a square-pillared antechamber. It was now late into the night, Loret was tired, and with only his candle to illuminate the scene, his imagination started to take over. He saw broken funerary boats, models of what the pharaoh would need in the next world, gilded images of the king, and bits of *ushabti* servant statues. Then the candle light fell on something for which he was not prepared.

> *I went forward [between the two columns] with my candle and, horrible sight, a body lay there upon the boat, all black and hideous, its grimacing face turning towards me and looking at me, its long brown hair in sparse bunches around its head. I did not dream for an instant that this was just an unwrapped mummy. The legs and arms seemed to be bound. A hole exposing the sternum, there was an opening in the skull. Was this a victim of human sacrifice? Was this a thief murdered by his accomplices in a bloody division of the loot, or perhaps killed by soldiers or police interrupting the pillaging of the tomb?*[3]

What Loret had seen was the mummy of a prince, disturbed so soon after his burial that the oils and resins used in embalming were still liquid. The robbers had placed the body in one of the model boats, where the oils solidified and glued the mummy into it.

Regaining his composure, Loret continued his descent, eventually arriving at a burial chamber that contained a lidless stone sarcophagus. Peering over the top, Loret saw a coffin with a garland of flowers at its head and a wreath at its foot. The mummy of Amenhotep II had been found.

Loret's long evening was not yet over; another shock waited. He began examining the four side chambers off the burial chamber. These small rooms contained statues of the pharaoh, vases for the seven sacred oils that the pharaoh would need, meat and fruits to sustain him in the next world, and wooden models of boats so he could journey there. It was in one of these chambers that Loret received his next shock:

> We passed to the rooms to the right. In the first one we entered an unusually strange sight met our eyes: three bodies lay side by side at the back in the left corner, their feet pointing towards the door. The right half of the room was filled with little coffins with mummiform covers and funerary statues of bitumined [resin-painted] wood. These statues were contained in the coffins that the thieves had opened and rejected after having searched in vain for treasures.
>
> We approached the cadavers. The first seemed to be that of a woman. A thick veil covered her forehead and left eye. Her broken arm had been replaced at her side, her nails in the air. Ragged and torn cloth hardly covered her body. Abundant black curled hair spread over the limestone floor on each side of her head. The face was admirably conserved and had a noble and majestic gravity.
>
> The second mummy, in the middle, was that of a child of about fifteen years. It was naked with the hands joined on the abdomen. First of all the head appeared totally bald, but on closer examination one saw that the head had been shaved except an area on the right temple from which grew a magnificent tress of black hair. This was the coiffure of the royal princes [called the Horus lock]. I thought immediately of the royal prince Webensennu, this so far unknown son of Ameno-

phis II, whose funerary statue I had noticed in the great hall, and whose canopic fragments I was to find later. The face of the young prince was laughing and mischievous, it did not at all evoke the idea of death.

The last corpse nearest the wall seemed to be that of a man. His head was shaved but a wig lay on the ground not far from him. The face of this person displayed something horrible and something droll at the same time. The mouth was running obliquely from one side nearly to the middle of the cheek, bit a pad of linen whose two ends hung from the corner of the lips. The half-closed eyes had a strange expression, he could have died choking on a gag but he looked like a young playful cat with a piece of cloth. Death which had respected the severe beauty of the woman and the impish grace of the boy had turned in derision and amused itself with the countenance of the man.

A remarkable fact was that the three corpses, like the one in the boat, had their skulls pierced with a large hole and the breast of each one was opened.[4]

The similar condition of the three mummies in the side chamber and the one in the boat was caused by methodical tomb robbers. In their search for jewelry, they had hacked at the wrappings on the heads first. After quickly stripping the outer linen, they then hacked at the chest searching for the heart scarab, thus causing the damage to the royal bodies.

Loret had no clear idea of the identities of the four mummies, and his judgment was certainly confused that night. The naked body he described as a man is clearly that of a young woman. To this day the identities of three of these bodies remain uncertain. The one sure identification was made almost a century later and required both modern technology and a lucky find in Tutankhamen's tomb; this bit of detective work will be discussed in the chapter "Missing Mummies." The four mummies that so moved Loret were not the only ones he found that night.

One of the side chambers had been sealed with limestone blocks, with only a small opening near the ceiling. Loret climbed to the top and with his candle was barely able to make out nine coffins, neatly arranged—six against the wall and three

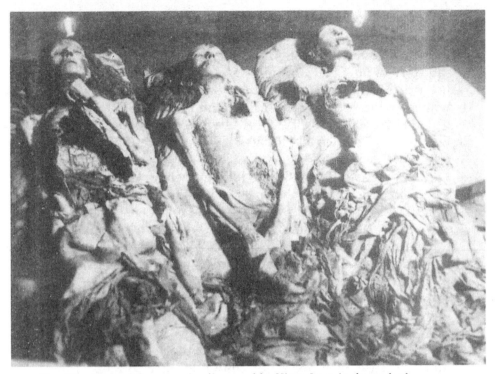

FIG. 38. *Three of the mummies discovered by Victor Loret in the tomb of Amenhotep II. Three quarters of a century after their discovery, the one on the left was identified as Queen Tiye, wife of Amenhotep III.* PHOTOGRAPH COURTESY DENNIS FORBES

in front of them. That was all he could see, and he realized that the wall would have to be taken down before the coffins could be studied. But first the tomb had to be cleared.

Unlike the Deir el Bahri cache, the tomb of Amenhotep II was cleared carefully and all the find spots recorded. Loret mapped the tomb, superimposing a grid to record the positions of more than 2,000 objects. Only after all this was he finally able to examine the nine coffins behind the wall. He saw then that he had discovered the mummies of Tuthmoses IV, Amenhotep III, Merenptah, Siptah, Seti II, Ramses IV, Ramses V, Ramses VI, and an unidentified woman. These were the pharaohs missing from the Deir el Bahri cache. Now most of the pharaohs of the Eighteenth through Twentieth dynasties had been found.

Just as at Deir el Bahri, these mummies had been gathered together by a Twenty-first Dynasty king to protect them from further desecration. Written on the mummy of Seti II was the sad story of how the convention of kings in the tomb of Amenhotep II came to be. On the sixth day of the fourth month of winter, in the twelfth year of the reign of Pinedjem I, that king had the despoiled royal bodies rewrapped and placed in the tomb of Amenhotep II for safekeeping, where they remained until Loret's discovery.

Loret prepared the mummies for shipment to Cairo—but, just before loading them on the boat, he received an order from the Ministry of Public Works to replace the mummies in the tomb and seal it. Again politics had superceded archaeology. Many Egyptians viewed archaeologists as foreigners robbing their heritage. They believed their kings should lie undisturbed where they were found. It would be years before these pharaohs would rest with their ancestors and descendants in the Egyptian Museum, and then only nine of the ten made the trip.

It was eventually decided that the nine mummies found in the side chamber could be sent to Cairo to join the Deir el Bahri cache because they were not found in their original burial places. The mummy of Amenhotep II would remain where it was found, in its sarcophagus. Howard Carter, as Inspector of Antiquities, was given the job of arranging the mummy so tourists could see it easily. As an added attraction, the three mummies that so startled Loret, as well as the poor prince stuck in the model boat, were to be left where they had been found, making the tomb more a house of horrors than an archeological site.

Maspero had been out of the country when the Deir el Bahri cache was moved to Cairo, but he was in Egypt when the decision about the mummies from Amenhotep II's tomb was made, and he had no intention of missing this royal transfer. Indeed, Maspero was so taken with the event that he orchestrated it to recreate an ancient funeral procession, but in reverse, going from the tomb to the Nile. In his romantic account of the event, he describes how the ancient route was followed and how he lined up the workmen to form a procession with an overseer in charge. The overseer Maspero chose was a Copt named Baskharoun, who had worked in the museum—first at Boulaq and then at Cairo—for twenty-five years. It was important to Maspero that he was a Copt because they are the descendants of the ancient Egyptians. They alone had not intermarried with the Arabs who entered Egypt with the rise of Islam, so old Baskharoun looked like an ancient Egyptian, and Maspero noted this. "Take off his blue shirt, his turban, his full trousers, and his red babouches, and dress him in the striped waist-cloth, the close-fitting cap, the rush sandals, and you will obtain an Egyptian of the best period, one of those, if you like, who helped seal up Amenothes in his vault."[5]

One hundred people formed the procession; Maspero supplied water-carriers and even carpenters in case of an accident that required repairs. The men carried the heavy coffins in relays over the five miles to the Nile, where Maspero's dahabieh, the *Miriam*, was anchored. When the coffins reached the banks of the Nile at 4:00 P.M., an event occurred that Maspero could never have orchestrated but that must have pleased him considerably. The *Miriam* was anchored in the middle of the Nile; as one of the men entered the launch with a coffin, he slipped and the coffin fell, upsetting the rowers and other bearers. But the coffin was stopped just before it hit the water, averting a tragedy. A similar scene is depicted on a tomb wall Maspero had seen: it shows the captain in a launch that is upset when it's hit by a funerary bark's rudder. Maspero comments that what he had just witnessed ". . . is the exact scene that the ancient artist had drawn three thousand years before."[6] Maspero must have been a very happy man as he sailed with his royal cargo downstream to Cairo.

Tomb 55

The next royal mummies would be discovered one at a time. Of all the royal bodies unearthed, none caused more excitement and controversy than the one found in Tomb 55 of the Valley of the Kings by Theodore Davis.

Davis, a wealthy American businessman from Rhode Island, held the exclusive concession to excavate in the Valley of the Kings in the early 1900s. With no training in archeology, Davis relied on "assistants" to conduct his excavations, and found his greatest pleasure not from his discoveries, but in the lavish publications about them, for which he paid. In 1907 Davis was assisted by Edward Ayrton, a young man who had worked with Petrie.

Davis and Ayrton were searching the Valley of the Kings systematically when they discovered a tomb near that of Ramses IX. All tombs in the Valley of the Kings are numbered, and this one received the new number 55; it is formally known as KV 55. Before they reached the actual tomb, they uncovered a group of pots buried in a pile of limestone chips. Clearing the area to ground level, they found the beginning of a flight of steps cut into the bedrock. When this was cleared they came to a doorway covered with more limestone chips. (The Valley of the Kings is littered with millions of such flakes, which the ancient workmen chipped out of the cliffs to create the royal tombs.) Behind the doorway, a second set of steps descended into the tomb, at the bottom of which stood a dry wall built of large limestone flakes. The wall had obviously been constructed to reseal a tomb that had been opened in ancient times.

The crowd gathered for the opening of the tomb included Gaston Maspero, Arthur Weigall, the Inspector of Antiquities for Upper Egypt, and Howard Carter, who was then inspector for Saqqara. Also present was Joseph Lindon Smith, an artist who had worked for several Egyptologists, and his wife Corinna. Nearly all of those present have left accounts of what happened on that clear January day in 1907. No two of these accounts agree.

What is clear is that when the blocking wall was taken down a typical Eighteenth Dynasty descending corridor was revealed, nearly but not quite filled to the ceiling with limestone chips. To deter tomb robbers, the descending passageway to a burial chamber was often filled completely with chips. The fact that a space remained near the ceiling suggested that this was a plundered tomb.

First to enter the tomb was Joseph Lindon Smith, whom Maspero selected for this honor because of his slight build and ability to squeeze through the narrow passage. On top of the chips rested a large gilded wooden door. Smith drew a quick sketch of the inscriptions he could see and showed it to Maspero, who read the name of Queen Tiye, wife of Amenhotep III and mother of the heretic pharaoh Akhenaten. The panel was in such fragile condition that the gentle breeze that entered the tomb for the first time in 3,000 years caused the gold leaf to flake off and fall to the ground. The panel could not be moved. A wooden plank was placed next to it, over which Smith carefully crept downward into the tomb. The tomb was clearly unfinished. What had once served as the burial chamber was an unpainted, roughly hewn room about eighteen feet square. More wooden panels lay on the floor and against a wall. In a niche cut in one wall, Smith could see four beautiful alabaster canopic jars with finely sculpted lids in the form of a woman's head. What drew Smith's attention among the jumble was a badly damaged but beautiful coffin lying with its lid ajar near one wall. The coffin, like the rest of the contents of the room, had suffered water damage from rain dripping through a crack in the ceiling. The coffin had once rested on a wooden funerary bier that had collapsed, causing even more damage to the coffin and knocking off its lid. The final indignity occurred when a rock fell onto it from the ceiling.

The coffin was of the type known as "*rishi*," which is Arabic for "feathered." Thousands of inlays of paste and semiprecious stones formed the protective wings of a falcon encircling the coffin. Even more impressive than the coffin itself was the fact that inside it lay a body—obviously undisturbed, since on its head remained a golden vulture, symbol of the pharaoh's power.

No one recorded how long Smith remained in the tomb, but it must have seemed forever to the group waiting outside for his report. When he finally emerged, he described things as best he could. Maspero asked a few questions and sent him back to look for water damage and to sketch the objects. Smith sketched the coffin, then returned to make a second report. Everyone was impatient to enter the tomb but had to wait for workmen to clear the passageway and put down more boards to accommodate Maspero's girth.

Davis's butler was sent to bring a picnic from the dahabieh. Over lunch the group discussed the discovery. Davis was de-

lighted because he was convinced they had discovered the tomb
and body of Queen Tiye. After lunch they were able, at last, to
enter the tomb, and Davis became even more certain that he
had found a great queen of Egypt.

Because the wooden panels were too fragile to be moved, one
of them was drawn by an artist. All but two have since disintegrated, but from what was observed in the tomb in 1907 it
was clear that the panels were the remains of a gilded shrine
that had once enclosed the coffin of Queen Tiye. In size, this
shrine was similar to the middle of the three enclosing Tutankhamen's coffin. Tiye's shrine was apparently made for her by her
son, Akhenaten, for it depicted him with his mother worship-
ping the Aten, the solar disc. Some time after the burial, someone had entered the tomb and hacked out Akhenaten's image
from the shrine, but left the figure of Tiye untouched.

Adding support to Davis's theory that the body in the coffin
was Tiye's were the four canopic jars with female heads as lids.
Davis was ecstatic, although Maspero remained cautious, mov-
ing about the tomb carefully, looking at each object in turn.
According to Joseph Linden Smith's account,

> Maspero studied inscriptions on a number of small objects that
> bore the name of Amenhotep III and of his wife, Queen Tiyi,
> and said with conviction that the tray of cosmetics, boxes,
> tools, and offerings in enameled stone or glazed pottery were
> tomb furnishings belonging to the Queen. At this information
> Davis tried to get Maspero to identify the tomb positively as
> Queen Tiyi's, with her mummy in the coffin. But Maspero re-
> fused to commit himself; he declared it was unquestionably a
> "reburial" and conclusions should be "cautious." . . .
>
> Ayrton, on his hands and knees in the vicinity of the coffin,
> found a gold-covered long boarding with lions' heads at both
> ends. This was confirmatory evidence that a raised couch had
> originally supported the coffin. The one canopic jar visible in
> the alcove niche had a head with a face like Queen Tiyi's as
> seen in the panel figure, and Davis was thrilled. He kept mur-
> muring ecstatically, "We've got Queen Tiyi."
>
> When Weigall submitted it as his opinion that, from the text
> on the coffin lid, the mummy was Akhenaten himself, Maspero

frowned. He said he saw indications that certain parts of some of the inscriptions on the lid had been replaced by other words on patches of gold foil, which was puzzling, and several cartouches had been cut out deliberately. He said there was nothing inconsistent in finding the son's name in his mother's tomb, and that the furniture in the tomb unquestionably belonged to at least two persons. And he kept reiterating that the evidence would continue to be "conflicting and confusing and hasty conclusions are to be avoided." He added: "I believe in the end the identity of the owner of the coffin may prove to be a surprise." [7]

Everyone believed that the identity of the occupant of the coffin in Tomb 55 would be settled once the body and any inscriptions the bandages or jewelry contained could be examined, but Maspero realized that this would have to wait. The fragile condition of the lid, which was ajar but still on top of the coffin, meant that the skilled hands of a conservator were required to remove it. Also, everything had to be photographed *in situ* before anything could be moved from the tomb. Several days passed before a conservator and photographer arrived from Cairo. In the meantime the identity of the body was hotly debated, with Davis convinced it was Queen Tiye and Weigall convinced it was Akhenaten himself.

When the day of the unwrapping of the mummy finally arrived, those present had a sense of the event's historical importance. They would be the first persons in more than 3,000 years to look at the face of this famous queen, or king, of Egypt. Present at the unwrapping were Maspero, Weigall, Ayrton, Joseph Lindon Smith and his wife Corinna, Theodore Davis, and Davis's mistress, Mrs. Anderson. Also present was Harold Jones, an artist who worked for Davis, and Arthur Quibell of the Antiquities Service, who arrived later. After the group entered the tomb and gathered solemnly around the coffin, the lid of which had been removed by the conservator, Maspero asked Joseph Linden Smith to do the unwrapping because he had ". . . the gentle hands of an artist."

Smith first removed the gold sheets covering the mummy from neck to feet. They were each the size of a piece of typing paper, and thick enough that they did not bend as he removed them. The body had been encased in gold, probably as a ritual preservative. Smith soon discovered that, unfortunately, the preservative didn't work.

As Smith removed each sheet of gold he handed it to Maspero for inspection, and Maspero pronounced each of the twelve "uninscribed." The gold sheets now removed, the mummy was exposed. The left arm lay across the breast and the right along the side, a pose normally reserved for royal women. Davis was ecstatic with this evidence supporting his Queen Tiye theory. Also visible were three gold bracelets on each wrist. Maspero asked Smith to feel under the wrappings in the area of the neck and upper chest for the pectoral that should have been there. When Smith delicately began the procedure, they were confronted by a scene like something from the end of a horror film.

> But no sooner had my hand touched the surface of the mummy than it crumbled into ashes and sifted down through bones. So it was with the entire body until nothing remained except a pile of dust and disconnected bones with a few shreds of dried skin adhering to them. The water that had got into the tomb explained the cloth resembling the consistency of the ash of a cigar. In feeling around I found pieces of a broad necklace of gold pendants, inlaid plaques, lotus flowers of gold, and numerous minute beads.[8]

Smith next felt something hard under the small of the mummy's back. When Maspero asked him to remove it, it proved to be another gold sheet. For the first time Maspero became excited, peering intently at the sheet. Unlike the others, this one was inscribed with a cartouche; though it had been obliterated at some later date, Maspero thought he could see the remnants of the name Akhenaten. Now there was evidence for Weigall's Akhenaten theory.

The bones were now exposed, but none present had the expertise to determine if they were those of a male or female. Quibell, who had just joined the group, suggested that there might be a physician who could help among the tourists visiting the area. All agreed to this idea, and Quibell left, eventually to return with Dr. Pollock, a local doctor, along with a "prominent American obstetrician" whose identity has been lost to history. The results of their examination in Tomb 55 was described in a letter Davis later wrote.

> *In the presence of the doctor and surgeon, Mr. Ayrton and one or two other persons, the mummy was opened and the bones exposed. In fact the mummy had absorbed so much dampness that it could not be unwrapped, but it yielded to the touch and disintegrated to such an extent that there was no difficulty in exposing the bones from end to end. The pelvis was admitted to be the criterion of sex. Both the doctor and surgeon instantly agreed that it was the pelvis of a woman. The surgeon made the most thorough examination and explained to us why it was a woman's pelvis and what the difference was between a male and female pelvis.*[9]

Davis's Queen Tiye theory had won, at least for the moment.

The bones in the coffin were carefully wrapped, packed, and sent to Dr. G. Elliot Smith, Professor of Anatomy at the Cairo School of Medicine. As mentioned before, the various accounts of almost everything about Tomb 55 differ. Joseph Lindon Smith's account emphasized that the bones were sent to Dr. Smith with no word as to which tomb they came from, so that he could be unbiased in his evaluation.[10] Cyril Aldred, however, says "... he [Elliot Smith] found to his intense surprise that they were those of a young man."[11] If Elliot Smith had no expectations, clearly he couldn't have been surprised. In any event, Elliot Smith's report contradicted the evaluation of the "prominent American obstetrician." The debate raged on even into the letters section of the London *Times*. At first it seemed as if Weigall had won. If the body was that of a male, it would almost certainly be Akhenaten's. The problem was that Smith did not just declare that the body was male, he went on to say that the bones were those of a young man not more than twenty-five years old. From the Egyptological records it is certain that Akhenaten lived into his thirties. So if Elliot Smith was correct, the coffin contained neither Queen Tiye nor Akhenaten.

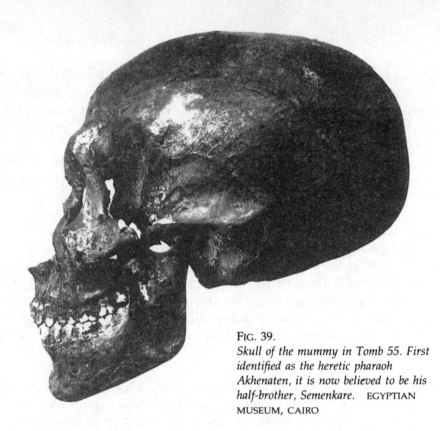

FIG. 39.
Skull of the mummy in Tomb 55. First identified as the heretic pharaoh Akhenaten, it is now believed to be his half-brother, Semenkare. EGYPTIAN MUSEUM, CAIRO

Nevertheless, both sides claimed victory. Theodore Davis published the results of his excavation of Tomb 55 under the title "The Tomb of Queen Tiyi," but included Smith's brief statement that the body was that of a young man. This, however, was not the end.

Smith's major work on the royal mummies is his volume of the *Catalogue General* of the Egyptian Museum that describes all the royal mummies known at the time of its publication in 1912. The book includes a very brief report on the body, stating its age and that its head was unusually shaped, perhaps indicating hydrocephaly, and notes an elongated chin, both features of Akhenaten's depictions on monuments. But what about the age problem?

Because of that, another candidate has sometimes been suggested—Akhenaten's younger brother (or half-brother), Semenkare. For a while it was generally accepted that this answered the puzzle. He is depicted on monuments with features similar to Akhenaten's, and he did not live into his thirties. All the facts fit. In recent literature on the question, experts now agree that the body is that of a male; they do not, however, agree on the crucial age question. A disease known as Froelich's Syndrome clouds the issue.

Froelich's Syndrome is a glandular disorder that causes hydrocephaly along with underdeveloped genitals and a feminizing of the physique, just as Akhenaten is shown in his colossal statues. The disease retards bone development so that the bones of a man of thirty-six or so could seem to be those of a man in his early twenties. Thus the body in the coffin could indeed be that of the heretic pharaoh who tried to turn Egypt from polytheism to monotheism. The explanation is *nearly* perfect, but there is one problem: Froelich's Syndrome invariably causes sterility. Akhenaten had six daughters, and possibly a son.

With the exception of this problem, the explanation fits the data so well that many Egyptologists are willing to say that the daughters born to Nefertiti, Akhenaten's beautiful wife, were not his. Others prefer to say the daughters were Akhenaten's, so the body in Tomb 55 must be Semenkare's.

G. Elliot Smith's successor, Dr. D. E. Derry, also examined the bones but concluded that the skull shape did not indicate hydrocephaly and that the bones were indeed those of a man in his early twenties, and thus could not be Akhenaten's remains. Derry's analysis was made *after* the discovery of Tutankhamen's mummy, so he was able to note something that no one before him was able to: there was a remarkable resemblance between the skull from Tomb 55 and Tutankhamen's. Since Tutankhamen, Akhenaten, and Semenkare may have been half-brothers, the resemblance is not surprising. It does not help establish the mummy's identity.

In the eighty-seven years since the discovery of the mummy in Tomb 55, more articles have been written about its identity than any other royal mummy. As of this writing there is no agreement among the Egyptological community about the identity of the body, although currently Semenkare is favored. This is because of the first modern, thorough examination of the Tomb 55 skeleton, performed in 1963 by Dr. R. G. Harrison, a professor of anatomy from the University of Liverpool.[12] Harrison's analysis, based on a wide range of scientific measurements and observations, yielded some surprises.

Because the skeleton is almost complete, with only a portion of the sternum missing, it is possible to analyze many of its anatomical features. Careful measurements and X-rays of the skeleton to examine the interior of the bones established that no evidence exists of either hydrocephaly or a pituitary disorder, as had been so often hypothesized. The body is that of a normal male, without significant abnormalities.

It was also possible to obtain a reliable age estimate for the occupant of Tomb 55. Throughout the twentieth century, anatomists have been gathering empirical data about what the normal range of measurements for physical features is for specific populations, such as the cephalic index (ratio of width to length of skull), ages at which epiphyseal union (when cartilage at the ends of bones turns to bone) occurs, normal angles of the pelvic bones for males, etc. Such data permit a precise determination of sex and abnormalities, if any, and an accurate estimate of age.

As we age our cartilage turns to bone, while bones near each other fuse. This is one reason why we become less flexible as we grow older. In the case of the body in Tomb 55, based on the fusion of the bones in the sternum the age at the time of death could be placed at 19 to 20 years. From the collar bone the estimate is 20 to 22 years, and from the sacrum less than 23 years. Teeth also are good indicators. The fact that the third molar had not fully erupted indicates an age of between 18 to 22 years. These findings are confirmed by the pelvic bones, which suggest an age of 20 to 21. Given all this evidence, it is clear that this is a normal male who died very near the age of 20, and thus cannot have been Akhenaten.

This leaves Semenkare as the leading candidate. Harrison had a medical artist do a facial reconstruction based on all the skull measurements and also on frontal and lateral photographs of it. The artist was not aware of the possible identities of the skull, and thus was unbiased when doing his drawings. The reconstruction did not match Akhenaten's depictions, but strongly resembled Tutankhamen, as depicted on the second of his three nested coffins. All indications are that it was Semenkare, Tutankhamen's half-brother, who was buried in Tomb 55.

Although it has been studied extensively, because of its poor condition Semenkare's body provides no clues to the procedures carried out during a pharaoh's mummification. But when Tutankhamen's mummy was discovered fifteen years later, the situation was quite different.

Tutankhamen

When Tutankhamen's mummy was discovered, there was no doubt about its identity. During his excavations in the Valley of the Kings, under a rock Theodore Davis found a faience cup bearing Tutankhamen's name. Near that find spot he found a pit containing wine jars, bandages, a small mask, and other minor objects also bearing Tutankhamen's name. Davis concluded that he had found what little remained of a reburial of Tutankhamen. He published his discovery under the title *The Tombs of Harmhabi and Touatankhamanou*, and it is here that he made his famous statement, "I fear that the Valley of the Tombs is now exhausted."[13]

Tutankhamen's tomb was the one every Egyptologist knew was missing, and for which everyone was looking. Now that Davis believed he had found Tutankhamen's reburial site, he saw no reason to continue searching. He relinquished his concession, opening the door to Howard Carter. As an experienced excavator, Carter knew that Davis had merely found an embalmers' cache from Tutankhamen's burial, not a tomb. Carter, with Lord Carnarvon's support, eagerly took up the search.

The story of the discovery of Tutankhamen's tomb has been told many times and is well known. It should be noted, however, that the discovery of the tomb was in no way a stroke of luck. Carter and Carnarvon knew exactly what they were looking for and how to find it. Working from a detailed map of the valley prepared by Carter, they intended to clear every unexplored meter down to bedrock. After years of methodical work Carter and Carnarvon discovered the tomb that gave the world its single totally undisturbed pharaoh's mummy.

The first step leading down into the tomb was discovered on November 4, 1922, but it would be more than three years before Carter was able to see the boy king face to face. The tomb had four chambers, and the antechamber, which preceded the burial chamber, was packed with the goods a pharaoh needed in the next world. Chariots, statues, game boards, linens, jewelry—all had to be photographed, catalogued, and conserved in the tomb before removal. Sometimes it took as long as a week to coat a fragile wooden object with wax so it could be moved. It was not until February 16, 1923, that the task of clearing the ante-chamber was completed. Only then could the burial chamber be entered. Carter found evidence of at least two ancient minor robberies, but hoped that the thieves had not reached the body of the king and that behind the resealed wall of the burial chamber rested Tutankhamen's untouched body.

The official breaking through of the burial chamber wall took place on February 17, 1923—and when Carter and Carnarvon finally peered in, it seemed to them that they were face-to-face with a wall of gold. The small burial chamber was almost completely filled with a gilded wood shrine that, both hoped, encircled the body of Tutankhamen. When the excavators entered the chamber and examined the door to the shrine, they must have had their first serious doubts about finding the king's body intact. The expected seals were missing; perhaps thieves had violated the grave of the dead king. The bolt slid easily, and for the first time in 3,000 years the doors to the seventeen-by-eleven-foot shrine opened. That shrine enclosed another, covered with a linen pall; also of gilded wood, it bore religious texts the king needed for his resurrection. Unlike the first shrine, however, the two doors to this shrine were sealed.

The seals were broken, and the doors opened to reveal yet another gilded shrine, also with sealed doors. When these doors were opened the fourth and last shrine was revealed. It was clear that this was the last, the one containing the body of the king. Carter was greatly affected by being the first person in the presence of a pharaoh who died more than three millennia ago. He writes:

The decisive moment was at hand! An indescribable moment for an archaeologist! What was beneath and what did that fourth shrine contain? With intense excitement I drew back the bolts of the last and unsealed doors; they slowly swung open . . . and there filling the entire area within, effectively barring any further progress, stood an immense yellow quartzite sarcophagus . . . intact, with the lid still firmly fixed in place, just as the pious hands had left it. It was certainly a thrilling moment. . . . [14]

Carter had found the king for whom he had been searching so long.

Work on the sarcophagus had to wait until the shrines could be dismantled and removed from the chamber. Because of the confined space, this was an extremely difficult feat of engineering. The job had been easier for the ancient workmen, who had assembled the shrines from fresh, strong wood. Carter had to deal with the dry, brittle wood that now remained.

Still visible, painted in black and white inks on the shrines, were ancient instructions as to how to assemble them. On the front of the side panels was the hieroglyph 𓄿, meaning "front." On the rear was 𓄿, meaning "rear." These hieroglyphs matched those on the roofs of the shrines—our equivalent of "Insert tab A in slot A." The workmen had been told to orient them with the doors opening to the west so the king could emerge into the next world. However, the ancient workmen got it backward; the doors opened to the east. Because the sun died in the west and was reborn each day in the east, the west was associated with death. Cemeteries were on the west bank of the Nile, for instance, and a common euphemism for the dead was "westerner." Tutankhamen would have walked into this world rather than the next.

Once the shrines were dismantled and removed, the massive lid to the sarcophagus could be carefully examined and raised. The sarcophagus was carved from a single block of yellow quartzite, while the lid, which was not the one originally intended for the sarcophagus, was of pink granite painted to look like yellow quartzite. A crack across the middle had been repaired with plaster and painted to conceal the damage. The crack made it difficult to raise the lid, but eventually a block and tackle were brought in and ropes placed under the lid so it could be hoisted. Carter was one step closer to his goal—Tutankhamen himself.

> *Many strange scenes must have happened in the Valley of the Tombs of the Kings since it became the royal burial ground of the Theban New Empire, but one may be pardoned for thinking that the present scene was not the least interesting or dramatic. For ourselves it was the one supreme and culminating moment—a moment looked forward to ever since it became evident that the chambers discovered in November, 1922, must be the tomb of Tut Ankh Amen, and not a cache of his furniture as had been claimed. None of us but felt the solemnity of the occasion, none of us but was affected by the prospect of what we were about to see—the burial custom of a king of ancient Egypt thirty-three centuries ago. How would the king be found? Such were the anticipatory speculations running in our minds during the silence maintained.*
>
> *The tackle for raising the lid was in position. I gave the word. Amid intense silence the huge slab, broken in two, weighing over a ton and a quarter, rose from its bed.*[15]

The group working in the tomb peered into the sarcophagus, but as if through a mist; they could not make out any details. Then they realized that they were looking at a linen shroud covering the coffin in the sarcophagus. When the shroud was rolled back, they were confronted with more than they could have hoped for. A seven-foot coffin of unsurpassed workmanship, bearing the likeness of Tutankhamen, came into view. On the forehead of the boy-king were the cobra and vulture, symbols of Upper and Lower Egypt—the pharaoh's dominion. Around these symbols of power was a small funeral wreath. Carter was evidently moved by the scene; it is one of the few times in his three-volume work about the tomb that he becomes overly sentimental.

... but perhaps the most touching by its human simplicity was the tiny wreath of flowers ... around these symbols, as it pleased us to think, the last farewell offering of the widowed girl queen to her husband, the youthful representative of the "Two Kingdoms."

... Many and disturbing were our emotions awakened by that Osiride form. Most of them voiceless. But in that silence, to listen—you could almost hear the ghostly footsteps of the departing mourners.

Our lights were lowered, once more we mounted those sixteen steps, once more we beheld the blue vault of the heavens, where the sun is Lord, but our inner thoughts still lingered over the splendor of that vanished Pharaoh, with his last appeal upon his coffin written upon our minds. "Oh Mother Nut! spread thy wings over me as the Imperishable Stars."[16]

Carter's wait was not over. It was now February 12, 1924, and the next day would prove a pivotal point for the remainder of the excavation.

There had been bad feelings between the two excavators, Carter and Carnarvon, and the Egyptian Antiquities Service, almost from the day the tomb was discovered. One source of conflict had been the handling of publicity. To avoid the nuisance of hundreds of reporters pouring into the Valley of the Kings, Lord Carnarvon decided to sell the exclusive rights to the story to the London *Times*. This allowed the team to deal with one reporter only, but it also alienated all the other members of the press. Reporters from the Egyptian newspapers, whose country owned the tomb and on whose soil the excavators worked, were not permitted to interview Carter or Carnarvon; only the foreign reporter from the London *Times* was allowed this privilege. This situation was viewed by the Egyptians as British colonialism at its worst.

When Carter invited his colleagues' wives to be present at the opening of the outer coffin, the Egyptian Antiquities Service refused permission. If Egyptian reporters were not to be allowed access, then neither would the wives of Carter's colleagues. The message to Carter was: This is not your tomb, but ours. By this

time Lord Carnarvon had died of complications from an infected mosquito bite, and Carter was left to handle the situation
alone. Carnarvon had possessed a soothing charm that enabled
him to smooth things out; Carter was a meticulous excavator
but he lacked charm, and that caused him political difficulty.
He posted a notice at the Winter Palace Hotel stating that he
and his colleagues could not work under such restrictions, and
that he was closing the tomb. The Egyptians responded by
sending guards to lock Carter out of it. It was now clear whose
tomb it was. There was little Carter could do, so he left on a
lecture tour of America. The Egyptian government knew that
Carter was the best man for the excavation and eventually an
agreement was worked out, but it was not until October, 1925,
that the lid of the outer coffin was removed.

Removing the three coffins nested inside one another was a
delicate task that consumed most of the 1925–1926 season. The
outer lid included silver handles for lowering it onto the coffin;
These proved strong enough for raising it. The second, equally
beautiful, anthropoid coffin was revealed; it too bore floral
wreaths. This coffin, however, gave Carter his first inkling that
the mummy might not be in the best condition. Some of the
inlays in this coffin had fallen out, a sign of moisture's destruc-
tiveness.

Because of the delicate condition of the second coffin, it was
decided to remove the entire ensemble rather than just the lid.
This was done, but no one could explain the incredible weight
they seemed to be lifting. With the entire group of coffins suspended above the sarcophagus, planks of wood were placed on
the stone sarcophagus and the coffins lowered onto them.

The problem now was that the second coffin had no handles
but fitted inside the outer one with less than a half-inch to spare
on any side. Carter screwed strong eyelets into the outer coffin,
removed the planks, and lowered it back into the sarcophagus
rather than raising its contents. The second coffin, still holding
the innermost, remained suspended until a wooden platform
could be placed under it. With room to maneuver now, the lid
of the second coffin could be raised. The reason for the unexpected weight was discovered—the third, innermost, coffin was
solid gold.

The details on the gold coffin were obscured by a black coating, the remains of magical unguents that had been poured over it. These liquids had run into the bottom of the second coffin, gluing the two together. But the handles on the lid of the gold coffin allowed it to be lifted. At last the mummy of the king was uncovered. Carter wrote:

> *At such moments the emotions evade verbal expression, complex and stirring as they are. Three thousand years and more had elapsed since men's eyes had gazed into that golden coffin. Time, measured by the brevity of human life, seemed to lose its common perspectives before a spectacle so vividly recalling the solemn religious rites of a vanished civilization. But it is useless to dwell on such sentiments, based as they are on feelings of awe and human pity. The emotional side is no part of archaeological research. Here at last lay all that was left of the youthful Pharaoh, hitherto little more than the shadow of a name.*[17]

Like the gold coffin, the mummy itself had been ritually dowsed with buckets of unguents, which explained the evidence of moisture noted in the second coffin. The famous gold mask protected the head of the pharaoh, but the rest of the body was in poor condition. An autopsy would prove to be difficult.

To soften the unguents, Carter took the coffins and mummy out into the sun, and mentions this in his daily notebooks:

> Nov. 1st. *Removed the Royal Mummy to No. 15. It took ten men to bring it out of the tomb and carry it up. Placed in the sun for a few hours . . . Heat of the sun not sufficient today to make any real impression upon the pitch-like material which has stuck fast the mummy and coffins.*
> Nov. 2nd. *Found that heat of the sun was of no avail in freeing the mummy from its coffin. In consequence, the examination of the Royal Mummy must necessarily take place as it lies.*[18]

Dr. Douglas Derry, who was then an anatomy professor at the Egyptian University, was given the responsibility for working with the body. He first tried to chisel the mummy free, then used heated knives, causing considerable damage to the body. Finally, Derry cut the mummy in half at the third lumbar vertebra so it could be removed in sections.

Unwrapping began on November 11, 1925. Derry, who more than a decade earlier had studied the bones in Tomb 55, was assisted by Dr. Saleh Bey Hamdi, Director of Sanitary Services in Alexandria. Present were Pierre Lacau, Director-General of the Department of Antiquities, Harry Burton (a photographer loaned to Carter by the Metropolitan Museum of Art in New York to document the excavation), and several Egyptian officials. No wives were present.

The task was extremely difficult because of the fragile condition of the bandages. The unguents poured over them had caused a chemical reaction, and they were darkened, actually burned, by a slow spontaneous combustion. Because the bandages could not be unrolled, heated wax was brushed over their outer layer so it could be cut away in a large piece. When the wax had cooled, Derry made a longitudinal incision and peeled back the first layer of linen. The unwrapping continued for hours, with each successive layer revealing amulets and jewelry incorporated in the wrappings. In all, 143 splendid objects were removed with the bandages. Finally the mummy was revealed.

The feature that shocked Derry was the similarity between Tutankhamen's skull and the one he had examined from Tomb 55, which was then generally agreed to be Akhenaten's. So striking was the similarity that Derry made a chart to emphasize the near-duplication of cranial measurements:

	AKH•EN•ATEN.	TUT•ANKH•AMEN.
Length of skull	190.0	187.0
Breadth " "	154.0	155.5
Height " "	134.0	132.5
Forehead breadth	98.0	99.0
Height of face: Upper	69.5	73.5
" " : Total	121.0	122.0
Breadth of jaw	99.5	99.0

| Circumference of head | 542.0 | 547.0 |
| Height calculated from limb bones | 1.66 metres (5 ft. 5¼ in.) | 1.68 metres (5 ft. 6 in.)[19] |

Because the mummy's arms and legs were disarticulated from their joints, Derry could clearly see the tops and bottoms of the long bones. The ends of these bones, the epiphyses, are not completely part of the long bone in early life, but instead ossify gradually. At birth they are attached by cartilage that converts to bone after growth stops. Since the average point at which the epiphyses join to the long bone is known, the degree of this union is a reliable criterion of age. In the case of Tutankhamen, the kneecap could be lifted off easily to examine the lower end of the femur. The epiphysis was separate from the shaft, and movable. Tutankhamen was indeed a boy king. Derry wrote:

> *This part unites with the shaft about the age of twenty. At the upper end of the thigh bone the prominence known as the great trochanter was almost entirely soldered to the main bone, but on its inner side a definite gap showing the smooth cartilaginous surface where union was still incomplete, could be well seen. This epiphysis joins about the eighteenth year. The head of the femur was fixed to the neck of the bone, but the line of union was clearly visible all round the articular margin. This epiphysis also unites about the eighteenth or nineteenth year. The upper end of the tibia was also united, but the lower end appeared to be quite fused. As this latter portion of the tibia is generally found to fuse with the shaft at about age eighteen, Tut Ankh Amen, from the evidence of his lower limbs, would appear to have been over eighteen but below twenty years at the date of his death.*[20]

Arm bones can also indicate age, and they too agreed with the estimate from the leg bones.

Because of its poor condition, the mummy of Tutankhamen yielded few secrets or surprises. The most interesting discovery was a fact about the embalming process. The incision through which the internal organs were removed, in this case on the

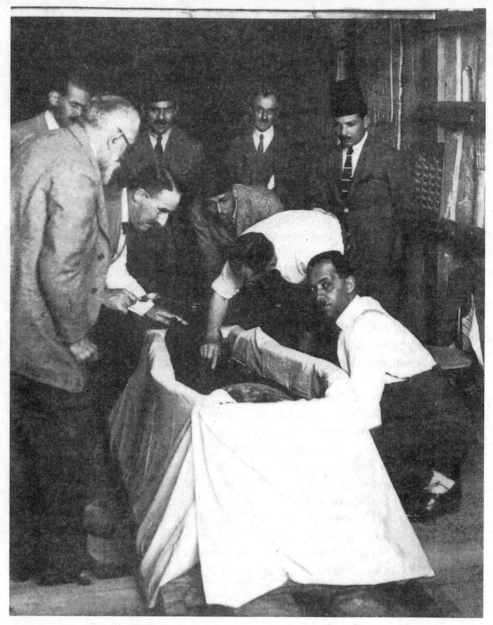

FIG. 40.   *The unwrapping of Tutankhamen. Howard Carter is leaning over with magnifying glass in hand; Dr. Douglas Derry is pointing into the coffin; Dr. Saleh Bey Hamdi, the only other physician on the team, is kneeling facing the camera. The man with the beard is Pierre Lacau, director of the Department of Antiquities.*   GRIFFITH INSTITUTE, ASHMOLEAN MUSEUM, OXFORD

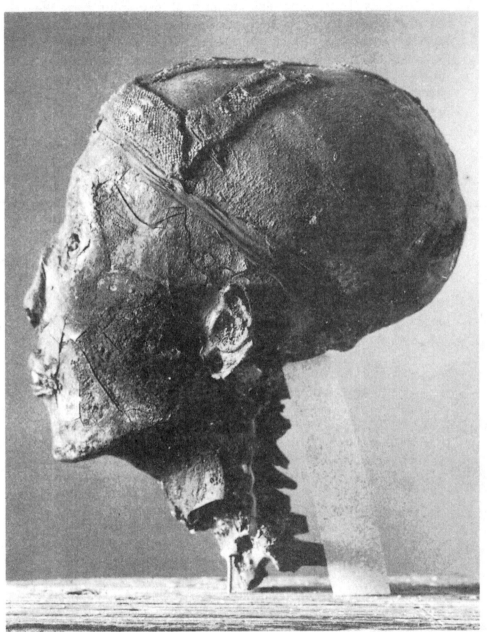

FIG. 41. *Head of Tutankhamen, which yielded measurements surprisingly similar to those of the skull from Tomb 55 (see Fig. 39).* PHOTOGRAPHY BY EGYPTIAN EXPEDITION, METROPOLITAN MUSEUM OF ART

left, as is usual, was higher than normal, beginning near the navel and descending at an angle toward the hip bone. The incision was open and the flaps pushed inward, which probably occurred when the body cavity was packed with resin-soaked linen. Surprisingly, there was no gold plaque covering the incision, although one was found within the wrappings on the left side of the body.

Carter had hoped that Derry would be able to determine the cause of Tutankhamen's death, but because of the limited facilities in the Valley of the Kings, where the autopsy took place, and the poor condition of the mummy, this was not possible. The mummy of Tutankhamen has never left the valley. Because the King was found undisturbed in his original tomb, it was agreed he should remain there. Even so, preparing the coffin for the permanent storage of the mummy presented problems. The gold coffin was still stuck to the wooden one in which it rested, but Carter invented a risky yet ingenious method for separating the two. It was such an amazing venture that it is worth quoting it in full from his notebook:

> Nov. 27th–Dec. 14th. *It was found that this pitch-like material could be melted under great heat, and that was really the only means of successfully getting the coffins and mask apart. Thus, so as to apply sufficient heat as was necessary without causing damage . . . the third coffin was completely lined with plates of zinc which would not melt under a temperature of 500 centigrade. We then reversed the coffins by turning them upside down upon trestles, covered the outside (second) coffin with heavy wet blankets for protection against fire, and placed under the hollow of the third coffin primus paraffin lamps burning at full blast. The temperature was naturally carefully watched so that it did not exceed the melting point of the zinc plates. It took some three hours before any real effect in the way of movement took place. The moment signs of movement became apparent, the lamps were turned out and the coffins left suspended upon the trestles when after an hour they began slowly to fall apart—the movement at first almost imperceptible owing to the tenacity of the material which when heated was of an exceedingly plastic nature and of the consistency of*

FIG. 42.
Tutankhamen's unwrapped mummy lying in a tray filled with sand. It still rests in his tomb in the Valley of the Kings. PHOTOGRAPHY BY EGYPTIAN EXPEDITION, METROPOLITAN MUSEUM OF ART

thick treacle, which even when the coffins came apart was very difficult to remove—even with quantities of various solvents—among which the final cleaning was done by means of acetone.[21]

The second and third coffins were transported to the Egyptian Museum in Cairo. Tutankhamen's mummy, however, was allowed to remain in the tomb, in the outermost coffin, inside the yellow quartzite sarcophagus.

Despite the poor condition of the mummy, from all the funerary equipment found in the tomb a great deal was learned about the rituals that accompanied the burial of a pharaoh. One new discovery was how liberally unguents were used. Gallons of oils were poured on the body and inner coffin of Tutankhamen, and this was not the only place they were employed. Past the burial chamber was a small room, named "the Treasury" by Carter, that, among other funerary items, contained the canopic chest holding the pharaoh's internal organs. Here, too, unguents had been poured over everything. Most interesting was the container for Tutankhamen's internal organs.

The canopic chest was carved from a single piece of calcite, divided into four shallow compartments to hold the king's mummified organs. There are several precedents for such a chest, perhaps the earliest being Queen Hetepheres' of the Fourth Dynasty, which was unadorned. The four corners of Tutankhamen's canopic chest are carved with figures of the goddesses Isis, Nephthys, Selket, and Neith. Each was associated with one of the four sons of Horus, guardians of the internal organs. A carved calcite lid with the head of the king sealed each compartment. Unlike Queen Hetepheres', however, the internal organs of Tutankhamen were not merely resting in the compartments, but had first been placed in a unique set of four tiny gold coffins, miniatures of the second of Tutankhamen's full-sized coffins. Each small coffin was wrapped with linen, then anointed with unguents and placed into a compartment. A magical spell emphasizing the connection between the protective goddesses and the four sons of Horus ran down the front of these little coffins. For example, the spell on the coffin containing the king's intestines reads: "Words spoken by Selket: I have placed my two arms around that which is inside. I protect

FIG. 43.
Calcite canopic chest holding Tutankhamen's internal organs, still in situ *on its sled in the tomb.*

FIG. 44.
One of the four gold miniature canopic coffins that contained Tutankhamen's internal organs. PHOTOGRAPHY BY EGYPTIAN EXPEDITION, METROPOLITAN MUSEUM OF ART

Qebhsenuf who is in there. Qebhsenuf of the Osiris, the King, Neb-Kheperu-Re, true of voice." (It was believed that everyone, even pharaohs, would be judged before being allowed entry into the next world. The deceased would have to plead his case before a tribunal of gods and convince them that he was honest, good, truthful, etc. If he was successful, the gods would declare him "true of voice," a euphemism the ancient Egyptians had for those who died.)

Each miniature gold coffin depicted of one of the four goddesses with her protective arms (shown as wings) outstretched, accompanied by an elaborate magical spell. Nothing like these canopic coffins had ever been seen before, but there is evidence that they were not unique. One of Tutankhamen's had originally been made for his brother Semenkare, and traces of Semenkare's name can still be seen under Tutankhamen's. Thus Semenkare may have had a set, and the same may well be true of other kings of the late Eighteenth Dynasty.

The tomb of Tutankhamen provided archeologists with the burial of a king to study. However, those who were interested in the history of mummification were disappointed; nothing new was learned from the poorly preserved body of the boy king. But another intact grave of a pharaoh would eventually be discovered, and in many ways it would be as spectacular as Tutankhamen's.

The Royal Mummies of Tanis

As the clearing of Tutankhamen's tomb reached its last stages in 1929, Pierre Montet, a French Egyptologist, began his excavations at Tanis, in the Delta. Montet was convinced that Tanis was the city of the Pi-Ramses mentioned in the Book of Exodus. It would later be proven that this biblical city was actually eleven miles away at Qantir, but for ten years Montet excavated and mapped the site, discovering that Tanis had been the capital of northern Egypt during the Twenty-first and Twenty-second dynasties, when high priests took control of Thebes.

During the 1939 season an anomaly caught Montet's atten-

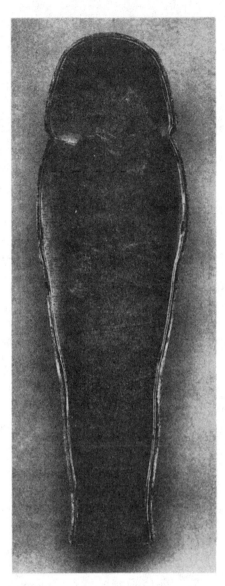

tion. At the site's southwest corner, an enclosure wall did not parallel the wall of the temple it encircled. Investigating the reason for the irregularity in the wall, Montet cleared a group of mud-brick structures and found a limestone tomb beneath them. Paintings on the walls indicated that it was the tomb of Osorkon II of the Twenty-second Dynasty. The tomb consisted of several rooms, one of which contained the remains of Osorkon II's successor and son, Takelot II. Another room contained the funerary equipment of his other son, Prince Hornakht. Although these tombs had been plundered, what remained was of such high quality that existing conceptions of the wealth of the northern Twenty-first and Twenty-second dynasties had to be revised.

Once the rooms were cleared, Montet found an adjacent tomb that had never been disturbed. He realized that this was his opportunity for a discovery to match that of Tutankhamen's tomb. When entry was gained, the wall reliefs indicated that it was the tomb of Pseusennes I, the founder of the Twenty-first Dynasty. There were hundreds of *ushabti* figures and numerous bronze vessels, but the object that dominated the burial chamber was a solid-silver coffin. Similar in style to Tutankhamen's gold one, but it had a falcon's head rather than the face of the king. Montet called for armed guards to watch the tomb; three days later, on March 20, 1939, in the presence of King Farouk, the lid was raised to reveal a gold facemask upon the head of the king. The hieroglyphs on the jewelry in the coffin indicated that the pharaoh was not Pseusennes but a previously unknown king, now called Sheshonq II. The jewelry and gold mask paralleled Tutankhamen's; another similarity was the four miniature silver coffins holding the king's internal organs. Unlike Tutankhamen's, they were not associated with the four protective goddesses, but only with Horus's sons.

The Egyptian Delta is a moist area, much more humid than Thebes. For this reason the body of Sheshonq II was far more decomposed than Tutankhamen's. The remains of Sheshonq were sent to Douglas Derry in the Anatomy Department of Cairo University's Faculty of Medicine.[22] He noted that water had entered the coffin, since the bones of the mummy's legs were covered with tiny rootlets that had penetrated the coffin where it was broken at the foot end. All the soft tissue was gone, but from the miniature coffins we can be sure that the internal organs had been removed. Examination of the skull revealed that the brain had been removed and that the roof of the nose had been broken, presumably for that purpose.

From the degree of ossification of the ribs and from the degree of skull-suture closure, it was determined that Sheshonq must have been more than fifty years old at the time of his death. His skull also revealed the cause of death: An injury to the head developed into a massive infection that spread to much of the cranium. There is no evidence of healing; Sheshonq died of septic infection.

If Sheshonq II was buried in a tomb originally intended for Pseusennes I, where then was Pseusennes I? Given the riches of the previously unknown king he had just found, Montet couldn't help but wonder what the grave of Pseusennes I would reveal. One year later he found out.

After clearing the tomb of Sheshonq II, Montet realized that the west wall actually contained two cleverly hidden doorways. He dismantled one and found a corridor with a large granite plug still place. There was just enough room between the block and the wall so that Montet could see into the chamber beyond it. He had found the intact tomb of the pharaoh Pseusennes I.

It took six days to remove the granite plug. Unlike Howard Carter, when Montet entered the burial chamber he brought along no distinguished visitors. No press attended. World War II was raging, which accounts for the almost total lack of publicity given to this great discovery. Also, Montet lacked a Harry Burton to produce a series of extraordinary photographs. The photographs that documented the discovery of this tomb have an amateurish, slightly out-of-focus quality. Still another reason why the world does not know of Montet's discovery is that he published primarily in French, thus limiting his audience.

The burial chamber was dominated by a massive pink granite sarcophagus; all around were canopic jars, *ushabti* servant figures, and gold and silver vessels. Unlike Tutankhamen's dry tomb, anything made of wood had crumbled in the moist Tanis ground. On February 21, 1940, Montet raised the lid of the sarcophagus. Inside was an anthropoid black granite sarcophagus

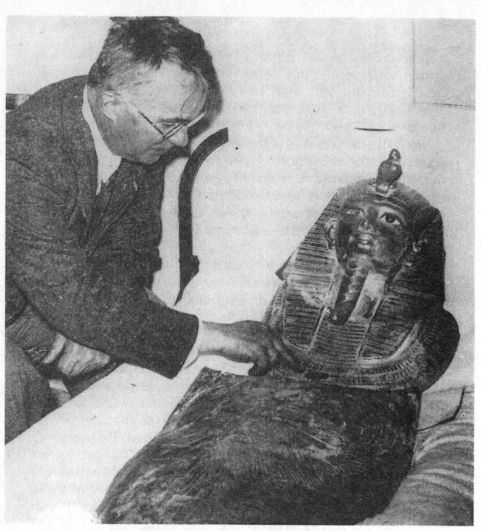

FIG. 47. *Pierre Montet with the mask of the pharaoh Pseusennes I.*

that recalled the nested coffins of Tutankhamen. When the lid
of the second sarcophagus was raised, a solid-silver coffin was
revealed. Inside was the decomposed body of Pseusennes I; the
damp had cheated Montet out of the chance to look into the
face of a king of ancient Egypt. The silver coffin contained a
beautiful gold mask and a fantastic array of jewelry, again par-
alleling Tutankhamen's. It took two weeks to record and remove the jewelry from the coffin. The king's fingers and toes
had been encased in gold stalls, and he was buried with gold

sandals on his feet. The finger stalls are the most elaborate ever found, with sculpted fingernails. Each finger wore an elaborate ring of gold and lapis lazuli or some other semiprecious stone. Over what must have been the embalmer's incision, but had now long disintegrated along with the rest of the king's soft tissue, was a rectangular gold plaque bearing the king's name and a procession of the four sons of Horus.

From the bones Derry determined that Pseusennes I was an old man when he died.[23] His teeth were in horrible condition, worn down and pitted with abscesses. The king's vertebral column showed evidence of extensive arthritis; judging from the bones of his feet, he must have been crippled during his last years. The mummy had been painted red, as was the custom for males in the Twenty-first Dynasty. (Just as in the tomb paintings, where red was used for males and yellow for females, the mummies of women during this dynasty were painted yellow.)

Montet had now found three tombs and two royal mummies, but his discoveries were not yet over. On April 16, King Farouk arrived to view the finds. When Montet told him that he had opened only one of two concealed doorways, the king asked Montet to open the second. Conservation of the objects already discovered would have to wait. This was Farouk's country and he was the king.

When opened, the second doorway revealed a granite plug, a clear indication that another unplundered tomb lay behind it. Montet had found the tomb of King Amenemope, the successor to Pseusennes I. The sarcophagus contained a badly damaged mummy,[24] but also an exquisite gold facemask and a whole complement of funerary jewelry.

War forced Montet to stop excavating for several years, but when he returned to Tanis he found the intact tomb of a general of Pseusennes I. The three pharaohs Montet added to the list of royal mummies were the last ever discovered. In the fifty years since then not a single pharaoh's body has been found, although many are still missing.

Because of their poor condition, the royal mummies of Tanis yielded no secrets about how kings were mummified. The same is true of the body in Tomb 55. The situation is only somewhat better with Tutankhamen's mummy because of the oils poured on it during burial rites. The real warehouse of information on how a pharaoh was mummified is the Egyptian Museum in Cairo, which contains all the royal mummies from the Deir el Bahri cache. Most of these mummies were unwrapped at the turn of the century, when a mummy-unrolling was more a social event than an attempt to answer specific scientific questions.

5
Holy Unrollers:
The Mummy Unwrappers

Ancient Egyptian tomb robbers searching for treasure were probably the first to unwrap mummies; later, modern unwrappers searched more for answers than for gold. After the Roman occupation of Egypt, Europe lost its ties with that part of the world, so by the Middle Ages mummification had become a long-forgotten process. It was not until the Renaissance, with its renewed interest in science, that attention was again focused on the subject. But few Egyptian mummies were available for study; most had been ground into medicine by apothecaries.

The use of mummies as medicine is the result of a confusion about the Persian word *mummia*, meaning "bitumen," the mineral formed from pitch. A tenth-century Persian manuscript stated that *mummia* could be collected only for the king, so it was guarded and harvested once a year in amounts no greater than something the size of a pomegranate. Abd al Latif, an Arab physician of the twelfth century, first described *mummia* as a mineral that dripped from mountains into water, where it coagulated on the bottom. Later travelers to Persia commented on the miraculous properties of *mummia*. Sir William Ousley visited Kieh Mummaiy (Mummy Mountain) and said the Persians valued *mummia* more than gold because they believed it healed cuts instantly and mended broken bones in minutes. So prized was *mummia* that in 1809 the King of Persia sent the Queen of England a sample as a gift. What she did with it is not recorded.

The word *mummia* came to be applied to preserved bodies in the Middle Ages, when travelers from Persia visited Egypt and saw the embalmed corpses of the ancient Egyptians. They mistook the darkened resins coating these bodies for their black *mummia*. So far only the coating of these corpses was mistakenly called *mummia*; designating the body underneath the coating by the same name was the result of a second confusion. By the end of the Middle Ages and through the seventeenth and eighteenth centuries, *mummia* was prized in Europe as a medicine. The 1583 edition of *Rates for the Custom House in London* lists "mummia by the pound." Since Persian *mummia* was so rare, and the more plentiful Egyptian resins had been designated by the same name, Egypt became the main supplier for European apothecaries. Along with the mineral came ground-up ancient bones and flesh as well, and soon the name extended to the lot. The confusion between the mineral and the human remains appeared in *The Physical Dictionary* in 1657: "Mumia, a thing like pitch sold at the apothecaries; some affirm it's taken out of old tombs." When seventeenth-century adventurers began traveling to Egypt, a supply of mummies for scientific study became available.

It should not be surprising that one of the earliest published accounts of a mummy unwrapping (1718) is authored by an apothecary, Christian Hertzog.[1] The mummy was headless, but within its thirty-five layers of bandages seventy-four amulets were uncovered, the record for that time. Because Hertzog was a druggist, it is a fair bet that the mummy was ground into powder and dispensed to his patients.

By the eighteenth century, more and more travelers visited Egypt, greatly increasing the supply of mummies and the frequency of unwrappings. These early unwrappings were simple affairs with a few physicians gathering somewhere to peel away the layers from an unnamed bundle in the hopes of verifying Herodotus' or Diodorus' accounts of mummification. One such group met on December 16, 1763, in the house of the London physician John Hadley.

> *Our intention was; to examine the manner in which this piece of antiquity had been put together; to compare it with the accounts given of these preparations by ancient authors; and to see, whether there were any traces left of the softer parts; and if so, by what means they had been preserved.*[2]

The poor preservation of the mummy surprised the group. From their readings of Herodotus and Diodorus they had expected a perfect specimen, but, to their disappointment, various bones were missing and no soft tissue remained. The biggest surprise was an onion bulb under the arch of the left foot. Even today no one knows why it was there.

Johann Blumenbach

Unwrappers grew more experienced as time passed; one of the first of a more scientific breed was the German physician and anthropologist Johann Blumenbach. Blumenbach visited England in 1792, unwrapping mummies everywhere he went. His first was a small mummy, less than a foot long and bearing a cartonage mask over the face area. When he unwrapped the mummy in the house of one Dr. Hartshorne, the attendant group, which included the president of the Royal Society, discovered that it contained nothing more than the linen wrappings from a larger mummy.[3] Small mummies were not uncommon in London at the time, so when word spread of these disappointing contents, other owners wondered whether their mummies were also fakes. A few days later Blumenbach unwrapped a fourteen-inch mummy belonging to a Dr. Lettsom, but this time he found the disarticulated skeleton of an ibis, which delighted those present.[4] Blumenbach was gaining momentum, and next went after three miniature mummies in the British Museum. Not only was he given permission to open one of the small mummies; he was also allowed to select one from a group of four large mummies to unwrap.

The small mummy he chose was a fake that contained only the arm bone of a child. The large one also proved disappointing, primarily because Blumenbach had read about both Hertzog's mummy containing amulets and Hadley's complete with the onion. The dejected Blumenbach mentions, "No idol or any artificial symbol whatever, was found in the inside of this mummy. Nor did it contain anything like an onion, such as have been now and then found about the parts of generation, or under one of the foot-soles of mummies."[5] His mummy did, however, have two artificial ears made of linen.

The British Museum permitted Blumenbach to examine yet another large mummy, but it too proved a disappointment: None of its soft tissue remained. This absence of soft tissue surprised most of the early unwrappers and led them to conclude that the flesh had been removed from the skeleton prior to wrapping. They did not realize that they were working with mummies two thousand years older than those seen by Herodotus and Diodorus, and that desiccated soft tissue could pulverize over millennia.

Having unwrapped half of the British Museum's collection, Blumenbach moved on to a mummy owned by John Symmons, which had been unwrapped four years previously. Symmons permitted Blumenbach to dissect the mummy and keep whatever parts he thought worthy of further study. The delighted Blumenbach dissected the poorly preserved cadaver, but what interested him most was the facial mask. Blumenbach took it back to Göttingen along with some selected mummy parts. After soaking the mask in water to separate its layers, the sharp-eyed doctor realized that something was wrong.

> *I discovered the various* fraudulent artifices *that had been practiced in the construction of this mask: the wooden part was evidently a piece of the front of the sarcophagus of the mummy of a young person; and in order to convert its alto-relievo into the basso-relievo of the usual cotton mask of a mummy, the plaster had been ingeniously pasted over the whole face, and lastly, this paper had been stained with the colours generally observed on mummies.*[6]

During his two months in England Blumenbach unrolled seven mummies and had learned that many of the mummies in Europe were fakes. The small mummies he had examined were of modern construction, their wooden containers joined with iron nails rather than the wooden pegs used by the ancient Egyptians. Reflecting on the fake-mummy industry, Blumenbach, now the most experienced mummy-unwrapper in the world, commented:

> *How many other artificial restorations and deceptions may*
> *have been practiced in the several mummies which have been*
> *brought into Europe, which have never been suspected, and*
> *may perhaps never be detected, may well be admitted, when we*
> *consider how imperfect we are as yet in our knowledge of this*
> *branch of Egyptian archaeology, which as a specific problem,*
> *few have hitherto treated with the critical acumen it seems to*
> *deserve.*[7]

Virtually all the mummies then in Europe had been purchased by travelers from Egyptian antiquity dealers. Serious study of mummification required a supply of mummies actually *found* in tombs, so there could be no doubt about authenticity. Napoleon Bonaparte's expedition to Egypt met this need.

Bonaparte's Mummies

Napoleon's Egyptian campaign launched modern Egyptology. When Bonaparte sailed to Egypt with his army in 1798, he also took more than 150 scientists—botanists, zoologists, mineralogists, chemists, engineers, linguists, everyone necessary to describe Egypt in scientific detail. The undertaking was so bold and captivating that history often forgets that Bonaparte lost the war. But while Napoleon's soldiers were suffering a war of attrition, his artists sketched, scientists measured, antiquaries excavated—and the birth of modern Egyptology took place. While the discovery of the Rosetta Stone provided the key to deciphering the ancient Egyptian language, the publication of the *Description de l'Égypte* by Bonaparte's scientists was also of great importance. Requiring more than two decades to complete, it was the largest publication in the history of the world, with 1,000 spectacular engravings that provided Europe with its first accurate depiction of ancient Egyptian monuments. The illustrations included mummies that the team had found in their tombs, guaranteeing their authenticity. With a seemingly unlimited supply of mummies, Bonaparte's men dissected unhesitatingly, and were able to observe different wrapping techniques used for mummies in different areas of Egypt.

The *Description de l'Égypte* beautifully reproduced, in color, the heads of a male and female mummy found at Gourna, near the Valley of the Kings. They noted that the brain of the woman had been removed through the nasal passages, just as Herodotus had described. The French decapitated the two mummies and sent the heads back to Europe. Josephine received the head of the woman. (When her Malmaison collection was sold in 1814, the head was bought as a souvenir of Napoleon's campaign by Vivant Denon, who had been with him in Egypt.)

Because Napoleon's scientists themselves found the mummies they unwrapped, they didn't have to worry about modern fakes; they did, however, discover their share of ancient ones. Several of the animal mummies they unwrapped were merely bundles of rags fashioned to look like animals. What appeared to be a mummified crocodile consisted only of a skull with the torso fabricated from bundles of linen held together with resin.

P. C. Rouyer, a pharmacist on the expedition, wrote a lengthy essay on mummification that was published in the *"Mémoires"* section of the *Description de l'Égypte*.[8] From first-hand experience of unquestionably ancient mummies, Rouyer was able to make some astute observations about the various methods of mummification, correctly citing desiccation as the crucial step, but falsely assuming that it was accomplished by heating the corpses.

The Napoleonic expedition alerted Europe to the wonders of Egypt. Soon French clothing, furniture, and architecture began to incorporate Egyptian motifs, including tables ornamented with gilded mummy-shaped legs. Quantities of antiquities, including mummies, were shipped to Europe, as travel between Egypt and Europe became more common for the upper classes. Frédéric Caillaud, a Frenchman trained in mineralogy, was one of those caught up in the wave of Egyptomania. In 1815, on the first of two trips to Egypt, he was hired by Mohamet Ali to find the lost emerald mines mentioned by medieval Arab writers. Captivated not by the minerals of Egypt but by its antiquities,

FIG. 48. *Nineteenth-century engraving of Napoleon examining a mummy at Giza.*

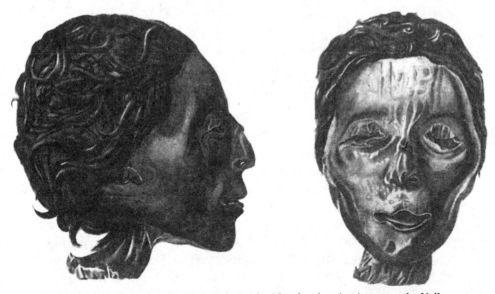

FIG. 49. *Head of a female mummy found by Napoleon's scientists near the Valley of the Kings. This illustration, from* Description de l'Égypte, *is the first accurate drawing of a mummy. The head was among Josephine's possessions when she died in 1814.*

FIG. 50. *Mummified crocodile. The head was real, but the body consisted of bundles of linen.* DESCRIPTION DE L'ÉGYPTE.

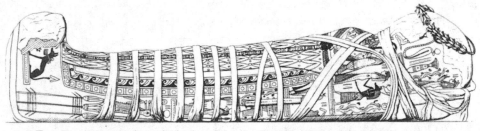

FIG. 51. *Mummy brought back to Paris by Frédéric Caillaud in 1823.*

Caillaud explored much of the country, making several important discoveries. On his second trip, in 1819, he discovered an intact mummy of the Greco-Roman period, which he carried back to Paris. On November 30, 1823, he unwrapped it before a fascinated audience.

Because he was trained as a scientist, Caillaud's careful observations are far better than those of many mummy-unrollers who came after him.[9] The mummy's name, Petamon, was written in Greek, as were details of his family history, including the fact that he was born on January 12, A.D. 95. The mummy still retained the metal olive branch that had been placed on its head

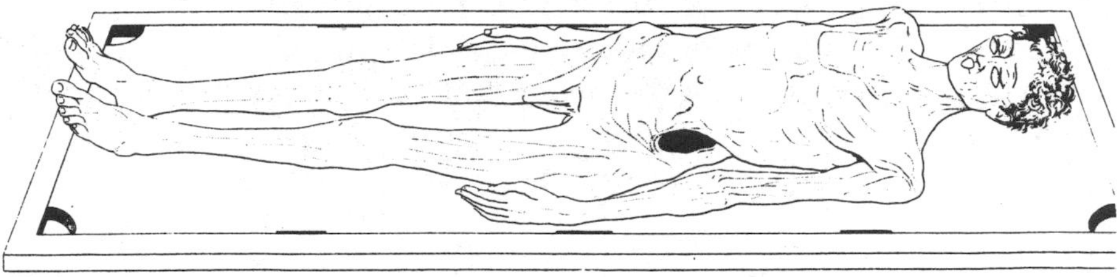

FIG. 52. *The unwrapped mummy as drawn by Caillaud. The eyes and mouth were covered with thin gold plates. The embalmer's incision was extremely high on the torso.*

on the day its burial, as well as preserved eyes and mouth covered with thin gold plates and gilded abdomen and arms. It was a fine mummy. The unusually high embalmer's incision is shown in a beautiful drawing of the unwrapped mummy. This unwrapping caused a sensation in Paris and was even reported in America's *Salem Observer* for June 19, 1824.[10] Mummy unwrapping had become a fad.

Captivating the public with tales of mummies and adventure was easy for Giovanni Battista Belzoni, a six-foot-six Italian circus strongman, hydraulic engineer, and raconteur. Belzoni originally came to Egypt in 1816 to sell Mohamet Ali an irrigation pump, but was forced into another profession when his assistant's leg was broken during the demonstration of his water wheel. Belzoni turned his attention to antiquities, where his ability to move large objects gained him commissions from Henry Salt, the British consul who was building an Egyptian collection. Belzoni made important discoveries in both the Valley of the Kings and the Valley of the Nobles. At Giza he opened the pyramid of Chephren, becoming the first in modern times to enter it. His vivid *Narrative of the Operations and Recent Discoveries Within the Pyramids, Temples, Tombs, and Excavations in Egypt and Nubia* made much of his sojourns among the mummies. Although the crude illustrations accompanying the text were inferior to those of Napoleon's professional artists, Belzoni's narrative had the thrilling ring of true adventure. The public loved it. A showman, Belzoni went to England to display a replica of the tomb of Seti I that he discovered. He also brought back a number of mummies, which provided the starting point for the career of the greatest of all mummy-unrollers, Thomas Pettigrew.

Thomas Pettigrew

The son of a naval surgeon, Pettigrew became a prominent physician (he vaccinated Queen Victoria). In 1820 Belzoni asked him to examine several mummies, and the project captivated Pettigrew. Soon after, he purchased a mummy that had been brought to England in 1741 by another physician, Charles Perry. Pettigrew leisurely unwrapped the mummy in the privacy of his home. It would be his only private unrolling.

Ten years passed before Pettigrew had his next chance to unroll a mummy. He purchased a Ptolemaic mummy for twenty-three pounds at the 1833 auction of Henry Salt's collection. His friend Thomas Saunders purchased another at the same sale for £36 15s. Both mummies were unrolled on April 6, 1833, to a packed audience in the lecture hall of Charing Cross Hospital, where Pettigrew was professor of anatomy. The combination of England's fascination with mummies and Pettigrew's social connections made the public demonstration a huge success, and soon mummy unrollings became the vogue.

A few weeks later, Dr. John Lee asked Pettigrew to unwrap yet another mummy from the Salt sale, so on June 24, 1833, Pettigrew gave another performance. He began with some remarks on Egyptian religion, the purpose and technique of mummification, and provided a running patter throughout the unrolling. He had read of Champollion and Young's decipherment of hieroglyphs, so he often could make out the name of deceased from the inscriptions on the mummy case. John Davidson, who attended the unwrapping of Dr. Lee's mummy, was so enthralled by the event that he asked Pettigrew to help him unwrap a mummy he owned. The "mummy of the month" was unwrapped on July 13, 1833, in front of a standing-room-only audience at the lecture hall of the Royal Institute. David-

FIG. 53. *Giovanni Belzoni, who started Thomas Pettigrew's career as a mummy unroller in 1820 when he asked Pettigrew to examine some mummies.*

son's mummy had been brought, along with a second one, from Thebes in 1821 by John Henderson. Pettigrew knew that the second mummy had been given to the Royal College of Surgeons. Smitten with mummy fever, he requested permission to inspect drawings of the mummy's two coffins. After having borrowed the drawings for a fortnight, he wrote to the librarian of the Royal College of Surgeons:

> *May I beg of you to communicate to the Council of the Royal College of Surgeons my thanks for their obliging attention to my request and for their munificence in the loan of the Drawings of the Mummy Cases which shall, agreeably to specification, be returned at the period mentioned. I will, however, take*

this opportunity of acquainting you that I have already been able to make out the name and occupation of the Egyptian and that I find him to have been one Horiesi, the son of Naspih-iniegori, an incense-bearing Priest in the Temple of Ammon and that he has been brought from Thebes. It would be very satisfactory to have the mummy unrolled and this may be done without any injury whatever to the case. I should be happy to undertake this task or assist any one in the performance, and should the Council think fit to direct this to be done, I should further be obligated by their appointment of an early day for the purpose, as my work is now in the Press and it is probably I might meet with something new in illustration of my subject.

Believe me to be,
Your very faithful Serv[t]
T. J. Pettigrew[11]

Pettigrew had just completed his book *History of Egyptian Mummies*, and it would be timely publicity if he could unroll one more mummy before it was published. Permission to unroll was granted.

Such a demand arose for invitations to the event that plans were made to accommodate those who could not get in. The diary of William Clift, Conservator at the Royal College of Surgeons Museum, notes:

Prepared *large* Notices against the Meeting to-morrow, to obviate as much may be the effects of disappointment to those who will not be able to gain admission:
"Gentlemen who may be disappointed in witnessing the unrolling of the Mummy this day, will have an opportunity of viewing it in the Museum every Monday, Wednesday, and Friday, from 12 till 4 o'clock. Jan. 16, 1834."[12]

Considerable preparations were necessary on the day prior to the unwrapping. The mummy cases had to be opened so Pettigrew would know what he was dealing with—in the past he had found mummies so covered in hardened pitch that he couldn't unwrap them and disappointed his audience.

By the time of the unwrapping the auditorium was so crowded that even the Archbishop of Canterbury and the Bishop of London had to leave because of lack of space. At one o'clock a procession led by the mace-bearer, president, and council of the Royal College of Surgeons filed into the theater, leading Pettigrew and his two assistants. Clift's account recreates the event:

Visitors in considerable numbers arrived very early and filled all the Seats; many were obliged to stand; and many others retired from all the doors who could not find admission.

The president took the Chair precisely at One o'clock, the time appointed. Mr. Pettigrew immediately began his address, describing the various methods employed from the earliest periods downwards—exhibited various parts of his own mummy—and a portrait copied from an original lately discovered on opening a Mummy in the British Museum sent by the late Henry Salt Esq. which is executed in a very superior manner, considering the period. . . .

The bandages were now removed as carefully as circumstances and time permitted. The outer smooth cloth being removed, exposed the circular hand-breadth rollers, which extended from head to foot several times in succession:—others oblique and diagonal very neatly but without much regularity or uniformity till we reached the very innermost layer or two which firmly adhered to the surface by a coat of asphaltum. On the breast, near the situation of the zyphoid cartilage, was a small protuberance, which when divested of the bandage, exposed a small carved Scarabous [sic] of a pale semi-transparent white colour—and on the upper part of the Sternum a cluster of four or five small Tally-shaped bodies enveloped in, and sticking to the body by, asphaltum. Part of the face was exposed, and showed that a pair of artificial eyes, apparently of enamel, had been placed on or substituted for the natural ones. Here the examination of this part ceased for the present. In removing the crumpled wadding between the thighs, a small clay model of an outer Mummy case rudely made and imperfectly if at all vitrified, and now partly decomposed was found beneath

FIG. 54. *Illustration for Pettigrew's* History of Egyptian Mummies *drawn by Charles Cruikshank, who later became famous as Charles Dickens' illustrator.*

the Scrotum, but no coins, ornament, or Papyrus was discovered.[13]

Pettigrew unrolled two additional mummies before the end of 1833, providing marvelous publicity for his book, which appeared in 1834. Many of the book's purchasers were those who had attended this presentation. Charles Cruikshank, who was later to become Dickens's illustrator, drew the plates. *History of Egyptian Mummies* provided the first comprehensive history of mummification and remained the standard reference for more than a century. Just as the unwrappings helped sales, the popularity of the book in turn accelerated unwrappings.

Pettigrew went on to give a series of six public lectures on ancient Egyptian funerary customs, culminating with "Recapitulation—Unrolling of an Egyptian Mummy." Tickets were one guinea for mummy-side seats and half a guinea for seats in the rear. Ladies were admitted. The series was so successful that Giovanni D'Athanasi, who had also been employed by Henry Salt to collect antiquities in Egypt, decided to capitalize on Pettigrew and the craze. He had brought a well-preserved mummy from Memphis, which was something of a curio since all the mummies unwrapped so far had come from Thebes. D'Athanasi distributed a handbill advertising the unrolling of "The Most Interesting Mummy that has yet been discovered in

SYLLABUS OF A COURSE OF LECTURES ON
EGYPTIAN ANTIQUITIES,

More especially as connected with the Processes of Embalming;

By T. J. PETTIGREW, F.R.S. F.S.A. F.L.S., &c. &c. &c.
Author of a "History of Egyptian Mummies," &c.

These Lectures will be delivered at the EXETER HALL, STRAND, at Half past Eight o'Clock in the Evening precisely, c piously illustrated by Specimens and Drawings,

AND IN THE FOLLOWING ORDER:

Monday, Feb. 13.—LECTURE I. INTRODUCTORY, ON THE FUNERAL CEREMONIES OF DIFFERENT NATIONS. Reverence paid to the dead—Burial in the earth—Earliest example on record—disposal of the dead by fire, a practice among the ancient Greeks, Romans, Germans, Gauls, &c.—Roman Urns—Ashes of the dead dispersed to the winds, or taken in the beverage of the living—Burial in water, in snow, and ice—Perfuming of bodies by the Romans—Painted bodies of the Macrobians and Ethiopians—Preservation of the Persians, Syrians, and ancient Arabians, by honey and wax—Chinese method of treating their dead. Guanches of the Canary Islands—Mode of preservation—Examples—Peruvian Mummies—chiefly desiccated bodies, not embalmed—Articles found in the Mummy Pits—Examples of the Ancient Peruvians—Desiccated bodies of Palermo—their arrangement—mode of preparation—Examples of great preservation from burial in sawdust—Burman Priests—singular account of their mode of embalming—exhibition—destruction—curious ceremony on the occasion.

Thursday, Feb. 16.—LECTURE II. EGYPTIAN TOMBS. Wisdom of the Egyptians—Antiquity of the Egyptian Mummies—extraordinary perfection of the art to be accounted for by referring to their theology—immortality of the soul—transmigration—Mummies as guests at feasts—as pledges for the loan of money—deposit of treasure in the tombs—various articles found—examples of several earliest tombs—pyramids. Architecture and Sculpture of the Egyptians—Temple of Karnack—bears the name of Osirtesen I. the cotemporary of Joseph—Monotony of Egyptian buildings—colossal character—Head of Remeses the Great—Subjects represented in the temples and in the tombs—their variety—Egyptian Funeral Procession—ceremonies—instances of the denial of sepulture—examination of the characters of the dead—Assessors—Sacred Boat or Bari—QUEENS' TOMBS—Tombs of the Valley of Dayr el Medeenah—under the protection of the Goddess Athor—Invention of the arch—Amunoph I. Catacombs and pits of Abd el Qoorneh and Drab Aboo Negga—Gate or Gates of the Kings—ROYAL TOMBS—number known—Tomb of Osirei, commonly known as Belzoni's tomb—Alabaster sarcophagus—not likely to have been the receptacle of the body of a monarch—Some of the representations given in this tomb—Tomb of Remeses III. The Harper's—illustration of Egyptian manners and customs—Tomb of Remeses V. Astronomical subjects—Tomb of Remeses VII.—peculiar character of its sculptures—Tomb of Remeses II. the supposed Sesostris of the Greeks—Tomb of Pthah-Septhah—Western valley—Tomb of Amunoph III.—TOMBS OF PRIESTS AND PRIVATE INDIVIDUALS.—Largest sepulchre hitherto discovered, that of Petamunap—Sale of tombs by the Priests—CATACOMBS.—At Alexandria—Saccara—Ghizlis—Gournou or Qoorna—Thebes—Mummy pits—Position of the Mummies. Concluding remarks on the Representations in the Tombs.

Monday, Feb. 20.—LECTURE III. ON MUMMIES, AND THE PROCESSES OF EMBALMING. Etymologies of the term Mummy—various applications of it—Natural Mummy of the Mountains—its scarcity and value—Mummy used in medicine—introduced by Elmagar—generally employed in the 15th and 16th centuries—cessation of the practice. EMBALMING—definition—art now unknown to the Egyptians—accounts given by Herodotus and Diodorus Siculus—variations in the modes—principal kinds—order pursued—peculiarities observed—substances employed—Mummies of the poor Nubians—Finest specimens of embalming—Destruction of Mummies in the search for treasure—Mummies of Thebes—Abydus—Memphis. The embalmers—the swathers—Extraction of the brain and other viscera—instruments employed—Account by Porphyry, supported by Plutarch—its improbability—Aromatics—Resinous substances—application of heat—Gilding of Mummies—Tongue plate—Body of Alexander furnished with a covering of gold close work—Staining of the nails with henna—Position of the Mummies—horizontal—arms crossed—Preservation of the hair—plaited—examples—rarity of the Mummies of Children—Mummy of a Fœtus—its case—Cessation of the practice of embalming—Christian Mummies—Insects found in the head of a Mummy—Medicaments employed in embalming—resinous and bituminous matter—asphaltum—Cedria—Balm—different kinds: of Judæa—Syria—Egypt—Mecca—Colocynth—Myrrh—Aloes—Cedar dust—Natron—its analysis—Honey—Wax.

Thursday, Feb. 23.—LECTURE IV. BANDAGES, CASES, AND SARCOPHAGI. Necklaces in contact with the body—Scarabæus—Rings—Enamelled eyes—Mouthpiece of the time of Remeses the Great—Ear-Rings—Silver nails—Deities of the Amenti—Bandages of different colours—Græco-Egyptian Mummies—covering of painted cloth—Bandages formed of linen—satisfactory proof—researches of Dr. Ure and Mr. Thomson—different substances with which the bandages are coloured—Bitumen—Aloes—Goudron—Tannin—Scount—Carthamus—length of bandages—compresses—all applied wet—limbs sometimes separately bandaged—quantity of bandage varies greatly—Hieroglyphical characters impressed upon them—generally at the end—Articles of dress occasionally found—old linen, mended and darned—Hieratic and Enchorial and Greek Inscriptions—Splendid Mummy from Memphis, in Signor D'Athanasi's collection—Amulets—leathern finger-ornaments in the Leeds Mummy—Garlands of flowers—Sandals—painted ones, with hieroglyphics—Symbolical representations under the heads of some Mummies—Varnished bandages—Portrait over the face of a Mummy—Idols and ornaments placed between the first and second layers of the bandages—great variety of necklaces—golden ornaments—quantity of gold in Egypt—metallic mirror, wooden cistern, alabaster vases, &c. found in a mummy case—Funeral tablets—breast-plates of kings—The Genii of the Amenti—idol found in the mummy of Horseisi—Bulbous roots—Rosemary—Eye of Osiris—Bracelets of gold and other materials—Diadem of gold and silver—Mosaic work—No money discovered in the tombs—Egyptian commerce—Rings of gold and silver—Medals struck under the Greeks, Romans, and Arabs—First current coin in Egypt—Coin of Ptolemy in a Mummy—Leaden Medals affixed to a Greek Mummy.—CASES. The Cartonage—its manufacture—beautifully painted—subject of the representations—Wooden coffins—sycamore—cedar—formed occasionally out of a single trunk—outer cases—hard wood—inscriptions—SARCOPHAGI. Lapis assius—different materials and forms—ordinary shape—rose-coloured granite—marble—limestone—alabaster—Egyptian breccia—basalt—slate—baked-earth—wood. Sarcophagus of Amyrtæus (Alexander's tomb) in the British Museum—"Lover's Fountain"—Alabaster Sarcophagus in Sir J. Soane's Museum—Description of the Wooden Sarcophagus of Osiri.

Monday, Feb. 27.—LECTURE V. ON THE PAPYRI, & ON THE HIEROGLYPHICAL LANGUAGE AND LITERATURE. Natural History of the Papyrus—its manufacture into paper—Egyptian literature—Rosetta stone—labours of De Sacy—Akerblad—Young—Salt—Champollion—Wilkinson—Burton, &c.—Hieroglyphical characters—Hieratic—Enchorial—Bilingual MSS.--Papyri—their contents.

Thursday, March 2.—LECTURE VI. Sacred Animals—Worship of various Animals throughout Egypt—difficulty of the enquiry—Egyptian Mythology—Embalming of the Sacred Animals—Quadrupeds—Birds—Amphibious Animals—Fishes—Insects—Embalmed Vegetables.

Monday, March 6,—LECTURE VII. RECAPITULATION—UNROLLING OF AN EGYPTIAN MUMMY,

Tickets of Admission to the Course, to which Ladies will be admitted, to be had of the Lecturer, No. 8, Saville Row; Mr. LEIGH SOTHEBY, Wellington Street, Strand; and at the Exeter Hall. Front Seats and Gallery, One Guinea. Back Seats, Half-a-Guinea.

FIG. 55. *Syllabus for Pettigrew's six-lecture series on mummies, which concluded with the unrolling of a mummy.*

GIOVANNI D'ATHANASI

Respectfully informs the Public, that

On the EVENING of MONDAY, the 10th of APRIL NEXT,

AT SEVEN O'CLOCK,

THE

MOST INTERESTING MUMMY

That has as yet been discovered in Egypt,

WILL BE UNROLLED

IN THE LARGE ROOM AT EXETER HALL, STRAND.

WHICH MAY BE NOW SEEN

At the House of Mr. LEIGH SOTHEBY, Wellington Street, Strand.

" Every Traveller who has visited Egypt, and indeed all those who have taken an interest in the Antiquities of that Country, are fully aware of the difficulty—nay, almost impossibility—of discovering at Memphis a Mummy in any thing like a perfect state, owing to the general destruction occasioned by the search of gold that took place in the Tombs during the period when Cambyses invaded Egypt. Though many of the most beautiful objects of antiquity, such as the minute Figures in Porcelain, the Alabaster Vases, and MS. Rolls of Papyrus, have been discovered at Memphis, yet, it is well known, that in no museum in Europe does there exist a perfect Mummy from that city.

" The circumstance, therefore, of this Mummy coming from Memphis, and being in so perfect a state, alone renders it very valuable ; but it is now, arising from a discovery made since its arrival in this country, rendered of the highest interest and importance.

" On removing the covering of fine linen which was placed on the body of this Mummy, it was observed, from a small piece of linen which obtruded through a fracture in that which appeared a thick layer of asphaltum, that it had on it some inscription. On a more minute examination, it was discovered that the folds of linen, then perceptible, were all written upon in the same manner, and that the layer of asphaltum was merely intended for their preservation. This thin layer of asphaltum was immediately removed from the upper part and sides of the body, leaving only, as now seen, a small portion towards the feet, as a specimen of its original state ; and the appearance which the Mummy now presents is such as has never been before seen. The numerous folds of cloth with which the body is surrounded are covered with HIERATIC, ENCHORIAL and HIEROGLYPHICAL INSCRIPTIONS and DESIGNS of all the Funereal Ceremonies. The piece of linen now placed round the Mummy is above eight feet in length ; it was taken from around the feet, and from the mark or character at the end, it would appear that the pieces placed on the breast and other parts of the body were a continuation of it—thus forming the subjects which are usually found in the MS. rolls of Papyrus. It is believed, that these, with the other inscriptions with which the whole of the bandages are covered, include the ENTIRE RITUAL of the ancient Egyptians.

" It would be difficult to enter into a description of the numerous designs with which the folds of linen are decorated. There is a greater variety of subjects here given than is to be found in any of the Funereal Manuscripts on Papyrus. On the piece of linen taken from around the feet, is a representation of a funereal ceremony, wherein the body of the deceased is being conveyed to its resting place on a *four-wheeled* carriage. This circumstance was particularly reverted to by Mr. Pettigrew, in the second of his very interesting course of Lectures on Egyptian Antiquities, at Exeter Hall, *Feb.* 16 ; when he observed, and supported in his opinion by the authority of Mr. Wilkinson, whose valuable researches into the history and customs of the ancient Egyptians cannot be too highly appreciated, that this, the representation of a carriage on *four wheels*, as used by the ancient Egyptians, was the first that has been discovered.

" The Sarcophagus, which is 5 *feet* 9½ *inches long,* 1 *foot* 9 *inches broad, and* 1 *foot* 3 *inches deep,* is, with the exception of the three lines of Hieroglyphics on the exterior of the cover, and a representation of the Four Deities of the Amenti at the head, without any ornament ; it is singularly shaped, yet more resembling the coffins of the present period. The Hieroglyphics alluded to are found to give the name of the deceased, and make mention of the City of Memphis ; thus corroborative of its having been found in that place."—*Extracted from Mr. Leigh Sotheby's Catalogue of Giovanni D'Athanasi's Collection of Egyptian Antiquities.*

Tickets, as under, with a description of the Mummy, may be now had of GIOVANNI D'ATHANASI, at No. 3, Wellington Street, Strand.

A limited number of Seats will be reserved, immediately around the Tables on which the Mummy will be placed, at *Six Shillings.*

Seats in the Balconies and Platform, *Four Shillings.*

All the other Seats in the centre of the Hall and Gallery, *Two Shillings and Sixpence.*

J. DAVY, Printer, 13, Queen Street, Seven Dials.

FIG. 56. *Handbill for Giovanni D'Athanasi's mummy-unrolling.*

Egypt." The charge was six shillings for seats near the operating table, four shillings for balcony seats, and two-and-sixpence for seats in the back. Before more than 500 people, Pettigrew began the unrolling but soon found trouble.

> *After some travel [sic], Mr. Pettigrew came to a complete asphaltic envelope, of extreme hardness and tenacity, into which the body had been plunged; and which resisted hammers, knives, and chisels. By much perseverance it was partially removed; and about the neck scarabei, cornelians and other stones were found. . . . Finding it impossible to make greater way in removing the obstacles interposed by the preparation, it was announced that the task would be carefully completed elsewhere, and the results submitted to the view of the public.*[14]

Despite this disappointing performance, Pettigrew soon was offered another mummy to unwrap—the "Jersey Mummy." John Gosset had bought this mummy in Egypt but died on the way home to Jersey. The mummy was donated in his memory by his father to the Jersey Museum, where Pettigrew unwrapped it. Prior to the unwrapping, Pettigrew delivered his six-lecture series. He concluded with the unrolling, and this time he did not disappoint his audience.

The mummy contained amulets of the four sons of Horus, a heart scarab, and a pectoral, all of which Pettigrew removed from the wrappings with a magician's flair. His sense of the dramatic is preserved in a newspaper account.

> *The lecturer now exclaimed "Here at length is something to repay one's caution (applause): in a preceding lecture I mentioned the scarabeus as an ornament found frequently between the bandages: I will now lift this portion of the covering, and you will see a very fine one." Here the mummy was carried round, and every one rose to see the ornament on the breast. . . . The work of unrolling now again proceeded until the joyful announcement was made that something new was discovered which had never before been found on a mummy. Mr. P. now exercised his scissors very freely, and soon released the scara-*

beus which was found to be fixed above a plate of metal . . .
found to be fashioned in the form of a hawk. . . . [15]

Pettigrew's account of this unrolling[16] is detailed, and his description of the coffin and hieroglyphic inscriptions is quite good. He did not realize, however, that what he thought was a Ptolemaic mummy actually dated from the Twenty-first Dynasty.

Over the next few years Pettigrew continued to unroll mummies, now often assisted by his son, Dr. W. V. Pettigrew. By the end of his career, Pettigrew had unrolled dozens of mummies, delighted thousands of witnesses, and advanced the study of mummification considerably. He is the first to note that mummification techniques varied over the different periods of Egyptian history. His interest extended far beyond merely looking for amulets in wrappings, and his medical training made him an astute observer of physiological characteristics of the mummies he unwrapped. His extensive experience made him uniquely qualified for his last and greatest performance, the mummification of the Duke of Hamilton.

Thirty years before his death, the duke had purchased a black basalt sarcophagus for his eventual burial. On the grounds of Hamilton Palace he erected a mausoleum that the *Times* of September 7, 1852, described as ". . . the most costly and magnificent temple for the reception of the dead in the world—always excepting the Pyramids." Following the duke's instructions, Pettigrew not only mummified his Grace, but also officiated as the high priest at his burial. (The mummy mania inspired Edgar Allen Poe to write "Some Words with a Mummy," which appeared in the April, 1845, issue of the *American Weekly Review*. The story, featuring a character modeled on Pettigrew, satirizes the mania for unwrapping mummies.)

The Granville Mummy

Pettigrew was not the only mummy-unroller in England. As early as 1821, Augustus Granville unrolled a mummy pur-

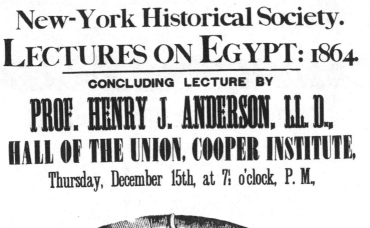

New-York Historical Society.
LECTURES ON EGYPT: 1864.

CONCLUDING LECTURE BY

PROF. HENRY J. ANDERSON, LL. D.,
HALL OF THE UNION, COOPER INSTITUTE,

Thursday, December 15th, at 7½ o'clock, P. M.,

To be followed by the

Unrolling of the Mummy.

FIG. 57.   *Advertisement for an American unrolling.*

chased in Thebes in 1819 for four dollars. The mummy, an ex-
ceptionally well-preserved female, probably of the Persian
period, was unrolled painstakingly over a period of several
weeks in Granville's home. The dissection of the pelvic area
alone occupied two hours a day for a week, and enabled Gran-

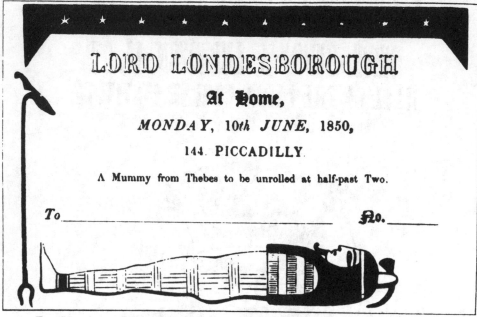

FIG. 58. *Invitation to Samuel Birch's unwrapping of a mummy belonging to the Earl of Londesborough. Guests were treated to the sight of the mummy's silver gloves, uncovered during the unrolling.*

ville to conclude that the probable cause of death was a uterine disease (recent research, however, suggests that the tumor Granville found was in fact benign). Granville's publication[17] is remarkable for its time, reviewing the known literature on the subject and carefully describing the details of his autopsy, but it is not free of error.

Because of the texture of the body, Granville concluded that wax was the main ingredient used in the mummification. The body, he said, was immersed in a solution of wax and resin and cooked slowly over a fire for several days. He also concluded that his mummy was wrapped in cotton. Even in Granville's time it was generally known that cotton did not exist in ancient Egypt. Their cloth was linen, a product of the flax plant. So prevalent and important was flax that one of the phonetic hi-

eroglyphic signs depicts a piece of twisted flax: ⧘. For some unknown reason, Granville claimed that if old linen and cotton

were rubbed with glass or ivory, the cotton would be unchanged but the linen would gain luster.[18] The test "proved" to
Granville that this mummy was wrapped in cotton. In spite of
these errors, the Granville mummy is an important part of the
history of the study of mummification, although for quite a
while its exact location was unknown. It was rediscovered in a
storage room in the British Museum in 1992 and soon will be
studied again.

Granville's theory that mummies were waxed was finally put
to rest by the "Leeds Mummy," the first ever submitted to a
professional chemical analysis. In 1828, utilizing a team approach, the Leeds Philosophical and Literary Society enlisted
the aid of physicians, anatomists, and a chemist. The chemist,
E. S. George, reported that although he was aware of Granville's
conclusion about wax, the Leeds mummy contained not wax,
but adipocere—a fatty substance produced by dead bodies.[19]
This is probably what Granville mistook for wax. Adipocere is
a common feature of cadavers buried in moist areas and actually resembles soap. (The "Soap Lady" in the Mutter Museum
of the College of Physicians of Philadelphia is that institution's
main exhibit. Buried during the nineteenth century, this obese
woman's fat turned to adipocere, preserving her body like a
huge bar of soap.)

Samuel Birch

While no one would ever replace Pettigrew as the master
mummy-unroller, Samuel Birch, Keeper of Oriental Antiquities
at the British Museum, became his successor by default. While
his knowledge of Egyptology was far greater than Pettigrew's,
Birch lacked medical training and his reports of unrollings all
suffer from this. His terminology is imprecise—he calls the abdominal cavity the "stomach"—and rarely offers interesting observations about pathology. In 1850, unwrapping a mummy
belonging to the Earl of Londesborough,[20] he stated that the
embalmer's incision was "under the left arm." It is difficult to
imagine how internal organs could be removed through such a

FIG. 59. *Discovering mummies for the Prince of Wales in 1862.*

slit. Within the wrappings Birch found a *Book of the Dead* and several amulets, but most interesting were the silver gloves on the mummy's hands. Birch describes the *Book of the Dead*, amulets, and gloves in some detail, but tells us little about the physical state of the mummy.

It is unfortunate that it was Birch who became the next high priest of the unrollers; he had little interest in mummies, but because of his museum position he was often called upon to examine them. Birch had a unique opportunity to examine the Prince of Wales' mummies. The prince had sailed up the Nile in 1868 in the grand style, with one boat solely for transporting his wines. When royalty visited Egypt, it was usually arranged that something memorable was to be found. A large number of coffins and mummies were "discovered" for the prince near the colossi of Memnon at Thebes. About thirty coffins and mummies were hoisted from a tomb cut ninety feet into the bedrock and given to his highness as a souvenir by the Viceroy of Egypt.

The prince returned to England with twenty of the best, and this group was examined by Birch at Clarence House. His report devotes more than twenty pages to translations of writings on the coffins, discussions of funerary rituals, hieroglyphs, etc., but only one sentence describes the mummies themselves: "The process of embalming which had been used varied in the different mummies, some having been preserved by the bitumenical process, others simply dried and salted, or prepared by wax."[21] The mummies and their coffins were eventually distributed among various museums and friends of the prince who accompanied him to Egypt. A unique opportunity was lost because the wrong man had been given the job.

Birch's reports on his excursions into mummy unwrapping are all similar—much on coffins and language, but little on the mummies themselves. In his report of unwrapping the Duke of Stafford's mummy, he discusses the cartonage and Egyptian religion in great detail, but hardly mentions the mummy.[22] Prior to Birch, mummies had usually been unrolled by physicians, but now a dangerous precedent had been set. The next non-physician unroller was the Director of the Egyptian Antiquities Service, Gaston Maspero, who did more damage to important mummies than all his predecessors combined.

Gaston Maspero

The Deir el Bahri cache of royal mummies found in 1881 had the potential of providing considerable data on royal mummification techniques. Maspero was in France when the mummies were transported from Thebes to Cairo, so it was Émile Brugsch, his assistant, who began their unwrapping. Chastising him in the official report, Maspero says, "Within the first few weeks of their arrival at Boulaq, Mr. Émile Brugsch could not resist the desire to see for the first time one of their faces, and opened, without permission, and during my absence, the mummy of Tuthmose III."[23] Occupied with translating the coffins' inscriptions and the dockets on the mummies, Maspero waited several years before unwrapping the mummies. When

FIG. 60.
Mummy of Tuthmose III, showing where the Abd er Rassouls tore at the chest in search of the heart scarab. This was the first mummy unwrapped from the Deir el Bahri cache, and Brugsch was severely chastised by Maspero for doing so without his permission.

he began to do so it was as if in a frenzy, tearing through one mummy after another.

By order of the Khedive of Egypt, on June 1, 1886, the mummy of Ramses II was unwrapped. Attending were the Khedive, his entire council of ministers, various doctors, archaeologists, artists, and others. In his report Maspero attempts to create the impression that everything was done scientifically and with caution. He explains that every measurement was taken by two of those present, then verified by two other attendants.[24] In truth, the proceedings must have been frantic. Maspero unwrapped *three* mummies that day, two kings and a queen—the start of a good poker hand, but bad Egyptology. The next week, in a single day Maspero unwrapped the mummies of Seti I, Seqenenre Tao II, and Ahmose I, a far cry from Granville, who fifty years earlier had taken a week to dissect the pelvic area of his one mummy. One can only wonder what

Maspero's hurry was. In less than one month, from June 9 to July 1, twenty-one mummies of the Deir el Bahri cache were stripped of their wrappings.

Most of the mummies that escaped Maspero's hands were later unwrapped by Grafton Elliot Smith, a physician who had the necessary training, but who also worked too quickly. During 1905, Smith unwrapped nine mummies, including those of Tuthmose IV, Ramses IV, Ramses V, Ramses VI, Siptah, and Seti II. Smith's account of these unrollings in the museum's *Catalogue General* is almost obsessively brief, allotting each pharaoh a mere page or two.[25] His descriptions provide a few insights into royal mummification, such as position of the abdominal incision, but at times he is clearly more interested in the features of the royal visage than how the pharaoh was mummified. Fortunately, the era of whirlwind unrolling was drawing to a close. Science was becoming specialized, and it would soon be realized just how much information could be extracted from the study of a mummy. It was the dawn of paleopathology.

6
Paleopathology:
The Dead Are Our Teachers

The reasons for unwrapping are as varied as the unwrappers, ranging from the search for gold to morbid curiosity to the desire to learn mummification techniques. Paleopathology is a relatively new addition to this list.

The term "paleopathology" was first coined in 1892 by R. W. Schufeldt, a German physician.[1] The term, derived from two Greek roots (παλιος, "ancient," and παθος, "suffering"), means the study of diseases, or pathological conditions, in ancient people. The initial investigations centered on bones, for the obvious reason that they are both the best-preserved parts of the body and the easiest to study. More recently, advanced technology has permitted sophisticated studies even of soft tissues. The focus of paleopathology has changed considerably over the years, and now even the cloning of mummies is under consideration.

The broad aim of paleopathology is to understand how diseases begin, spread, and die out. To understand a modern infectious disease and predict its course, we must know as much of its history as possible. This is the role of paleopathology. By analyzing Egyptian mummies and comparing the frequency of their pathological conditions with those of modern man, we may gain insights as to whether our modern style of living is the cause of specific diseases. For example, arterial disease is frequently attributed to the stresses and strains of contemporary life, or to our modern high-fat diets. If ancient Egyptians also suffered from arterial disease, such theories would be placed in doubt. The answer to this question was made possible in the early part of this century by Sir Armand Ruffer.

Ruffer's Early Work

Ruffer, the son of a French baron, studied first at Oxford and later with the great Louis Pasteur. While researching a serum for diphtheria he contracted the disease, and, like so many ailing Europeans of his day, went to Egypt to recuperate. He fell in love with the country and stayed, becoming professor at the Cairo Medical School. Ruffer was in Egypt when large numbers of mummies were being excavated, knew Gaston Maspero and soon acquired an interest in applying his medical skills to the difficult study of ancient mummies.

Ruffer devised a technique for studying microscopic features of soft tissues. The problem with ancient tissues is that they are so brittle that they crumble if sliced thinly enough to be put under a microscope. In a note in the *British Medical Journal* for 1909, Ruffer discusses the difficulties he experienced in his first attempts with fragments of mummies from the Twenty-first Dynasty.[2] But he developed a method to soften the tissues by soaking them in a solution of alcohol and 5 percent carbonate of soda. This softened the tissue enough for sectioning and microscopic investigation. The solution, still known as "Ruffer's Solution," opened a new field of study.

Using this technique, Ruffer examined hundreds of tissue samples taken from mummies. One of his first puzzles was a sample of what looked like a human organ caked with mud given to him by Petrie from the tomb of an Egyptian prince named Ranefer that was discovered at Meidum. When Ruffer put a section under a microscope, he could clearly see the characteristic arrangement of liver cells.[3]

Through his newfound ability to see the microscopic structure of ancient tissues, Ruffer discovered that some aspects of the health of ancient Egyptians were remarkably similar to that of modern Egyptians. For example, one surprising similarity emerged when Ruffer developed a technique to examine arteries microscopically. Buried deep in tissues, arteries are quite difficult to dissect out. Ruffer was given an assortment of broken arms and legs from mummies of various periods in 1910 on which to conducted his research. He soaked entire limbs in his solution to soften and rehydrate the tissue so the arteries could be dissected out; the arteries then were placed in the solution for twenty-four hours more and cleaned. Soaking them in glycerine for a few weeks finally allowed them to be sectioned for microscopic inspection. Ruffer was shocked to discover that the ancient Egyptians suffered from arterial diseases similar to ours, with calcification like that found in autopsies of modern cadavers.

Even in Ruffer's day, the causes cited for arterial problems were high-fat diet, modern stress, and tobacco. None of these could be attributed to the ancient Egyptian, so Ruffer notes:

> I cannot therefore at present give any reason why arterial disease should have been so prevalent in ancient Egypt. I think, however, that it is interesting to find that it was common, and that three thousand years ago it represented the same anatomical characters as it does now.[4]

Ruffer also found that ancient Egyptians suffered from a modern Egyptian blight, bilharziasis. Small worms, which live in the irrigation canals and near the banks of the Nile where the water slows, bore through the soles of the feet of farmers and fishermen working in the water and enter the body, causing severe damage or even death. Ruffer found a quantity of calcified eggs of *Bilharzia haematobia* in the kidneys of two mummies, thus establishing that the disease is not solely modern.[5]

Ruffer also studied teeth of mummies from Egypt and Nubia.[6] For this he was in the right place at the right time. The Aswan Dam was being raised and would create a huge lake behind it, flooding many ancient Nubian sites. Surveys and excavations were hastily arranged before the impending flood, and many mummies became available for study.

Thus Ruffer was one of the first investigators to learn of the unexpected amount of wear on the teeth of both Egyptians and Nubians. Even the dentition of children less than ten years old

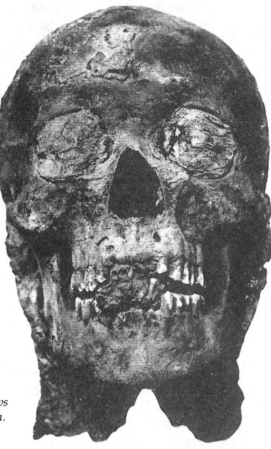

FIG. 61.
The mummy of Amenhotep III shows
poor teeth and periodontal condition.
EGYPTIAN MUSEUM, CAIRO

showed considerable wear. In adults the teeth often were worn down to the pulp, exposing the pulp cavity to infection. Such exposure would cause great discomfort, and because the ancient Egyptians had no remedy for infection, death could result. Vulnerability to tooth decay was not limited to the poor. The mummy believed to be that of Amenhotep III exhibits such rotted teeth and poor periodontal condition that he must have experienced constant pain. The degree of dental wear is generally related to diet; this seems to be the explanation of the ancient Egyptians' worn teeth. Sand infiltrated their food, especially their stone-ground bread, literally grinding down the teeth.

Ruffer's work on teeth, published posthumously in 1920, was his last. In December 1916 he left Egypt for Salonika, intending to reorganize the Sanitary Service for the Greek Provisional Government. On the way back to Egypt, his ship was lost at sea. Yet after only ten years work in the infant field of paleopathology, Ruffer had placed it on firm, scientific ground.

He was followed by two other pioneers in the field: Sir Grafton Elliot Smith and Warren Dawson. Dawson's great contribution was *Egyptian Mummies*, which he co-authored with Smith in 1924. It was the first book since Pettigrew's 1834 *History of Egyptian Mummies* devoted exclusively to the scientific study of mummies. Although much of Smith and Dawson's work has been superseded by modern techniques, much of it remains valuable.

Grafton Elliot Smith was an Australian anatomist appointed as professor of anatomy at the Cairo School of Medicine during Ruffer's tenure there. He too examined the mummies uncovered during the archeological survey of Nubia. His greatest contribution, however, was a systematic and careful study of the royal mummies in the Cairo Museum. Toward the end of his career, his ideas became rather eccentric; he championed, for instance, the theory that Egypt was the source of nearly all the customs of the civilized world.

During the half-century following the studies of Ruffer, Dawson, and Smith, paleopathology remained an individual pursuit, with isolated physicians applying their skills on mummies. But with scientific knowledge increasing at a fantastic rate, especially in the field of medicine, specialization became essential. No one physician could read the literature in all fields; the general practitioner became outmoded, and teams of specialists the rule. A similar trend befell the study of mummies. No one physician could be expected to command all the skills required to perform an autopsy on a mummy, to analyze the various tissue samples, or to have expert knowledge of botany, chemistry, and biology. Thus the Paleopathology Association was formed in the 1970s.

Instrumental in its establishment was an autopsy on a mummy loaned by the Pennsylvania University Museum to a group of scientists at Wayne State Medical School. The mummy was designated "PUM-II" (mummies are named after the museum or university that owns them, and this was the second of the Pennsylvania University Museum's mummies to be examined; PUM-I, examined earlier, proved to be poorly preserved, with little soft tissue remaining). Because of the complexities that arose in this examination and the varieties of skills required to resolve them, the autopsy clearly showed the need for teams of specialists.

The mummy had been X-rayed before the autopsy, a standard procedure so the team would know what to expect before unwrapping. The X-rays showed that PUM-II was a young man whose mummy was well preserved. The team's Egyptologist, William Peck of the Detroit Institute of Arts, began the work by unwrapping yards and yards of linen, which must have seemed endless to the rest of the team, primarily physicians eager to see the body. Indeed, they had to be very patient; the body under the linen had been coated with resin, and it was now so hard that hammers, chisels, and a Stryker saw had to be used to break through to the tissue.

As the saw began to cut through the hardened resin, heating it, the resin gave off a fragrant odor. It was startling to smell something from millennia ago, and the team working on PUM-II mentioned this experience in their report in *Science*.[7] One doesn't expect olfactory connections with the past, though their occurrence is not unknown.[8] When the Metropolitan Museum of Art washed the linen of Wah, a nobleman who died almost four thousand years ago, the fragrance of frankincense and myrrh filled the room.

When PUM-II finally emerged from his resin coat, he proved to be a rather handsome man of thirty-five or so with regular features—even his eyelashes remained intact. X-rays had indicated that his right leg and foot were deformed, raising the speculation that he may have suffered from osteomyelitis, the same bone disease that ended Mickey Mantle's baseball career. The abdominal cavity contained four packets of his internal organs.

The autopsy continued throughout the day, with some difficulty because the hot resin that had been applied to the body had penetrated most of the bodily cavities. For more than eight hours the team worked on the body of this long-deceased Egyptian. Samples of different tissues were collected, including the eyes, one with its lens still recognizable. It was months before most of the samples were analyzed, but there were some important finds.

The lung tissue showed a high silica content; PUM-II had pneumoconiosis, a lung disease almost certainly caused by inhaling desert sand throughout his relatively short life.[9] The deformity of his foot proved not to be pathological, but had been caused by the vigorous wrapping of the embalmers. The deformity of his right leg, however, was indeed pathological, caused by noninfectious periostitis. Along with his other problems, PUM-II, like many other ancient Egyptians, had arteriosclerosis. In addition, at some time during his life an acute middle-ear disease caused a perforated eardrum.[10] The most surprising discovery, however, came not from the body, but from PUM II's wrappings.

It is generally believed that the Egyptians did not have cotton until modern times. To everyone's amazement, however, when PUM-II's wrappings were analyzed by the U.S. Department of Agriculture, a ball of cotton was found wrapped in a piece of linen. Cotton was being grown in India at this early time, but this was the first example from ancient Egypt. (The cotton may, however, merely be a modern contaminant of PUM-II.)

Because disease is often correlated with unusual levels of trace elements in the body, analyses were made of these elements in the tissues of PUM-II.[11] For example, anemia is caused by iron deficiency, while a lack of zinc retards growth in adolescents. Still another technique that would prove to be important was an attempt to analyze the blood of PUM-II[12]; when later perfected, blood analysis would establish relationships between various pharaohs of Egypt. Perhaps even more important for the future, the team attempted to extract proteins from the tissues of PUM-II.[13] This was an essential step toward the extraction of DNA from a mummy, which occurred a decade later and could lead to the cloning of a mummy in the very distant future.

PUM-II is an important part of the history of paleopathology. New techniques that improved on Ruffer's work were developed for the microscopic study of mummified tissues. Because each organ has a different pattern of cell organization—tissue from a liver is clearly distinct from heart tissue—different procedures had to be worked out for each tissue sample. When a pathologist works with modern tissue, the first step is usually to place it in formalin to "fix" it, which kills any organism that may contaminate the sample and stops all enzyme activity. This step does not have to be taken with mummified tissues because the dehydration during embalming has "fixed" the tissue so no further decomposition can occur. However, because the tissue is dehydrated, it must first be rehydrated. When this is done it can be embedded in wax to hold it firm so that it can be sectioned by a microtome, a high-tech slicing machine. The thin slice is then placed on a glass slide and the remaining wax removed. The sample is not yet ready for viewing; it must first be stained with special dyes so that the features of the tissue under study will appear clearly under the microscope. The usual dyes are not always useful for mummified tissues, and different dyes had to be tried. Many of the new techniques were worked out by A. T. Sandison and Theodore Reyman, who are still active in the Paleopathology Association.[14]

PUM-II, however, was only a beginning; it was followed by PUM-III,[15] PUM-IV (a child), ROM-I,[16] and others. With each succeeding autopsy, techniques were refined and more discovered about diseases in ancient Egypt. Jeanne M. Riddle used electron microscopy to examine the blood of PUM-III to reveal its basic structures, such as blood cells, in a series of spectacular pictures.[17] Far more powerful than a standard optical microscope, the electron microscope reveals incredible detail. Samples less than one millimeter in diameter are embedded in plastic and sliced into sections less than a thousandth of a millimeter thick by an ultramicrotome using a diamond knife. An electron beam passing through the section then produces the image. Built into the electron microscope is a camera that can photograph desired features of the sample.

The research progressing in America was mirrored in England, where two major collections of mummies had been assembled, one in the Manchester Museum and one in the British Museum. In 1975 an autopsy was performed on England's equivalent of PUM-II, a mummy merely called "No. 1770." A team of scientists led by Egyptologist Dr. Rosalie David at-

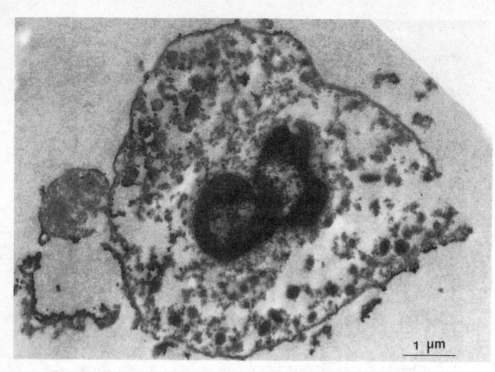

FIG. 62. *Transmission electron micrograph of neutrophil present in a blood clot found in PUM-III. The nucleus and some of the cytoplasmic neutrophilic granules can still be identified.* PHOTOGRAPH COURTESY DR. JEANNE M. RIDDLE

tempted to learn what they could about the life and death of No. 1770. They had, in fact, an interesting precedent for their research.

In 1906, Dr. Margaret Murray had unwrapped and performed preliminary autopsies on the mummies of two brothers housed in the Manchester Museum. This was certainly a pioneering and bold study, especially for a woman at the turn of the century, but resources and knowledge of how to proceed were limited, so not a great deal was learned. It was to be quite a different story with No. 1770.

From the very beginning there were puzzles about this mummy. X-rays showed that the lower portions of the legs were missing. One had been amputated below the knee, the other above the knee. The X-ray also showed that something was wrapped in linen between the mummy's legs. Because the X-rays indicated that No. 1770 was a teenage girl, it was sug-

FIG. 63.   *Dr. Margaret Murray (in apron) performing an autopsy on one of the two brothers.*   MANCHESTER MUSEUM

FIG. 64.   *Dr. Rosalie David examining mummy No. 1770.*   MANCHESTER MUSEUM

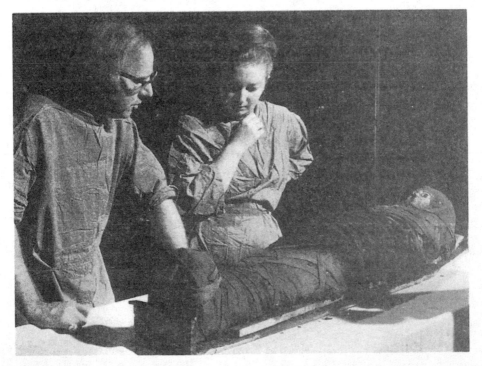

gested that she may have died in childbirth and that the package perhaps contained her foetus, or perhaps that the birth was out of wedlock and that the girl had been mutilated as punishment![18] This sort of speculation proves that scientists have as fertile imaginations as anyone else.

A careful examination of the leg bones was made when the mummy was unwrapped. The ends of the bones, where the breaks had occurred, showed no signs of the calluses that would have formed had the legs been amputated during the deceased's lifetime. It is possible that the legs were broken after death; indeed, the linen package between her legs proved to contain artificial feet encased in slippers, so the teenager would have all her bodily parts in the next world. The leg broken off above the knee had a wooden splint attached to it, as if to make it complete, but this raised another question. The splint attached directly to the bone, indicating that the surrounding tissue was already absent at the time of splinting. Therefore the body must have been decomposed when it was mummified. Confirming this view was the fact that traces of red and blue paint were found on the bones of the skull. Thus here too there was neither skin nor tissue present—otherwise the paint could not have been put on the bones. All these signs pointed to decomposition of the body before wrapping. The imagination of the autopsy team again roamed freely. Perhaps she had fallen in the Nile; a crocodile had chewed off her legs, and the body decomposed until it was recovered later. Then another bit of mystery emerged. There was no doubt that No. 1770 was a teenage girl—in fact she wore gold nipple-shields, as was common for mummies of the Roman period. However, the autopsy team found an artificial phallus between her legs, as was traditional for males. Was No. 1770 the world's first hermaphrodite? All the questions raised during the unwrapping were later answered by nonmedical scientific tests, again indicating the virtues of the team approach.

Samples of both the bones and the wrappings of No. 1770 were eventually submitted to radiocarbon dating, a technique that can be used only on once-living materials. Carbon dating is based on the fact that all plants and animals contain carbon and that carbon occurs in three forms, or isotopes. Because it is radioactive, only one isotope, Carbon 14 or C-14, is used for dating. While the plant or animal material tested was alive, it absorbed C-14. After death carbon is no longer absorbed; the unstable C-14 inside the body begins to decay and break down into nitrogen. The greater the time since the plant or animal died, the greater the time for decay and the less C-14 will remain in the sample. Dating requires about five to ten grams of matter, which is burned under carefully controlled conditions to determine the quantity of C-14. Because the rate of decay of C-14 is constant, the age of the sample can be calculated. For Egyptian samples this test is usually accurate to within a century. In the case of No. 1770, that was sufficient to solve the mystery.

The wrappings of No. 1770 proved to be from the Roman period, just as the exterior decorations had indicated, but the bones were well over a thousand years older than the wrappings.[19] The mummy had been rewrapped a thousand years after its original embalming. During that time the body had deteriorated, perhaps losing its legs, so by the time a second set of embalmers went to work on it there was little tissue left. Thus they placed the splint next to the bone and painted the skull. The body was probably so badly damaged that they could not tell whether it was male or female. Taking no chances, they gave it both nipple-shields *and* a false penis. The only mystery now is who No. 1770 was, and why she was important enough to be given such care ten centuries after her death.

Although No. 1770 was the only mummy as yet unwrapped by the Manchester researchers, they still had the remains of two brothers and a few other mummies previously unwrapped that now could be analyzed by modern techniques. The findings of the pathologists who analyzed these mummies confirmed what their American colleagues had found: The average ancient Egyptian was in very poor health.

When tissues from the lungs of Nakht Ankh, one of the two brothers, were examined under a microscope, it was discovered that one lung had partly collapsed and its blood vessels were surrounded by tiny particles. Nakht Ankh's lungs were like those of modern miners who inhale lethal doses of coaldust. When the particles were examined, they were found to be mainly silica, sand breathed into the lungs. Nakht Ankh had suffered from sand pneumoconiosis, just as do many modern Egyptians.

In the intestines of Asru, a woman who lived approximately three thousand years ago, numerous worms were found. These worms (Strongyloides), which live in contaminated soil, enter the skin through the feet and travel through the blood vessels to the lungs. Then they follow the air passages to the throat, where they are swallowed, thus reaching the stomach and eventually the intestines. They produce swellings in the lungs and intestines, and cause wheezing, coughing, and asthmatic symptoms, all of which probably plagued Asru.

A Guinea worm found in No. 1770 can grow up to a yard in length and cause fevers, itching, and considerable discomfort. The fact that so many worms have been found in such a small sample of mummies suggests that worms were common afflictions of the ancient Egyptian.

The teeth of the Manchester mummies showed the familiar patterns of extreme wear, but were high in calcium, and thus not susceptible to decay. Although the Egyptians did not suffer from ordinary cavities as we do, perhaps because of a difference in diet, the excessive wear their teeth received ground them down enough to expose the pulp and thus, as mentioned earlier, cause the root to become infected.[20] The abrasives that caused this wear could have come from two sources: sand blown into food during its preparation, or particles entering bread from the stones on which the grain for it was ground. Dr. John Prag of the Manchester Museum conducted an experiment to determine which source was the culprit. He ground corn on ancient grindstones for fifteen minutes and produced very coarse flour; when he added a bit of sand and continued grinding, however, he obtained a much finer flour.[21] Thus it is possible that the Egyptians intentionally added sand to the grain they ground. X-rays of ancient Egyptian bread have revealed large quantities of mineral particles; some had come from grindstones, but most was sand.[22]

During the 1970s fundamental procedures for investigating mummies were developed and a great deal learned about health in ancient Egypt, including the fact that the ancient

Egyptians were like their modern counterparts in some ways and in other ways very different. Indeed, they too suffered from arterial disease, worms, and sand in their lungs. However, unlike the modern Egyptians and modern people in general, they may not have suffered from cancer. While bone tumors have been found, no cancerous tumors have conclusively been discovered in the soft tissues of any Egyptian mummy. Thus mummies teach us that some forms of cancer—of the breast, lung, stomach, etc.—may be strictly modern diseases.

X-rays

While mummies yielded significant secrets in the 1970s, the development of paleopathology in the 1980s provided even more spectacular discoveries. One reason for this was the development of X-ray axial tomography.

X-raying a mummy is the first step in any autopsy. From x-rays one can often determine the sex and approximate age of the deceased and sometimes even the cause of death. The great virtue of the procedure is that it is nondestructive and all its data can be collected without unwrapping the mummy.

The first X-ray of a wrapped mummy was published by Flinders Petrie in 1898 as the final illustration in his excavation report of Dashasheh, a site eighty miles south of Cairo. The developed film showed the leg bones of a mummy that had been wrapped and perhaps rewrapped.[23] This first use of X-rays, only five years after their discovery, was not imitated immediately. Twenty-six years later, Smith and Dawson mention in their *Egyptian Mummies* that only one mummy in the Egyptian Museum in Cairo had been X-rayed, that of Pharaoh Tuthmose IV.[24] What they do not say is that this pharaoh was also the first to have ridden in a taxi cab. The mummy had to be taken from the Egyptian Museum to the hospital that owned the only X-ray machine in Egypt, and Smith and Howard Carter transported the mummy by cab. Soon after, full-body X-rays for mummies became common outside Egypt. But the most spectacular breakthrough came half a century later with the development of the CAT scan.

A CAT scan takes a series of X-ray cross-sections of the body so that a complete record of the subject can be made. A computer can then image the subject from any angle. The first application of this technique was on the brain of a fourteen-year-old weaver named Nakht who died around 3,000 years ago (he is known to paleopathologists as "ROM-I"). The CAT scan showed the internal structure of the brain, including ventricles. The most advanced stage of this technique is known as "axial X-ray tomography," and in the hands of a skilled technician it is an art form, producing beautiful images as well as vast amounts of information.

Scanning the body and recording the information takes less than half an hour, after which the information is transferred to tape. A computer can be programmed to present any view desired. The mummy of POST-I (autopsied at C. W. Post College) was scanned by Dr. Elliot Fishman, director of the Division of Computed Body Tomography at Johns Hopkins Hospital in Baltimore. We were particularly interested in the skull, so Dr. Fishman produced a videotape in which the skull appears to be rotating through 360 degrees; it can be seen from every angle, without the fragile specimen having to be unwrapped or handled. With computerized axial tomography, Egyptologists no longer have to wonder what amulets or jewelry remain inside the wrappings. Fragile mummies need not be destroyed by unwrapping; others that are wrapped beautifully may now remain intact.

Cloning

By far the most startling discovery made by studying Egyptian mummies is that it is possible to isolate and clone DNA taken from four-thousand-year-old bodies. News of the cloning of DNA from an ancient Egyptian mummy first appeared in the British scientific journal *Nature* in 1985.[25] It told of the work of a Swedish scientist, Svante Pääbo, whose research was based

FIG. 65. *Cerebral hemispheres of the brain of Nakht, a fourteen-year-old weaver.* PHOTOGRAPH COURTESY DR. PETER K. LEWIN

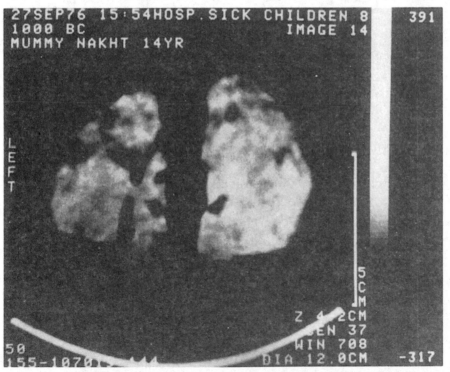

FIG. 66. *CAT scan of the brain of Nakht. The ventricular outline and white and gray matter can be identified.* PHOTOGRAPH COURTESY DR. PETER K. LEWIN

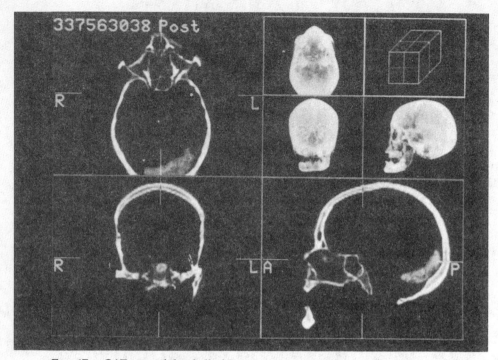

FIG. 67.   *CAT scan of the skull of Post-I as computer-processed to present images of the skull rotating through space.*   PHOTOGRAPH COURTESY DR. ELLIOT FISHMAN

on previous efforts to clone extinct animals.

DNA, or deoxyribonucleic acid, is the genetic material in every living cell. The molecule takes the form of a helix of two chains wound around each other, the famous "double helix." These chains consist of four kinds of links or units. The way these units are strung together, repeated, and alternated is what we call the genetic code. The human genetic code is composed of about six billion such units.

The first attempt to clone "old" DNA was made by a research group at Berkeley in 1984. From the skin of a quagga, a relative of the zebra extinct for more than a century, the team located and then reproduced the animal's DNA. Cloning old DNA had been impossible before PCR (Polymerase Chain Reaction) techniques were developed in 1983. The two steps for this process are: First the DNA sample is extracted and the two strands of the double helix are split into single strands. Next, the single strands are immersed in nucleic acid bases whose enzymes reproduce the missing strand; the amount of DNA is thus doubled. This process can be repeated indefinitely until enough DNA is produced for analysis. The fantastic possibility of creating a quagga from cloned DNA amounts to reconstituting an extinct species—which, of course, is not possible yet. It would require a complete DNA double helix that could be inserted into a modern zebra embryo, and that in turn implanted into a mother zebra. The DNA would then program the development of a quagga fetus that, if carried to term by the zebra, would be born as a quagga. However, of the six billion units of a quagga DNA chain, it was possible to reproduce only 200 units from the hundred-year old quagga skin.

A frozen woolly mammoth more than 40,000 years old found in 1977 in northeastern Siberia provided scientists with an opportunity to look at some far older DNA.[26] However, the Russian scientists permitted the mammoth to thaw before placing it in a fixative, and then oven-dried it,[27] destroying a great deal of the surviving DNA. Although some DNA was located in the mammoth's tissues, it was not enough to clone.[28]

With both the quagga and the woolly mammoth as precedents, Svante Pääbo attempted to isolate and then reproduce DNA from an ancient Egyptian mummy. After examining tissue samples from twenty-three Egyptian mummies, he found traces of DNA in tissues of one infant and two adults. The DNA he found in the cartilage cells from the outer ear of an adult female and in skin from the head of the adult male had both deteriorated too much for cloning. However, the cells taken from skin on the left leg of the infant, which was stored in the Egyptian Museum in Berlin, had remarkably well-preserved DNA. Using the PCR method, Pääbo grew more than 3,000 DNA subunits, as compared to 200 from the quagga clones.

This cloning of DNA from an Egyptian mummy raises exciting possibilities that may be realized in the 1990s. Clonings so far have used mitochondrial DNA, which is found in the body of the cell, not the nucleus. Mitochondrial DNA comes exclusively from the mother, while chromosomal DNA in the cell nucleus comes from both parents. In the future it should be

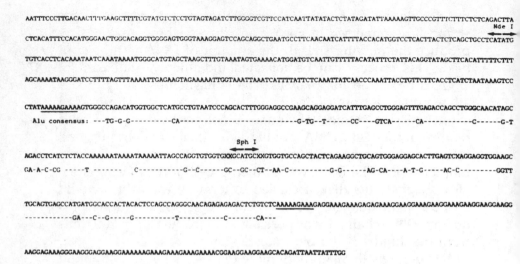

FIG. 68.   *DNA sequence of part of the clone of a 2,400-year-old mummy of a child.*   PHOTOGRAPH COURTESY DR. SVANTE PÄÄBO AND NATURE

possible to clone chromosomal DNA, yielding additional information, such as determining the parentage of royal mummies, which could settle identities conclusively. Devised by Professor Alec Jeffreys of Leicester University in 1984, the technique is based on the fact that DNA varies among individuals as much as fingerprints do. A child acquires half its nuclear DNA from each parent, so his chromosomes contain the DNA patterns of each parent. After electrophoresis has separated DNA strands cut by special enzymes, radioactive probes can identify the sequences. These tagged sequences are exposed on X-ray film to allow identification and comparison.

In fact, once sufficient DNA can be extracted and cloned, we may be able to settle the question of the true origins of the Egyptians. No one really knows from where they first entered the Nile basin. On an even broader view, molecular archeologists hoping to extract DNA from Neanderthal bones may be able to trace human evolution not just morphologically, from the shape of bones, but genetically, from DNA found *in* the bones.

Paleopathologists have done a great deal to apply medical technology to the study of mummies. Their focus has been primarily on disease in the ancient world, and while this is important work, it is not exactly what is needed for our human mummification project. To determine mummification procedures for a pharaoh, we need the technology of the paleopathologist and the orientation of the Egyptologist. The unique research on the mummy of Ramses the Great provides both.

7
Special Treatment: Ramses the Great

Ramses the Great is one of the few pharaohs who emerges from history with a personality. During the sixty-seven years of his reign he built so many monuments and usurped so many statues of his predecessors that the image of an egomaniac became impressed on the public's mind. Ramses' temple at Abu Simbel, fronted by four sixty-seven-foot colossal statues of himself, is as impressive as any monument ever built. Bound foreign captives cowering at the feet of the pharaoh line the entrance; the walls inside show Ramses single-handedly defeating the Hittite army at the battle of Kadesh. Other temple reliefs boast of his 200 children—and everywhere he carved his name deeper into the stone than any other pharaoh had so that no successors could erase it. Ramses knew about such practices, for during his reign he repeatedly erased the names of his predecessors from their temples and statues to replace them with his own, which earned him the nickname, among Egyptologists, of "The Great Chiseler." His numerous colossal statues impress even the casual tourist to Egypt. Although eleven pharaohs shared his name, Ramses II, "The Great," is the one posterity remembers.

Shelley's "Ozymandias" is about the fallen statue of Ramses at his mortuary temple. "Ozymandias" is the Greek corruption of Ramses' throne name—"User-Maat-Re." Thus Ramses became the paradigm of the egoistic monarch. More exhibitions have been devoted to Ramses II than to any other king of Egypt, despite the fact that no jewelry or wonderful objects from his tomb have been found. It is the man and his reputation that generate all the interest.

By the mid-1970s it had long been realized that the pharaoahs in the "Mummies Room" of the Egyptian Museum were literally falling apart. Comparing the photos of Ramses II in Elliot Smith's 1912 volume, *The Royal Mummies*, with the mummy's present state revealed clear signs of deterioration. Cracks in the skin were larger, the hole in the thoracic area had grown, and the skin texture had changed somewhat. All of this was to be expected, for the mummies had lain for decades in simple wood coffins inside glass cases that were not hermetically sealed. Thus, the mummies shared the air breathed by thousands of visitors, and were open to microbe infestations of various sorts. Neither temperature nor humidity had been controlled. Also, the mummies had been exposed to the sun's ultraviolet rays—which promotes the growth of certain bacteria cultures—that came streaming in through the museum's windows. The tombs in which the mummies had rested for thousands of years had been extremely dry, thus preserving the bodies. In the museum, the thousands of tourists visiting the mummies added their humidity, both from perspiration and breathing, to the environment, so it was not surprising that the mummies had deteriorated since being removed from their tombs a century before.

In 1975 the French government requested the mummy of Ramses for its "Ramses the Great" exhibition, but after an inspection of several royal mummies by a French physician, Dr. Maurice Bucaille, the Egyptian Antiquities Organization decided that a study of the stability and condition of Ramses would be necessary before he could be exhibited. Eventually the French government was asked to conserve the mummy of Ramses II,[1] so when he finally traveled to Paris it was as a patient, not as an exhibit.

The royal mummies housed in the Egyptian Museum have always enjoyed a special status, both good and bad. Since their hasty unwrapping at the turn of the century, first by Maspero and then by Smith, they have remained relatively untouched. While objects such as those found in Tutankhamen's tomb have been restored and conserved, the mummies were viewed as a different category, more as people than as artifacts, and thus no conservation measures were taken for them. The royal mummies had never been permitted to travel to exhibitions and had never been studied with modern scientific methods. Thus when the mummy of Ramses was permitted to leave Egypt for conservation and study, it was a major event. Because the mummy had originally been requested for an Egyptological exhibition, Egyptologists would be involved in the research, and something about mummification of the pharaoh would almost certainly be revealed.

The transportation of an ailing 3,000-year-old-mummy is not an easy task. Its fragile condition dictated the basic principle—move the mummy as little as possible. In the museum in Cairo Ramses had lain on a thin cloth mattress inside the bottom half of a wood coffin. The mummy remained in the coffin for the trip to Paris, with specially molded packing placed around his body. His destination was the Musée de l'Homme (Anthropology Museum), where a team of scientists had gathered to evaluate his condition and decide what conservation measures might be required.

Ramses arrived at Le Bourget Airport in Paris on September 26, 1976, receiving a full military reception reserved for former heads of state. His arrival was none too soon, for his condition required immediate treatment, although not everyone agreed on precisely what to do.

When the mummy reached the Musée de l'Homme, the first question was how to remove Ramses from his coffin. The traditional method would have been to pass belts under the body and lift it out. Given enough belts there would be relatively little weight at each pressure point, since the desiccated Ramses weighed less than forty pounds. Even this method, however, was considered too much of a risk, so it was decided to saw off the foot end of the coffin, then slip a thin Plexiglas sheet (actually Altuglas—similar material, different manufacturer) under the cloth mattress to slide the king out. Then the mattress was cut away in sections from under the mummy, each piece being numbered so it would be known what part of the body had rested on which section. Small fragments of Ramses had fallen onto the mattress over the years, and these samples could

FIG. 69
Lid of the coffin in which Ramses II was found at Deir el Bahri. EGYPTIAN MUSEUM, CAIRO; PHOTOGRAPH COURTESY DAVID MOYER

FIG. 70.
Mummy of Ramses II in its simple wood coffin. EGYPTIAN MUSEUM, CAIRO

be analyzed to see what sections of the mummy were worst off. These analyses took several months to complete, during which time a great controversy erupted.

A headline in *The New York Times* of November 8, 1976, read: RAMSES' ILLNESS WAS FABRICATED SCIENTISTS ALLEGE. Two scientists—James Harris, an American dentist who had written a book, *X-raying the Pharaohs* (1973), and an Egyptian, Ibrahim Nawawy, an official at the Egyptian Museum—claimed that the disintegration of Ramses II had been fabricated by French scientists for the mere prestige value of treating him in Paris. Six days later the *Times* carried a rebuttal by the French scientists, including a statement by Dr. Gamal Mukhtar, the Director of the Egyptian Antiquities Organization, who said that Ramses had gone to France only because he needed treatment. The results of the tests would show how right Mukhtar was.

Ramses was biologically infested. The bacteria identified on and in the mummy were the result of modern contamination, but posed no immediate threat to its condition. Fungi, however, were a real danger and were slowly destroying it—370 separate colonies consisting of 89 different species of fungi were identified. Some fungi were specific to the wood of the coffin, some were growing on the linen, others were localized in vegetable matter within the body, and some were on the body itself. Aspergillus was the most destructive fungus, thriving because of the combination of temperature and humidity to which the mummy had been exposed while on exhibit in Cairo. The pressing question became how to cure the patient.

Most of the established techniques for treating infested objects could have damaged the mummy: Heating could have burned the mummy's tissues and melted the resins impregnating the mummy; cold would contract the tissues, which later would expand, causing fractures; chemical treatment could affect tissues, and the Egyptian Antiquities Organization would not permit its use. Therefore only a few choices remained, the most obvious being gamma-ray irradiation.

Gamma-ray sterilization is common both in hospitals and in art conservation. Operating-room instruments are routinely sterilized by irradiation with gamma rays, but delicate works of art are also irradiated to kill all living organisms while leaving the art work unaffected. The technique is also used on meat and other food products. Given these successful uses, it was a reasonable tool for decontaminating Ramses the Great.

Although the chemical nature of an object treated by irradiation remains the same, occasionally a change in color occurs, and this concerned the scientists responsible for bombarding the mummy of Ramses II with gamma rays. One area of special concern was the resins inside the mummy and on its surface, and so numerous tests preceded the treatment of Ramses' remains. The Egyptian Museum provided resin from other Nineteenth Dynasty tombs for testing, which did not change color when subjected to gamma-ray sterilization. Fragments from other mummies were also tested, and even some parchment, because its texture was similar to Ramses' skin. From these tests it was determined that the mummy of Ramses could tolerate twelve hours and forty minutes of irradiation at 1.8 megarads. This treatment was administered over two sessions of six hours and twenty minutes each. When it was over, Ramses was cured: The bacteria and fungi which had infested the pharaoh's body were gone.

In addition to sterilizing the mummy, other tests and inspections were performed that shed some light on how Ramses was mummified. From the X-rays taken, it appears as if the internal organs had been removed, wrapped in linen, and then replaced in the body. I say "appears" because while the X-rays definitely show wads of some material in the abdominal cavity, they could not indicate exactly what that material is. It is unfortunate that no CAT scans were taken, since they reveal more than X-rays and may have been enough to settle the question. If it is the internal organs that we see on the X-rays, it would be unusual for a burial of the Nineteenth Dynasty; prior to the Twenty-first Dynasty the normal procedure was to place the internal organs in canopic jars, not inside the body. One possibility is that when the body of Ramses was moved from his plundered tomb in the Valley of the Kings to the cache at Deir el Bahri during the Twenty-first Dynasty, his canopic jars were found broken and their contents spilled on the tomb floor. The embalmers restoring the body could have wrapped and placed the organs inside the body, though this would have been a difficult procedure on a mummified body. The state of the internal organs is not the only area of uncertainty regarding Ramses' mummification.

The official report states that the heart is still in the thorax, but opposite its natural place.[2] One explanation for its being on the right side rather than the left may be that it was accidentally cut by the embalmers in the course of removing other internal organs and was improperly replaced. The X-ray seems to show metallic threads in the area, so Ramses' heart may have been sewn in place with gold thread. This, too, would have been an extremely difficult operation because the embalmers would have been working through the embalmers' incision in the abdomen, not through a chest opening as in modern heart surgery. It must be stressed, however, that one cannot be certain from the X-ray that it *is* the heart that one is looking at. If a CAT scan had been taken, perhaps it could have resolved the question with greater certainty. The heart, however, was almost always left inside the body in both royal and nonroyal mummifications, so it probably is the heart that appears on the X-ray.

If the heart indeed remains in the mummy, that fact contradicts a longstanding belief that Professor Loret of Lyons saw Ramses' heart at the beginning of this century. Apart from the X-ray, however, there is good reason to doubt this story—the thorax is completely closed on all sides and the abdominal cavity is blocked by whatever is inside the mummy, so the heart couldn't have been removed after the body was mummified.

One feature of Ramses' mummy that received considerable attention and study was the hair, for it was strikingly red-blond. A variety of analyses showed that the embalmers dyed the pharaoh's hair, probably with henna, so he would look young forever. The hair of an eighty-year-old such as Ramses would have turned white; however, traces of the hair's original color remain in the roots even in advanced age. Examined microscopically, Ramses' hair proved to have once been red. This has more than just cosmetic significance. People with red hair in ancient Egypt were associated with the god Set, the slayer of Osiris. Although Set killed the good god, and in the mythology is clearly presented as malevolent, the followers of Set were

accepted instead of being viewed as we might view Satan wor-
shippers. Ramses' father was Seti I, whose name means "fol-
lower of Set," and thus Ramses may have come from a family
of redheads. The study of Ramses' hair also provided another
finding, which was inflated well beyond its importance, perhaps for political reasons.

It has often been claimed that the ancient Egyptians were
black. Indeed, some writers have gone so far as to claim that
Cleopatra was black. In the case of Cleopatra, we are reasonably
certain that she had light skin because she is directly descended
from generations of the Greek Ptolemies. The truth is that some
Egyptians were black and some were not. Perhaps in reaction
to the claim that the Egyptians were black, the editors of the
official publication of the Ramses II studies (*La Momie de Ramses
II*) wrote in their summary of results:

> At the conclusion of this immense work, an important scien-
> tific conclusion remains to be drawn: the anthropological study
> and the microscopic analysis of hair, carried out by four labo-
> ratories: Judiciary Medecine (Professor Ceccaldi), Société
> l'Oréal, Atomic Energy Commission, and Institut Textile de
> France showed that Ramses II was a "leucoderm," that is, a
> fair-skinned man, like prehistoric or ancient Mediterraneans or,
> perhaps, the Berbers of Africa.[3]

When all the studies were completed, a picture of Ramses
emerged that was quite different from his popular image and
the way he portrayed himself on his numerous monuments.
Ramses was often depicted in battle as a youthful warrior riding
in his chariot, reins tied around his waist, shooting unerring
arrows at his enemies. In the public mind, Ramses became the
larger-than-life statues such as those at Abu Simbel. But
Ramses' mummy reveals an old man suffering from advanced
atherosclerosis—an X-ray of his pelvis shows calcification of
both femoral arteries. For at least the last decade of his life he
must have walked stooped, crippled by arthritis. His teeth show
great decay and all are worn down; there is a hole in the mandible caused by the spread of dental infection. An abcess
around his teeth was serious enough to cause death by infec-

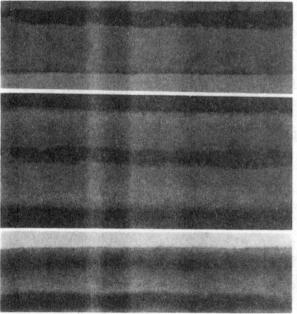

tion, and while we can't be certain that this caused his demise, we can be sure that Ramses' last days were spent in agony.

With the studies of the mummy completed, only cosmetic touches were needed. Ramses' ancient linen wrappings were dusted, washed, and rewrapped more neatly than when he had arrived in Paris. Minor cracks in his skin were filled with a compound of natural substances such as beeswax, turpentine, Vaseline, etc. At the end of his stay in Paris Ramses was in far better condition than on his arrival.

Last, his cedar of Lebanon coffin was restored and a small Altuglas bed was constructed in it to elevate the pharaoh's body so visitors could see it. A thin mattress of linen stuffed with cedar chips was placed on the bed. Final stereographic photos were taken of Ramses' head so a computer assisted portrait could be made—a final souvenir of his visit to Paris. Ramses was ready to go home.

All cosmetic work, photography, restoration of the coffin, and so on were done prior to the gamma-ray irradiation so that everything would be sterile for the trip home. Ramses' coffin was placed in a special Altuglas display case composed of only two molded pieces rather than the usual six rectangles glued together. Two pieces meant fewer seams, and thus less chance of leaks.

For the trip, the mummy, coffin, and case were all kept sterilized inside a clear plastic tent similar to those in which children born with immune deficiencies live. Inside were all the tools needed to complete the unpacking and installation of Ramses once he reached Cairo. All the objects could be manipulated by plastic gloves built into the sterile tent. This system was flown to Egypt on May 10, 1977, after Ramses' seven-and-a-half-month visit to Paris.

At the Egyptian Museum the plastic tent was inflated and, using the sterile tools and plastic gloves inside it, workers removed packing material from around the mummy. An electrically powered ventilation system maintained the air inside the display case at a slightly higher pressure than the outside atmospheric pressure so that contaminated air would not flow into the case if a leak developed. Because power blackouts are frequent in Cairo, a backup electrical system for the ventilation

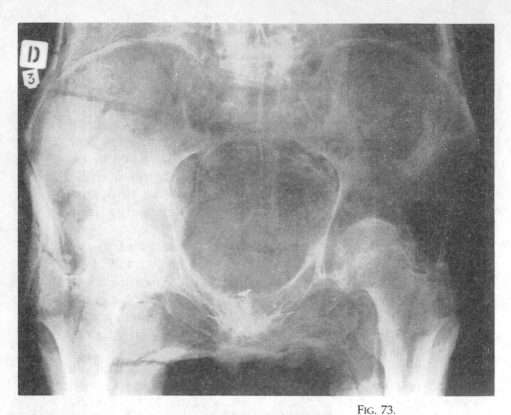

FIG. 73.
X-ray of Ramses II's pelvis showing calcification of both femoral arteries and their branches. COURTESY DR. CLÉMENT FAURÉ, HÔPITAL TROUSSEAU, PARIS

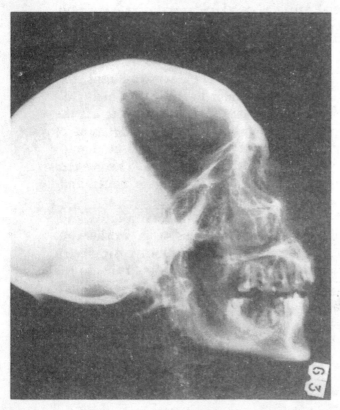

FIG. 74.
X-ray of Ramses II's mandible. The hole was caused by the spread of massive dental infection serious enough to have killed the pharaoh. COURTESY DR. CLÉMENT FAURÉ, HÔPITAL TROUSSEAU, PARIS

system was included. Two antibacterial filters were fitted with airlocks so bacteria would not enter the case when the filters were changed. Thus the mummy would not come in contact with contaminated air when the filters were changed every four years.

It would be nice to be able to say that this was the happy ending to "Ramses the Great's Most Excellent Adventure," but just as Ramses entered Paris with controversy, so he left it. Soon after his departure from France, criticism began appearing in the press concerning the way the French team had handled the mummy and its installation. There were allegations that the irradiation changed Ramses' skin and hair color. One American scientist said that the process had "roasted" the pharaoh. In truth, Ramses had not changed color, nor was he roasted; the irradiation had only changed the color of the display case. But some other dangers remain. The one defect in Ramses' new case is that it was not designed to control temperature and humidity, so the mummy remains subject to these fluctuations. Another problem is maintenance. As of 1993 there was no record of the antibacterial filters ever having been changed. Thus, the originally antiseptic atmosphere may have been polluted years ago.

The refurbished mummy of Ramses II was displayed briefly in President Anwar Sadat's "War and Peace" room at the Egyptian Museum in late 1979, but the public has not seen it since. If an overall evaluation of the Ramses project were to be made, it would have to be rated a partial success. The lack of humidity and temperature control, and the contamination by outside air, did not augur well for the fate of poor Ramses. In 1987, the Egyptian Antiquities Organization turned to the Getty Conservation Institute, an adjunct of the Getty Museum, for more help in preserving the king's mummy.

With vast financial resources left by oil billionaire John Paul Getty, the Getty Conservation Institute has earned a reputation as the premier conservation facility in the world, using both the best materials and the best scientists that money can buy. A history of successful work with Egyptian antiquities, most recently in conserving the extremely fragile tomb of Ramses' wife, Queen Nefertari, adds to its list of successes. Presently the Getty is investigating the cause of the Sphinx's deterioration in order to suggest measures to arrest its decay.

Since the problem of how to preserve Ramses II is no different from that of how to preserve any other mummy in the Egyptian Museum, the Getty's project became how to preserve *all* the royal mummies. The answer was surprisingly simple—nitrogen.

When the French chemist Antoine Lavoisier first isolated the components of air, he called nitrogen "azote" ("without life") because nothing could live in an atmosphere of nitrogen. Nitrogen makes up 79 percent of air's volume, and the percentage becomes even greater in sealed tombs, where the oxygen is removed from the atmosphere when it bonds with metal objects to form metallic oxides. The high percentage of nitrogen may account for the wonderful state of preservation of the objects in Tutankhamen's tomb (indeed, when the tomb was first opened, Lucas tested it for bacterial growth and found it to be sterile). So the Getty's solution to the problem was to seal the mummies hermetically in an atmosphere of nitrogen, sterilizing them. The Getty borrowed a mummy from the Egyptian Museum for six months and conducted various tests to see if this solution would work. The test was a complete success, so a case was designed that controlled temperature and humidity while maintaining the mummy in an atmosphere of pure nitrogen. The first case was delivered to the Egyptian Museum in 1989.

In 1994, I spoke with Dr. Nasri Iskander, the conservator at the Egyptian Museum responsible for the mummies. He told me that the museum had built enough cases to place twelve royal mummies on display, and that Ramses the Great would be included. Sometime in 1994 Ramses and his relatives should once again be receiving visitors.

Although Ramses' is the only pharaoh's mummy to have undergone careful scientific investigation, little new was learned about royal mummification from it, and in this sense the study was disappointing. The X-rays indicated that Ramses' heart was left in his body, but on the wrong side. The internal organs appear to have been removed, preserved, wrapped, and then placed inside the body—a technique common in the Twenty-first Dynasty but unusual in the Nineteenth. The one new and interesting detail is the cosmetic concerns of the embalmers who dyed Ramses' hair so he would appear youthful. Aside from this, there are no indications of any exceptional treatment afforded a king's mummification.

After our study of the mummy of Ramses the Great, our sources are almost exhausted. We have examined the mummies of kings and commoners, seen what the Greeks visiting Egypt said about mummification, and scanned ancient papyri looking for clues. While we have a good understanding of the procedure, it is far from complete. There is, however, one last group of mummies that must be studied—animals.

8
Animal Mummies

The ancient Egyptians mummified all kinds of animals, from bulls to mice, literally by the millions. This seemingly strange practice fascinated both ancient and modern writers, but most of them misunderstood it, assuming that there was a single reason for animal mummification, while in fact there were four distinct purposes: 1) Pets were buried out of fondness; 2) Animals were buried as food for deceased humans; 3) Animals were ritually killed and mummified as offerings to the gods; and 4) Certain sacred animals were mummified when they died of natural causes. Perhaps the most misunderstood situations are those where animals are found in human tombs.

The Egyptians were fond of animals, frequently depicting household pets in paintings and reliefs on their tomb walls. The pet-beneath-the-chair motif shows the master of the house seated with a pet cat beneath his chair. Dogs and monkeys were also frequently shown as pets. Because the Egyptians believed that the next world was a continuation of this one, and that you could "take it with you," it is not surprising that they had their pets mummified and included them in their tombs.

Several animals were found in the Deir el Bahri cache, almost certainly pets. One, a gazelle, was encased in a wooden coffin in the shape of its body, but another pet proved to be a surprise. Within a coffin containing Queen Makare of the Twenty-first Dynasty was a wrapped bundle. An inscription on the coffin suggested it was Princess Mutemhet, and Maspero poignantly conjectured that "The Queen Makare, wife of the High-Priest and King, Pinedjem I, died, giving to the world the infant which

FIG. 75.
Coffin containing the pet gazelle of Princess Esemkhet. EGYPTIAN MUSEUM, CAIRO

FIG. 76.
Mummy once believed to be Princess Mutemhet, but actually a pet baboon. EGYPTIAN MUSEUM, CAIRO

was buried with her." The mummy remains wrapped, listed in Smith's *Catalogue General* volume *The Royal Mummies* as a princess. However, when the princess was X-rayed in 1968, she turned out to be a female baboon.[1] Maspero had misread the inscription; "Mutemhet" was merely one of the queen's own names, the baboon almost certainly her pet. The gazelle in the Deir el Bahri cache belonged to her half-sister, Esemkhet.

Describing the death of pets in Egypt, Herodotus says:

> *All the inhabitants of a house where a cat has died a natural death, shave their eyebrows, and when a dog dies they shave the whole body including the head. Cats which have died are taken to Bubastis, where they are embalmed and buried in sacred receptacles; dogs are buried in sacred burial places in the cities where they belong.[2]*

As we shall see, Herodotus has conflated two different kinds of animal mummies: pets, and those given as offerings to the gods.

Herodotus was not the only traveler to be confused about animal mummies. Belzoni, the Italian strongman turned archaeologist, discovered a cache of animal mummies while he was excavating in the area of the Valley of the Kings in 1816. Not sure of their purpose, all he could do was describe them:

> *I must not omit, that among these tombs we saw some which contained the mummies of animals intermixed with human bodies. There were bulls, cows, sheep, monkeys, foxes, bats, crocodiles, fishes, and birds, in them: idols often occur; and one tomb was filled with nothing but cats, carefully folded in red and white linen, the head covered with a mask representing the cat, and made of the same linen. I have opened all these sorts of animals. Of the bull, the calf and the sheep, there is no part but the head which is covered with linen, and the horns projecting out of the cloth; the rest of the body being represented by two pieces of wood, eighteen inches wide and three feet long, in an horizontal direction, at the end of which was another, placed perpendicularly, two feet high, to form the breast of the animal. The calves and sheep are of the same structure, and large in proportion to the bulls. The monkey is in its full*

form, in a sitting posture. The fox is squeezed up by the band-
ages, but in some measure the shape of the head is kept perfect.
The crocodile is left in its own shape, and after being well
bound with linen, the eyes and mouth are painted on this cov-
ering. The birds are squeezed together, and lose their shape ex-
cept the ibis, which is found like a fowl ready to be cooked, and
bound round with linen, like all the rest.[3]

Belzoni knew the Valley of the Kings contained tombs for
kings, tombs for queens, and even some for commoners, but he
didn't realize that there were even tombs for pets.

In January 1906, Theodore Davis came upon a pit tomb that
surprised him. The tomb lay at the bottom of a twelve-foot shaft
cut into the bedrock. Davis described his descent into the tomb
in his usual colorful style:

I went down the shaft and entered the chamber, which proved
to be extremely hot and too low for comfort. I was startled by
seeing very near me a yellow dog of ordinary size standing on
his feet, his short tail curled over his back, and his eyes open.
Within a few inches of his nose sat a monkey in quite perfect
condition; for an instant I thought that they were alive, but I
soon saw that they had been mummified, and that they had
been unwrapped in ancient times by robbers. Evidently they
had taken a fragment of the wooden monkey-box on which they
seated the monkey to keep him upright, and then they stood
the dog on his feet so near the monkey, that his nose nearly
touched him. . . . I am quite sure the robbers arranged the
group for their amusement. However this may be, it can fairly
be said to be a joke 3000 years old.[4]

Because the tomb is near that of Amenhotep II, Davis suggested
that these animals were the king's pets. They could equally well
have been the pets of the original owner of the tomb, whoever
he may have been.

Near this tomb waited another that Davis' excavator, Edward
Ayrton, described as ". . . completely filled with animals, all of
which had been originally mummified and done up in cloth
wrappings." Ayrton's description of the contents is min-

FIG. 77.   *Mummified baboon and dog eye-to-eye. Probably a tomb robbers' joke for
eternity.*   PAINTING BY HAROLD JONES; PHOTOGRAPH COURTESY
DENNIS FORBES

imal, but sufficient to show that the tomb housed some strange
occupants. One mummy was of a large cenocephalic ape wearing a necklace of blue disc beads; another was of a large monkey whose wrappings had been torn from its head; there were
also an unwrapped ibis, three mummified ducks, and ". . . some
bundles of intestines made up in the form of little human figures; one of these had near it a mask of beautifully colored
stucco, representing a human head, which had probably originally fitted it. This was certainly of the XVIIIth Dynasty."[5]

The contents of the tomb do not make much sense. While all
were animals, they were not all were buried in the tomb for the
same reason. Monkeys, ibises, and baboons were associated
with various gods, ducks were not. Ducks were eaten, the other
animals were not. The wrapped intestines could be a canopic
hoard, but Ayrton does not say if he found the expected four
bundles, nor does he describe them in detail. The mask is intriguing, but unexpected considering the other items in the

tomb. If the contents of the tomb still exist together somewhere, they are worth further investigation.

Because Belzoni, Davis, and Ayrton had no interest in mummification, they left no comments about the process used to preserve the ibises, cats, dogs, etc., they unearthed. Viewed more as curiosities than objects of serious study, they were noted and cast aside. Fortunately, many animal mummies brought to Europe and America as souvenirs by nineteenth-century travelers are still available for study. Over the past twenty years my Egyptology classes have performed a series of autopsies on animal mummies to determine the methods used to embalm them. The first mummy studied was a cat, but this proved too emotional for the "cat people" in the class, so all subsequent autopsies were on fish mummies, to which students seem not so attached.

Hundreds of fish mummies have been found, but it is not known for certain *why* they were mummified. Most of the fish mummies are Nile perch, *Lates niloticus*. A painting in the tomb of Khabekhnet, a son of Sennedjem, shows a *Lates* being mummified by Anubis. While we do not know why this species was mummified, we may well know the reason for mummifying a different species, the *Bagrus bayad*.[6] Plutarch tells us that when Osiris was cut into pieces by his evil brother Set, his phallus was thrown into the Nile and eaten by three fish of different species. One he calls the "Phagrus," which is probably our *Bagrus*. Thus, this fish may have been sacred because of its association with Osiris and perhaps was mummified for this reason.

Our autopsies on several examples of the *Bagrus* showed minimal concern for preservation. In almost all cases the fish were in poor condition, with little soft tissue remaining. It seems as if these fish did not have their internal organs removed and were only partially dehydrated, if at all. As a result, upon burial insects began to destroy the soft tissue. As is often the case, shoddy embalmers' work was covered by careful wrapping, with eyes and mouths beautifully painted on the linen. Our results suggested that mummified animals did not receive anything near the care that human mummies received.

Often confused with mummified animals are foodstuffs provided for the *ka* (soul) of the deceased, to sustain him until he

FIG. 78. *Anubis mummifying a Nile perch. Tomb of Khabekhnet, Thebes.*

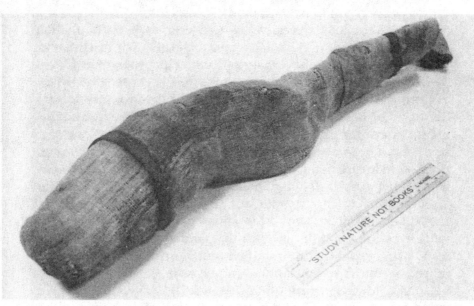

FIG. 79. *Mummified* Bagrus bayad, *one of the fish that devoured the phallus of Osiris*

Fig. 80.   *Removal from Tutankhamen's tomb of white egg-shaped coffins*
containing ducks and other food—the boy king's last "order to go."

enters the next world. All kinds of foods have been found
in tombs, including breads, fruits, meats, and fowl. Tutankhamen's tomb contained numerous duck- and egg-shaped
wooden boxes, painted white, that held joints of meat and fowl.
These are not mummified, but rather food placed in coffin-like
boxes to sustain the deceased.

Most animal mummies played a role in the religion of the
ancient Egyptians, but it is difficult to say exactly what that role
was. The main question is whether or not the Egyptians worshipped these animals. Most Greek and Roman sources say that
they did, while most Egyptologists today say that they did not.
The evidence for both sides is worth considering.

Egyptologists generally agree that animals were not considered divine by the Egyptians, although some deities were represented in animal form. For example, cats were associated in
some way with Bast, a feline goddess depicted as a cat, but the
ordinary pet cat was not treated as a goddess. To strengthen

their position, Egyptologists point out that animals such as cats, ibises, falcons, etc., were raised just to be killed and presented as offerings to the gods. Surely animals raised for slaughter could not have been considered gods. This is a reasonable position, but it still does not prove that the Egyptians never worshipped animals. There is considerable ancient evidence to the contrary.

Certainly the ordinary house cat, or its feline relatives raised for ritual slaughter, were not considered gods. The Egyptians understood that there was just one goddess, Bast, not thousands of them mewing and chasing mice. However, compelling evidence suggests that the Egyptians did worship bulls. This evidence was provided first by ancient Greek writers, and later confirmed more dramatically by Auguste Mariette's first excavation in Egypt.

Sacred Bulls

The Louvre had sent the young Mariette to Egypt in 1850 to purchase Coptic and Syriac manuscripts from the patriarchs of the Coptic Church. When negotiations bogged down, Mariette had plenty of time to visit antiquities dealers in Cairo. In these shops he saw several similar sphinxes, and when he asked where they came from, the reply was always "Saqqara." In his book on the Serapeum, Mariette records that he reached his decision to excavate at Saqqara on October 17, 1850, when he climbed to the top of the citadel to view Memphis, Dashur, Giza, and Saqqara. All thoughts of Coptic manuscripts were forgotten. The next day he hired donkeys and mules, bought provisions and a tent, and nine days later was walking the sands of Saqqara. He stumbled on a head much like those on the sphinxes displayed in the Cairo shops. Clearing away the sand, he uncovered fifteen sphinxes. He recalled the description of Strabo, the ancient geographer, who described a place called the Serapeum, where the Apis bulls were buried, and mentioned that it was preceded by an avenue of sphinxes. By November 1, Mariette had spent the money he had been given to buy manuscripts on thirty workmen to search for the Serapeum.

The word "Serapeum" is a corruption of a corruption. It is based on the conflation of two gods' names—Osiris and Apis.

In ancient Egyptian, Osiris's name was written ⌇⌇ ⌇ and pronounced "*Usir*." "Osiris" is the Egyptian word with the Greek ending tacked on. In Egyptian the other god, ⌇ ⌇ ⌇ ⌇ was pronounced "*Ap*," but was pronounced "Apis" by the Greeks. During Egypt's Greek period, the two gods merged to become Usir-Ap; then the Roman added the "eum," to indicate that this was the place of Usir-Ap, the "Serapeum." Herodotus, who seems to have missed nothing, described the cult of the Apis:

> *This Apis—of Epaphus—is the calf of a cow which is never afterwards able to have another. The Egyptian belief is that a bolt of lightning comes down to the cow from heaven, and this causes her to have the Apis. The Apis calf has special markings. It is black with a white diamond on its forehead, the image of an eagle on its back, the hairs on its tail are double, and a scarab is under its tongue.*[7]

The cult of the Apis was central to Egyptian religion of the Late Period, and Mariette was fixed on finding the burial place of the Apis bulls, but doing so proved far more difficult than he initially thought. He uncovered sphinxes that only led to more, in fact to 130 by the time he was finished. Along the way he uncovered other unsuspected antiquities—a semicircle of Hellenistic statues of Greek philosophers, including Plato, a beautiful statue of the god Bes, now in the Louvre along with one of the sphinxes, and many other statues and smaller antiquities. Finally, he arrived at the courtyard of a small temple built by Nectanebo II, the last native Egyptian king. Reliefs declared that the temple was dedicated to the Apis.

Mariette thought the entrance to the tombs might lie beneath the paving stones of this temple, and pried them up. He was wrong about the entrance, but found hundreds of small bronze and faience amulets of various gods. Word soon spread of Mariette's discovery, but, as is usual in Egypt, it was exaggerated

Fig. 81.
Early drawing of the Serapeum showing a sarcophagus of an Apis bull.

and the trove became "thousands of gold statues." The Egyptian government ordered Mariette to cease all excavations; later, after considerable deliberations, he was permitted to continue. In November 1852, after removing tons of debris, Mariette finally found the entrance to the Serapeum, and became the first person in modern times to enter the burial place of the Apis bulls.

He entered a high, spacious corridor about an eighth of a mile long, lined on both sides with twenty-four open chambers. They contained huge granite sarcophagi carved to receive the mummies of the Apis bulls who had died between the beginning of the Twenty-sixth Dynasty (663 B.C.) and the end of the Greek period (30 B.C.). All the fifteen-ton lids of the sarcophagi had either been removed or broken, and the bulls they contained had been plundered.

Another gallery was discovered; it contained Nineteenth to Twenty-second dynasty burials in wooden coffins. In the middle of this gallery stood a huge rock too heavy to budge, so Mariette blasted it with explosives. In the ground under the rock was a single intact coffin containing what appeared to be the mummy of a man. A gold mask covered the face, while amulets suspended from a gold chain hung on the neck. Two jasper amulets bore the name of a famous son of Ramses II, Kha-em-Wase. Eighteen human-headed amulets bore the inscription "Osiris-Apis, great god, lord of eternity." When Mariette opened the mummy, he found only a mass of perfumed bitumen and a mixture of small bones. It is likely that this was not the grave of Kha-em-Wase, but the partial remains of another Apis made to resemble the venerable high priest of Ptah.

Mariette found yet a third, even earlier gallery of Apis burials dating from the Eighteenth Dynasty. Here an unplundered chamber contained two large rectangular coffins painted black. In wall niches were two statues of the pious prince and high priest Kha-em-Wase. Again, the coffins yielded a surprise; inside wrappings that appeared to be Apis bulls lay a jumble of small bones, and no trace of any bull's head. Gold amulets with Kha-em-Wase's name were mingled with the bones. These curious findings have led to a great deal of speculation about the fate of the Apis bulls. Some have suggested that the bulls were drowned before attaining a specified age.[8] This seems unlikely, and classical authors tell of Apis bulls dying of old age.[9] Besides, the drowning hypothesis does not explain the curious condition of the bull's incomplete remains. One possibility is that when the Apis died, part of it was eaten by the pharaoh to ingest its power. There is a famous text inscribed in King Unas's pyramid (Fifth Dynasty) that is called the "Cannibal Hymn" because it states that Unas devours the bodies of the gods, Unas feeds on the lungs of the wise ones, Unas smashes the vertebrae, etc. Thus, it is possible that when an Apis died, it was ritually eaten by the king. If this explanation is correct, the practice did not continue into the Late Period, in which there is proof that the Apis was mummified.

Many years after Mariette excavated the Serapeum, a unique papyrus of the Late Period was discovered. Now called the "Apis Papyrus," this demotic text describes in detail the ritual for embalming, wrapping, and burying the Apis bull. Included are instructions to the priests for setting up the embalming tent.

> *They must enter the lake with Isis and Nepthys before him,*
> *with two vases of natron in their hands, ten* mnht *bandages.*
> *. . . They must go into the Kiosk to the god and open his*
> *mouth, in the four places of the Kiosk, absolutely alone. They*
> *must perform for him all the ceremonies which are in the festi-*
> *val ritual. . . . They must perform the Opening of the Mouth*
> *for him with all its things set out.*[10]

This is clear evidence that, at least in the Late Period, the Apis was not eaten. Hard evidence comes as well from the temple at Memphis where the Apis bulls were mummified. Huge alabaster embalming tables were found with drains to channel the animals' blood and bodily fluids. In addition, Herodotus says that when the Persian king, Cambyses, invaded Memphis, he saw that the Egyptians considered the Apis a god and he killed the bull and ate it. Cambyses ate the Apis bull because such a thing was almost unthinkable and was a great insult to the Egyptians, another indication that the Apis was never eaten by the pharaoh.

Mariette found more than the remains of Apis bulls in the Serapeum. He mentions a gallery containing tombs of cows. Possibly this was the burial place of the mother of the Apis, who was also venerated. Mariette was not particularly interested in cows, so his description is frustratingly brief, although he does mention that he found a tomb in one of the burial chambers of a cow for a person who had the title "Priest of the Mother of the Apis." H. S. Smith, one of the modern excavators of the animal cemeteries at Saqqara, has written a marvelous

FIG. 82. *Embalming tables at Memphis used for mummifying the Apis bulls. A basin for catching blood is clearly visible.* PHOTOGRAPH COURTESY DAVID MOYER

fictional account of what the funeral of the mother of an Apis must have been like. Under the title of "Two Athenians at the Funeral of a Mother of Apis," he gives us a tourist's view of the proceedings.

> The funeral procession took the Serapeum road, the great bier and its canopy being borne on the shoulders of priests, moving at a slow dignified pace. By the time it arrived at the House of Rest, the sun was high in the sky. The bier was borne in state

up to the shrine of Isis, Mother of Apis in the temple enclosure
of Hepnebes. Here only the priests were allowed to enter, the
mourning crowd remaining in the great courtyard below. . . .
When the bier was brought forth from the shrine a great shout
of rejoicing went up from the crowd: "Oh Isis Mother of Apis,
may she remain and endure forever." Then the bier was car-
ried down into the House of Rest. Here the necropolis masons
once more took over. With great care the bier, the mummy,
and its canopy were lowered into the open sarcophagus and
laid to rest and a final prayer said: "Oh Taese, Mother of
Apis, may you be praised forever and ever!" Then the thirty
necropolis masons swung the huge sarcophagus lid, which had
been left in the main gallery, round into position in front of
the vault. Gradually they pushed it forward, a few inches at a
time, against the great friction, into its place up on the sar-
cophagus.[11]

Mariette's excavation ended in 1853, but he was able to ship
more than 230 crates of antiquities to the Louvre. Later he commented that he returned home with no Coptic manuscripts, but
sent back a temple stone by stone.

Because the Serapeum was robbed in ancient times, and be-
cause Mariette did not publish details of the appearance of the
bulls, our knowledge of the method used to mummify the Apis
is based primarily on the Apis Papyrus mentioned above. The
Apis cult was only one of three bull cults existing in ancient
Egypt. The Mnevis bull was worshipped and buried at Heli-
opolis, a place called "On" in the Bible. Only two burials of the
Mnevis have been found, so little is known about this cult.
About the third cult, however, more information is available.
The Buchis bull was worshipped at Armant, called "Southern
On," because it was the sister city of Northern On, or Heliop-
olis. The site of the burial of the Buchis has been thoroughly
excavated and described in detail, and provides the best picture
of mummification as practiced in all the bull cults.

Like the Apis, the Buchis was selected for its markings. According to the ancient writer Macrobius, the Buchis changed
color every hour and its hairs grew backward, that is, opposite
to the normal direction. Not only was the mother of the Buchis

honored, but often the owner of the land on which the bull was born was ceremonially recorded. When a Buchis was found, it was installed at Thebes and then rowed in a sacred bark back to Armant, where it lived. Armant became an especially important city during the Ptolemaic period, so much so that Cleopatra VII built a small temple there to honor the birth of her son Caesarion.

The place of the burial of the Buchis bulls, called "the Bucheum," was discovered and excavated in the 1920s by an Egypt Exploration Society team led by Sir Robert Mond and Oliver Myers. The cemetery was similar to the Serapeum, with long galleries cut into the rock and chambers at right angles. The sarcophagi are a bit different, however, in that the lids often are made of several pieces that span the top of the sarcophagus. These pieces are marked with directions instructing the workmen how to form them into a single lid.

When found, the mummies were in poor condition and the excavators were hampered by what they described as, "Evil circumstances of unusual strength and number [that] combined to prevent us from obtaining much valuable information about the mummies."[12] While not so ominous as the authors indicate, the conditions were indeed unfortunate. The water table had risen significantly since ancient times, so that many of the galleries were now submerged. Those that were dry had been plundered. Further, the stone into which the tombs had been cut was friable and had collapsed on the mummies. In spite of all this, we know more about the mummified bulls from the Bucheum than those from the Serapeum because the excavators of the Bucheum were professionals interested in every detail that could be gleaned from the data, while the young and eager Mariette had no training, and archaeology had not yet become a science in his day.

The excavators learned that the Bucheum bulls were mummified in a recumbent position. To accomplish this the embalmers had to cut the tendons in the bulls' legs. Then the mummy was fastened to a board with from twenty-one to twenty-three bronze clamps. The Apis Papyrus also specified that the embalming board be four and a half cubits long by one and two-thirds cubits wide, with twenty-two clamps. Since this almost exactly matches the size of the boards used for the Buchis, it appears that the Apis and Buchis bulls were mummified in similar manners.

The mummification techniques described in the Apis Papyrus parallel the physical evidence from the Bucheum. The bulls were not eviscerated; rather, the internal organs were removed by the "second method" described by Herodotus—through dissolving fluids injected in the anus. The Apis Papyrus states:

> *A lector (priest) goes before the anus. He must lay a cloth over himself and the god. He must take the cloth and all things that he finds there as far as his hand can go. He must wash it with water and stuff it well with cloth. He must lay out the stuff and the wrapping which the five priests, who are in the ships, have taken, and which contain the things of the anus. He must anoint them with ointment and wrap them in cloth.*[13]

This description explains why the internal organs of Apis and Buchis bulls have never been found—they were dissolved.

It is ironic that no papyri exist providing details of human mummification, of which there were millions, though we possess a papyrus for the mummification of Apis bulls, of which there were at most hundreds. There may be a simple explanation for this. Human mummification was a continuing industry; someone always could be found to pass on his skill to an apprentice. On the other hand, the mummification of the Apis was not an ongoing industry. There was only one Apis or Buchis at a time, so it was possible for the last person who mummified an Apis or Buchis to have died by the decade or so when the next one needed mummification. Thus it was essential for the ritual and procedure to be preserved in writing.

Once embalmed, the bull had to be wrapped. This too is described in the Apis Papyrus.

> *They must anoint the god with ointment and let him lie on a board while a basis of four stones is under the god. . . . They must cause the* skr-cloth *to go under the god.*
>
> *They must overlay the middle with* nbti-bandages *and the* mtr-cover. *They must tie it with a* sbn-bandage *from front to*

FIG. 83. *Apis bull exhibited at the New-York Historical Society, 1869.*

> *back and* vice-versa. *They must again knot the* skr-*stuff from outside under the god as it is outside.*
>
> *They must do all this while the father and prophets stand there before the cloth is cut up. When the stuff is cut they must raise a lamentation. They must bring the bier before the god and make him rest thereon.*[14]

After the wrapping, the Buchis was decorated for burial. We know from remains found in the Bucheum that the bull's eyes were inlaid, sometimes with stone, sometimes with glass, while the head was encased in a plaster mask covered with gold leaf. On top of the mask sat the crown that the Buchis had worn while alive, a solar disc with ostrich plumes flanked by two cobras:

Numerous *ostraca*—pottery or stone fragments used as common notepaper because papyrus was too expensive—found within the tombs provide an additional source of information about the Buchis bull cult. The *ostraca* in the Bucheum record the materials used in the embalming and details of daily routine.

The Serapeum was open to the ancient public so it could pay its respects, and the same seems true of the Bucheum as well.

Ostraca discuss payments for the harp players, public singers, and dancers who came to the Bucheum on festival days. Others detail payments weavers received for preparing the cloth for the Buchis' mummification.

The cults of the Buchis, Apis, and Mnevis bulls were among the most important of Egyptian animal cults, but they were not unique. At Kom Ombo in Upper Egypt and at Karanis in the Fayoum during the Ptolemaic period there were crocodile cults that were attached to significant temples. These cult animals were worshipped as gods and mummified. However, the vast majority of animal mummies were never worshipped, but instead bred as sacrificial offerings to the gods.

Animal Offerings

When someone wished a favor of a god, he would leave an offering in the god's temple. The offering could be a bronze statue of the god, food, or, if a particular animal was sacred to the god, a mummy of that animal. Statues were placed in special areas of the temples, but they accumulated in such profusion that periodically space had to be made for new ones. Because the old statues were sacred offerings they couldn't just be thrown out, so they were buried within the sacred grounds of the temple. The great "Karnak Cache," found at the beginning of this century beneath the ground of Karnak temple, contained more than 14,000 ritually buried statues. Mummified offerings, however, were treated differently.

Rather than merely placing mummified animals within a temple—which would have seemed just as inappropriate to ancient Egyptians as it does to us—they were buried in special cemeteries at the cult centers, such as those for cats at Bubastis in Lower Egypt, or those for ibises and baboons at Tuna el Gebel in Middle Egypt. These were offerings from the common man—a mummified cat or ibis cost far less than a bronze statue. An extensive animal-mummy industry must have existed because literally millions of animal mummies have been found, not household pets who died of natural causes, but animals

FIG. 84. *Romantic nineteenth-century depiction of the festival of the Apis.*

Fig. 85.
Mummified kitten. MUSEUM OF FINE
ARTS, BOSTON

raised to become offerings. This is not mere speculation; the mummies themselves tell the story.

Perhaps the most familiar image of all animal mummies is the cat. So numerous were these that at the end of the nineteenth century shiploads of mummified Egyptian cats were sent to England to be ground into the fields as fertilizer. (Out of one shipload of nineteen tons of mummified cats sent to England, only one cat skull remains today, in the British Museum.) The most famous cat cemeteries were located at Bubastis (the city of the cat goddess, Bast), but others spread up and down the Nile, with large cemeteries at Dendereh, Abydos, and Giza. Recently the British Museum X-rayed its collection of fifty-three wrapped mummified cats, which had been donated to it by Flinders Petrie at the turn of the century.[15] From this a picture of the animal mummy industry emerged.

Of the fifty-three examples, forty-four were aged twelve months or less. Clearly, in the business of raising cats for offerings, it was not desirable to feed and care for them for years. As soon as a cat was mature enough to be presentable, it was killed. The X-rays also revealed the method by which they were dispatched; many had had their necks broken.

The mummification technique for cats was relatively simple. The internal organs were removed and the body cavity stuffed with sand or some other packing material. To make the animal into a long, cylindrical package for easy wrapping, the front paws were pulled down in front of the body and the hind paws drawn up in front, as if the animal were seated. In this position, the cat was tightly bound. For more expensive models, faces were painted on the mummy in black ink. Dehydration occurred naturally rather than chemically after burial.

The most extensive animal cemetery is located at Saqqara. Vivant Denon, one of the team of scholars Napoleon brought to Egypt to study and describe the country, and who later became the director of the Louvre, saw the ibis galleries there in 1798. He mentions that a chamber containing more than 500 ibises had been discovered and that he was given two, which he describes in some detail:

> *The pots which enclose these birds, and serve for their sarcophaguses, are of red and common earth, of from fourteen to eighteen inches in height; their form bears a general resemblance to a sugar-pot; they are found in great numbers at Sakkarah, in subterranean chambers; these chambers are so dry, that the pots on being taken out appears [sic] still new, and that their antiquity might be doubted if the art of embalmment were not lost, and if the bird whose mummy is found had not left the soil of Egypt. . . .*
>
> *On proceeding to open the pot and the mummy it contained, the solder which fastened its lid, and which was made only of a kind of chalk, gave way with a slight effort. The enswathed bird was loose in the pot; and this explains the state of pulver-*

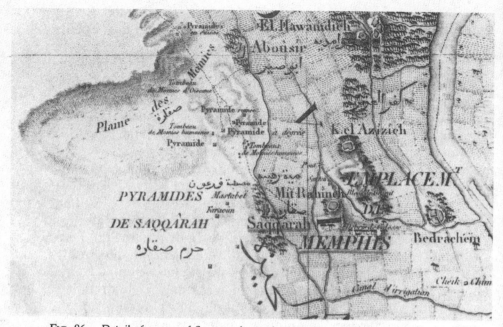

FIG. 86. *Detail of a map of Saqqara drawn by Napoleon's scientists. On the left of the map is an area labeled "Plaine des Momies" (Plain of Mummies). Just beneath the word "Momies" is the earliest mapping of the ibis cemeteries, marked "Tombeau de Momies d'Oiseau"—Tomb of the Bird Mummies.* DESCRIPTION DE L'ÉGYPTE

ization in which mummies of this kind arrive in Europe, after the jostlings of their journey. At first sight, the mummy of an ibis appears like that of a new-born infant; a fine cloth, of a bister-tint, and which appears to have been soaked in an aromatic fluid, after being crossed over the lower part of the body, covers the whole of one side; under this envelope, a double thread binds the mummy, horizontally and transversely, in the manner of a net, in all its parts; under this thread, the second envelope resembles the first, swathing the body in a similar manner; below this are little bandages, of an inch and an half in width, which like the thread, are wound round the bird in every direction.[16]

Denon was not the only member of Napoleon's team who became interested in the animal mummies. Mummified ibises

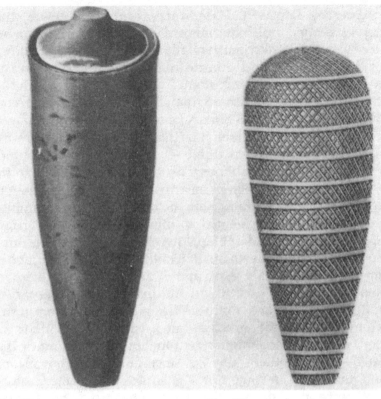

FIG. 87.
Pot containing a mummified ibis found at Saqqara by Napoleon's savants. DESCRIPTION DE L'ÉGYPTE

FIG. 88.
Elaborately wrapped ibis from inside a pot. DESCRIPTION DE L'ÉGYPTE

can be seen on several of the illustration pages of the *Description de l'Égypte.*

Despite their fame, the ibis cemeteries were not systematically excavated until almost 200 years later, in 1966, when Walter B. Emery began his search for the tomb of Imhotep, the architect of Zoser's step pyramid. The base of a now-lost statue found in the pyramid complex of King Zoser (Third Dynasty) listed Imhotep's titles as vizier, physician, and royal architect. In the Late Period he was deified as the Greek god of medicine, Aesculapius. Numerous ancient authors state that his tomb became a place of pilgrimage for the sick. Because Imhotep was the architect of the step pyramid of Saqqara, it is likely that he was buried nearby, along with Zoser's other courtiers. Knowing that pottery was often broken by pilgrims along their routes, Emery noticed a trail of broken pottery at Saqqara and concluded that the potsherds might lead him to Imhotep's tomb. His excavations uncovered several important Third Dynasty tombs. In the main pit of one he found more than 500 conical pots, each containing a mummified ibis. Emery, of course, knew the ibis was sacred to the deified Imhotep and that mummified ibises were brought as offerings to his tomb—but the tomb with the 500 ibises was not Imhotep's. Emery also found an entrance to the now-famous animal galleries nearby. The first gallery he entered had niches containing tens of thousands of mummified ibises that had been presented as offerings. Some were elaborately wrapped and had appliqué decorations sewn to the outer wrappings, often in the shape of Thoth, the ibis-headed god.

Emery continued his excavations and found a gallery of mummified baboons, each in a coffin placed in a niche carved from the soft limestone. Both the ibis and baboon were forms taken by the god Thoth and associated with Imhotep. In his six seasons at Saqqara looking for the tomb of Imhotep, Emery discovered several other galleries, including one for falcons. Within the rubble in some of the galleries were plaster casts of various human body parts—hands, feet, arms, faces, etc.[17] These were undoubtedly left by people with afflictions of those members, hoping to be healed. All the signs showed that Emery was near his goal. During the 1969–70 season he discovered the first written proof of a connection between the animal galleries and the cult of Imhotep. In a gallery of falcons he found a falcon coffin with a limestone stela on its top with a drawing of an ibis facing a falcon beside an offering table. Beneath the drawing, in black ink, was an inscription that convinced Emery he was near the tomb of Imhotep:

> May Imhotep the great son of Ptah, the great god and the good god who rest here give life to Petenfertem, son of Djeho, together with Paptah, son of Djeho, whom Tamneve bore. May their house and their children be established for ever. The blessing of the gods who rest here be upon him who reads this himself. . . . [18]

He hoped that following the galleries to their end would lead to Imhotep's tomb. However, parts of the galleries were totally blocked with thousands of mummified birds, whose clearing made slow work. Before the task was completed, Emery suffered a fatal stroke while working at the site. His colleague, Geoffrey T. Martin, finished Emery's partial excavation but had neither the time nor funds to complete the search for Imhotep. Martin drew the first detailed map of the animal galleries,[19] which showed that they continued for many a mile and contained more than one million mummies—and other galleries remained to be opened.

The extensiveness of the ibis galleries raises visions of the thriving industry that must have been connected with the mummies. Vast ibis farms must have existed to accommodate the demand. There probably were stalls along the pilgrimage route selling the wrapped and mummified birds. A pilgrim could select one according to his finances, after which it was probably placed in the pot and sealed in front of the customer. Then he would continue along to the place where his offering would be received by one of the priests of the gallery. The priest would accept the offering, see that it was reverently placed in a niche, and, for a small fee, say a prayer for the pilgrim.

This scenario is confirmed by a unique archive found during Emery's excavations in the ibis galleries. Called "the Archive of Hor," these writings by a priest of that name from the Sebennytos nome in Middle Egypt provide a glimpse of the activities around the ibis galleries in the second century B.C. Hor was born at about 200 B.C., moved to Memphis, and worked at the ibis galleries at nearby Saqqara. At times Hor experienced what he believed to be prophetic dreams, which he recorded on pottery fragments. He also used potsherds for drafts of official documents that would later be transcribed onto papyrus. Several dozen of his pottery fragments were found, from which something about life among the animal mummies can be reconstructed.

In one dream Hor says:

> *A great man called out to me, saying "come to me: I have found a house which is built, more than a house which lacks*

FIG. 89. *A highly romantic nineteenth-century rendering of* Feeding the Sacred Ibis *in which Karnak Temple serves as the background.* AFTER A PAINTING BY E. J. POYNTER

its roof-beams." He sat down in the middle of the dromos. He said to me, "Bring your clover, this food (for) the 60,000 ibises."[20]

The statement about bringing clover for the 60,000 ibises certainly suggests that live ibises were kept in the area of the galleries. Another pottery fragment refers to various officials in the galleries, one of whom is called the "doorkeeper," who Hor says must be reliable, for he supervises the birds and their young, and "Who until the sun sets will guard the ibis and keep it safe." The reference to the young of the ibis again indicates that it is live birds over which the doorkeeper watches, not mummies. Hor also mentions a "birth chapel," which may be a hatchery, and indeed caches of ibis eggs were discovered in the galleries.

While Hor is certainly to be believed about ibises raised in the neighborhood of the galleries, we cannot accept his figures without considerable doubt. First the number 60,000 comes from a dream; second, it seems too large for any one point in time. The galleries remained open for about four centuries, and a conservative estimate of the number of ibises buried in them is two million. This would mean that each century about half a million birds were deposited, on average, or about 5,000 per year. Thus there seems to be no need for 60,000 birds at any one time. These calculations are, of course, highly speculative, but they produce a picture of the Saqqara animal cemetery as a busy, bustling place with pilgrims coming and going, and a considerable volume of transactions taking place.

Several of Hor's records deal with reforms he urged for the managing of the mummy galleries. Apparently, many of the cemetery officials who were supposed to be present at various ceremonies were shirking their responsibilities, and the pious Hor wanted to put a stop to this. In his memoranda Hor refers to cemetery procedures. There was an annual mass burial of all the ibises offered over the course of one year. At this time the necropolis officials would gather in a procession terminating at a new gallery excavated to receive the burials. The procession included priests, the "servants of the ibises," as well as "the men who care for the bandages" (embalmers), and "efficient

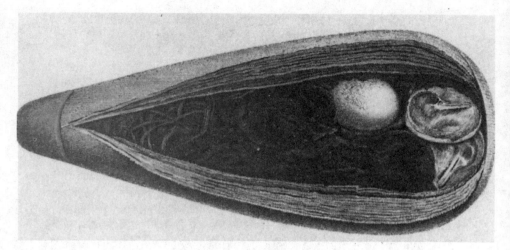

FIG. 90. *Mummy containing an ibis egg.* DESCRIPTION DE L'ÉGYPTE

FIG. 91. *X-ray of a complete mummified ibis. Not all pilgrims to Saqqara were sold whole ibis mummies.*

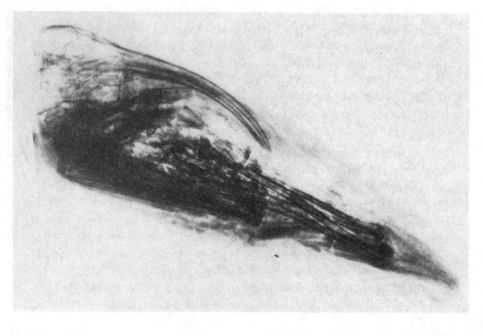

carvers"—probably the stonecutters who carved niches to hold the birds. Hor wanted to ensure that everyone who should have been present in fact attended, but he went even further in his desire for reform. He also wanted to make sure that the pilgrims were not cheated and says that there should be "one god in one vessel." Sometimes pilgrims were sold a few random bones wrapped with some rags made to look like an ibis. Many of the excavated pots contained such a mélange. Hor wanted to ensure that there was an ibis in every pot.

It is interesting that a priest named after the falcon god Horus ("Hor" was the Egyptian name, "Horus" the Greek version) was attached to the ibis galleries. However, wherever ibis galleries existed there were falcon galleries nearby. The ibis, sacred to the god Thoth, was considered a night bird, hence associated with the moon. The falcon was a day bird, associated with the sun. The falcon galleries at Saqqara have been less well explored than the ibis galleries and may yet yield some surprises when they are completely excavated.

Cats, ibises, and falcons were mummified by the millions, but many other animals were mummified in smaller numbers, and sometimes it is not so clear why. The cobra was the symbol of royalty, but all kinds of snakes were mummified. Even the lowly ichneumon, a kind of mongoose often called "pharaoh's rat" because it ate crocodile eggs, was mummified. Mongooses also eat snakes; according to one Egyptian myth, the solar god Re turned himself into an ichneumon to defeat Apophis, the evil serpent of the underworld. Thus ichneumons were mummified, placed in special coffins, and presented as votive offerings at temples.

The mummification of animals was not an arbitrary process. While we do not understand why certain animals were mummified, there was always a reason. Perhaps a lost myth explains why a given animal was sacred to a particular god; a now-forgotten cult may have worshipped the animal, or the animal may have been a beloved pet mummified to accompany his master to the next world.

Disappointingly, animal mummies have given us little information about techniques that might have been applied to humans. Animals were not given the careful attention afforded

FIG. 92. *Coffin containing an ichneumon.* COURTESY DR. W. BENSON HARER, JR.

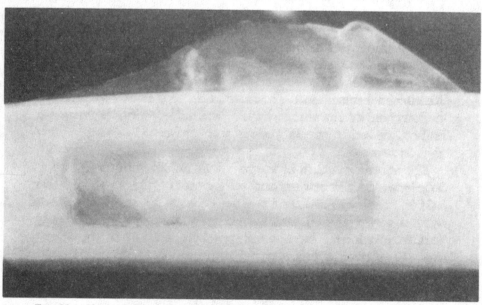

FIG. 93. *X-ray showing the ichneumon inside the coffin.* COURTESY DR. W. BENSON HARER, JR.

humans. As we have seen, mummies sold to pilgrims as offerings were only minimally treated, and even gods such as the
Apis bulls did not have their internal organs preserved. If a
more complete picture of mummification is to be drawn, it
will have to come from human mummies yet to be found and
studied.

9
An Inventory of Kings

The human mummies we have discussed so far are the successes—the ones that have been found. There are many royal mummies that may yet be found, and in order to know which it would be useful to know which pharaohs are already accounted for. But an inventory of the kings of Egypt is more difficult than one might suspect. A major problem lies with the New Kingdom mummies found in the two great caches—Deir el Bahri and the tomb of Amenhotep II. These mummies were disturbed more than once by robbers in ancient times, then rewrapped and reburied by priests of the Twenty-first and Twenty-second dynasties. Sometimes the coffin of a pharaoh had been destroyed and the mummy placed in a new coffin, or one originally made for another pharaoh. While preparing the bodies brought together from these caches, embalmers rewrapped the mummies of several pharaohs at one time, and confusions occurred. Thus the body in the coffin of Ramses IV may not be that of Ramses IV, and even the mummy labeled "Amenhotep III" may not belong to that pharaoh.

We do not have the same difficulty with pharaohs of the Old Kingdom, Middle Kingdom, or Late Period, but there are other problems with pharaohs of those eras.

Old Kingdom Pharaohs

Few royal mummies have survived from the Old Kingdom. Mummification techniques were initially primitive, so bodies were poorly preserved. Complete mummies are rare; usually what are found are body parts. In addition, a period of anarchy followed the collapse of the Old Kingdom during which the unguarded pyramids provided highly attractive targets for thieves. Every one was robbed and, in most cases, the mummy was destroyed in the process. Another reason there are so few mummies of Old Kingdom pharaohs is simply that they are older. An Old Kingdom mummy has had 2,000 more years to decay than has a Ptolemaic one.

The First Dynasty: The Earliest Kings

Prior to Petrie's excavation at Abydos, the kings of the First Dynasty enjoyed an almost legendary status. Their names were known through ancient writers, but little tangible evidence of their existence had been found. Petrie excavated a series of these kings' tombs (Hor-aha, Zer, Zet, etc.), but never found their mummies—only Zer's arm.

Because the kings of the First Dynasty had second tombs in the north, at Saqqara, debate still rages about which were the true burials and which were cenotaphs. For our purpose it doesn't matter; both the Saqqara and Abydos tombs were thoroughly plundered. We are not likely to find any bodies of the kings of the First Dynasty.

The Second Dynasty

No mummies of the pharaohs of the Second Dynasty have been found either, but hope still exists that some may be discovered. Several tombs (of Hotep-Sekmenui, Ra-Neb, Neteren, Sendji, Neterka, Neferkara, and Kha-Sekhem) have not been located. It is possible that these first kings were not buried at Abydos and that their tombs may have escaped plunderers. However, the last king of the dynasty, Kha-Sekhemui, did construct a huge tomb at Abydos. While his gold scepter was found there, no trace of his mummy remained.

The Third Dynasty

It is with the Third Dynasty that Egypt emerges from behind a mist. More monuments and artifacts survive, among them our next candidate for a pharaoh's mummy—King Zoser's foot.

Zoser's step pyramid—so called because of its wedding-cake appearance—at Saqqara, the first pyramid ever built, was undoubtedly his burial place. In 1926 Battiscombe Gunn cleared part of its burial chamber and found six vertebrae and part of the right hip of a man. He labeled them, but made no examination of them. In 1934 Jean-Philippe Lauer and James Quibell were completing the final clearance of the burial chamber and found more body parts, including the upper half of the right humerus, rib fragments, and most important, a left foot.

The foot is interesting because of what it tells about Third Dynasty mummification techniques, at least for royalty. As with most mummified remains found during the 1930s and 1940s, it was sent for study to Dr. Douglas Derry.[1] The foot had been wrapped in linen soaked in resin, and then sculpted realistically to indicate anatomical details, complete with tendons. The linen had not been placed over the foot and then molded; it was formed first and then placed on the foot. Finally, it was covered with a layer of fresh linen. Such modeling is not unique. The Fourth Dynasty mummy of the nobleman Ranefer from Meidum was covered by an extremely realistic layer of sculpted linen, and a few other Fourth Dynasty mummies recovered from tombs in the Giza complex also demonstrate this art. The practice of sculpting the mummy in its linen covering may have begun because the Egyptians had not yet learned how to dehydrate and preserve the bodies of their dead. This almost statue-like surrogate was the next best thing.

It is important to note that the human fragments found in Zoser's burial chamber are almost certainly his. The only entrance is through a very narrow hole made by ancient tomb robbers, which makes the introduction into the tomb of another body at a later period highly unlikely.

Zoser's successor, Sekhemkhet, is a real candidate for a missing mummy, but his special case is discussed in the next chapter.

The burial place of Huni, the last king of the Third Dynasty, is unknown. Some claim that he built the large and tower-like pyramid at Meidum, but no solid evidence links him with it.

The Fourth Dynasty

There is no question about where the pharaohs of the Fourth Dynasty were buried; their huge pyramids can hardly be missed. However, Sneferu, the first king of the dynasty, built so many pyramids that the question is, In which one was he buried? He almost certainly completed the Meidum pyramid. Although the pyramid is uninscribed, Eighteenth Dynasty graffiti on the walls of its adjoining temple state that the pyramid was Sneferu's. The remains of a wooden coffin were found in the burial chamber in 1890, but no traces of a mummy.

A better prospect for Sneferu's tomb is at Dahshur, six miles south of Saqqara. Here Sneferu built two pyramids, one of which is called the "Bent Pyramid" because the angles of the sides bend toward the top from fifty-four to forty-three degrees of incline. The second pyramid is called the "Red Pyramid" because it appears red when the sun shines on it. No trace of Sneferu's body was found in either pyramid, but Dr. Ahmed Fakhry, the pyramid's first scientific excavator, was convinced that King Sneferu was buried in the bent one. He was almost certainly buried in one of the two Dahshur pyramids, but because both were thoroughly plundered in ancient times, we are not likely to find his mummy.

The subsequent kings of the Fourth Dynasty built pyramids at Giza, and these, the largest ever built, were all robbed in

Fig. 94.
Fragment of the wooden coffin lid found in the burial chamber of Menkaure's pyramid. The lid was carved almost 2,000 years after the king's burial.   PHOTOGRAPH COURTESY DAVID MOYER

antiquity. It is interesting that in each of the burial chambers of the three largest pyramids at Giza, a stone sarcophagus remained relatively intact until modern times. In the case of the Great Pyramid this is not surprising, even though the pyramid has been open since the Middle Ages—the sarcophagus is larger than the only entrance into the burial chamber. Obviously, it was placed inside the tomb before the chamber was roofed, making removal extremely difficult. No mummy was ever found inside the Great Pyramid. Khufu's body was almost certainly destroyed long ago.

The second-largest pyramid, Khafre's, was opened in 1818 by Giovanni Battista Belzoni. He found a sarcophagus still in place in the burial chamber, but no remains of the king. Human remains were found, however, in the smallest of the three pyramids, that of Menkaure, the last Fourth Dynasty king to build at Giza. His pyramid was opened in 1837, by Colonel Richard Howard-Vyse, who found a beautiful basalt sarcophagus carved with the façade of a palace. He also found human remains and the lid of a wooden anthropoid coffin with the name "Menkaure" on it. All three—the sarcophagus, the mummy, and the wooden lid—were disappointments.

Because of the style in which it is carved, the lid cannot be from the Old Kingdom; it dates from the Saite period, almost 2,000 years later. Radiocarbon dating shows the human remains to be from the early Christian period. Neither lid nor mummy are Menkaure's. Saite period priests probably found the tomb of Menkaure plundered and piously made a new coffin for the reburial. Presumably this tomb was later robbed, but in the Christian era another body was placed in Menkaure's burial chamber. The only object in the burial chamber that truly was Menkaure's was the stone sarcophagus, yet it provided the greatest disappointment of all.

The sarcophagus, a masterpiece of Old Kingdom workmanship, was sent to the British Museum in 1838 on the merchant ship *Beatrice*. The ship stopped at Malta for supplies and then left that port on October 30, 1838, and neither the ship nor its precious cargo were seen again. It sank in deep water somewhere near Cartagena.

The remaining Fourth Dynasty pyramid stands five miles north of Giza, at Abu Roash. Many statue fragments of King Djedefre were found in the area, which strongly suggests that the funerary complex was actually used for this pharaoh's burial. The statues had been deliberately broken, so it is probable that the king's body was destroyed during some vengeful attack. Fragments of a granite sarcophagus were found in a burial pit beneath the pyramid, but no traces of the pharaoh's mummy. The last king of the dynasty, Shepsefkaf, built a tomb at Saqqara in the shape of a huge rectangular sarcophagus. But no body was found in the plundered burial chamber inside.

The Fifth Dynasty

The birth of the first three kings of the Fifth Dynasty are recorded in the Westcar Papyrus in the Berlin Museum. The tale tells how Dedi, a magician in the court of Cheops, foretold that the first three kings of the dynasty would be triplets. Their father was the sun god Re. It is possible that two of the kings,

Fig. 95.
Nineteenth-century drawing of the stone sarcophagus of King Menkaure found inside his pyramid. The body it contained was not his. The sarcophagus is now at the bottom of the ocean off Cartagena, where it sank in 1838 en route to the British Museum.
PHOTOGRAPH COURTESY DAVID MOYER

Sahure and Neferirkare, were, in fact, twins. The third, Userkaf, built a pyramid at Saqqara, but by the time it was excavated by C. M. Firth in 1928, the pharaoh's body was long gone.

The next four kings—Sahure, Neferirkare, Neferefre, and Niuseire—all built pyramids at Abu Sir, a few miles from Saqqara. We know that all were once buried in their pyramids because the Abu Sir Papyri record the administrative duties of priests whose job it was to make offerings to the souls of the pharaohs buried in those tombs. All the Abu Sir pyramids were robbed during the First Intermediate Period. It is unlikely that the bodies of these pharaohs will ever be found.

Still, two Fifth Dynasty kings qualify as missing mummies—Shepseshare and Menkauhor. Their pyramids have not been located, so there is a chance that their mummies still lie undisturbed in their burial chambers. Unfortunately, this is not the case with the last two kings of the dynasty, Isesi and Unas.

At South Saqqara rises a pyramid known as the "Haram esh Shuwaf" (The Watchman's Pyramid), the burial place of the Fifth Dynasty king Djed-Ka-Re Isesi. The pyramid was cleared in 1945 by Abdel Salam Husein and Alexandre Varille, both of whom died before they could publish the results of their excavations, so no complete report exists. It is known, however, that they entered the burial chamber and found approximately half of the king's mummy scattered about. Numerous fragments of a canopic chest, along with bits of viscera, showed that his internal organs had been removed.

No remains whatsoever were found in the pyramid of Isesi's successor, Unas, the last king of the Fifth Dynasty. This pyramid is the first with magical spells carved on the walls of the burial chamber. These spells were intended to protect the mummy, assure its safe journey to the next world, and guarantee that the pharaoh would be greeted by the gods and treated properly in the netherworld. The Sixth Dynasty successors of Unas—Teti, Pepi I, Merenre, and Pepi II—all had these texts inscribed in their pyramids. With one exception, however, their mummies were destroyed by tomb robbers.

In 1970 Jean-Philippe Lauer entered the burial chamber in the pyramid of Pepi I and found an intact canopic chest carved from a single block of pink granite from the Aswan quarries. Inside one of the four compartments was a complete packet containing one of the king's internal organs, all that remains of Pepi I. To this date, the packet has not been opened.

In fact, only one complete mummy of an Old Kingdom pharaoh has been found. Merenre, the son of Pepi I, was discovered by Maspero in 1881. Like all the other Old Kingdom pyramids, Merenre's had been robbed in antiquity. The pyramid had originally been sealed by three huge granite plugs, so the ancient Egyptian thieves had to break through a limestone wall into the space above the plugs, then tunnel through the ceiling down into the burial chamber. Later, in the Middle Ages, stonemasons removed the dressed stone from the burial chamber, creating a very precarious situation. The ceiling is an inverted V formed by pairs of thirty-ton granite slabs. Since the stones supporting the ceiling blocks had been stolen, when Maspero reached the burial chamber he discovered the blocks held in place only by their own weight. No fool, Maspero sent in his foreman, Mustapha, who found a beautifully polished basalt sarcophagus with its sliding lid still on top, although slightly ajar. Inside was the pharaoh's mummy. As Maspero put it, ". . . it had been despoiled by treasure hunters and was completely nude." He adds that the mummy was transported to the Boulaq Museum ". . . after several comic incidents."[2] (One wonders what these amusing events might have been.) The body was exhibited in the Egyptian Museum Royal Mummy Room as No. 5250, but is not listed in the 1912 *Catalogue General* volume on royal mummies and has not been on exhibit for many years.

It is unlikely that any more Old Kingdom pharaohs will be found. As we have seen, mummification had not been perfected, the tombs were obvious targets for robbers, who usually destroyed the mummies. But after the fall of the Old Kingdom, the Seventh through Tenth dynasties did not have true pharaohs ruling over Egypt. Stability was reestablished during the Middle Kingdom, and the pharaohs were well aware of what had happened to their predecessors' mummies. They took greater precautions.

Middle Kingdom Mummies

The Middle Kingdom consists of two dynasties, the Eleventh and Twelfth. During the Eleventh Dynasty, rulers from Thebes in the south gradually reunited Upper and Lower Egypt and restored stability to the country. The pharaohs of this dynasty, usually named Intef or Montuhotep, were buried in tombs at Thebes, whose dry climate would have preserved their bodies. But their tombs were all robbed, so not a single king's mummy survives from this dynasty.

Because of the great distance between Thebes and the Delta of Northern Egypt, these Eleventh Dynasty kings had difficulties managing the country. During the Old Kingdom the capital had always been situated in the north, at Memphis, where the center for administering the country was established. The kings of the Twelfth Dynasty moved the capital north again to It-Towey, which means "Seizer of the Two Lands." The exact location of It-Towey is not known, but it must have been near Lisht, about twenty-five miles south of modern Cairo.

The Twelfth Dynasty pharaohs built pyramids to protect their mummies, but not in the same manner as their forefathers. The economy of the Middle Kingdom did not allow building on the scale of the Fourth Dynasty kings, so the pharaohs of this dynasty built mud-brick pyramids faced with white limestone to give them a substantial appearance. The first two pharaohs, Amenemhet I and Sesostris I, built at Lisht. The site was not a good choice for two reasons. The water table has risen considerably since their construction, so burial chambers have been subjected to water damage. That of Sesostris I was even submerged at one time. The site was also distant from populated areas, making it easier for clandestine tomb robbing. Thus we do not have the mummies of these two pharaohs.

The next pharaoh, Amenemhet II, built his pyramid at Dashur, the same necropolis selected by the founder of the Fourth Dynasty, Sneferu. Later, Sesostris III and Amenemhet III also built pyramids on this site, but included innovations to protect their remains.

Pyramids of the Old Kingdom all had entrances on their north sides, leading to a descending passageway usually oriented toward the North Star. This star was a symbol of permanence because it seemed fixed in the sky while other stars rotated around it. The fact that the pyramids of the Old Kingdom all had entrances on the same side suggests that the location of the entrances was not a secret, a testament to the security that the pharaohs felt their tombs enjoyed. It was unthinkable during the Old Kingdom that anyone would violate a pharaoh's pyramid.

But because Sesostris III and Amenemhet III knew that the Old Kingdom pyramids had been robbed, they placed their entrances on the south side of their pyramids, and then covered them with facing stones. In addition to this precaution, they constructed a maze of dead-end passageways inside their pyramids to slow thieves in their search for the burial chamber. Huge granite sealing plugs blocked bare walls; passageways wound around to dead ends—but, despite all these precautions, tomb robbers succeeded. No traces of the mummies or jewelry of Sesostris III or Amenemhet III were found in their burial chambers. The precautions were more successful, however, in slowing nineteenth century archaeologists. Jacques de Morgan spent months during the 1894–5 season trying to find the burial chamber of Sesostris III.

Flinders Petrie had a similar experience excavating the pyramid of Sesostris II at Illahun during the 1887–8 season—he removed a significant portion of the north side of the pyramid before finding an entrance on the south side. The burial chamber, a new type, was carved out of a single piece of granite that weighed more than a hundred tons and was sunk forty feet into the bedrock. The pyramid was constructed over it. Petrie found a beautiful pink granite sarcophagus in the burial chamber, but that was all—thieves had gotten there first.

The success and persistence of tomb robbers has been commented upon more than once. It seems remarkable that they always succeeded, despite all the precautions to hinder them. Often the tomb robbers were the tomb builders, so they knew which corridors led to dead ends and which led to treasures.

Middle Kingdom rulers, aware that attempts would be made to rob their pyramids, and suspecting that the robbers might have intimate knowledge of the pyramids, frequently hid their jewelry in niches in the walls, away from their bodies. While this did not succeed in stopping thieves from ransacking their mummies, sometimes the jewelry escaped them, so we have discovered more royal jewelry from the Middle Kingdom than from any other period.

The only pharaoh of the Middle Kingdom to have built two pyramids was Amenemhet III. His pyramid at Dashur developed major structural problems, which may be why a second one was built at Hawara, in the Fayoum. Flinders Petrie excavated this as well, and again he had difficulty in finding the burial chamber. Like the pyramid of Sesostris II, the burial chamber was made of a single block of stone, this time yellow quartzite, sunk in the bedrock then covered by the superstruc-

ture of the pyramid. Inside the burial chamber stood *two* quartzite sarcophagi, but both were empty. Objects were found
inscribed for Amenemhet's daughter, Neferuptah, so the other
sarcophagus may have been intended for her.

The rulers of Dynasty XII are all accounted for, with the exception of the last two—Amenemhet IV and his sister Sobek-
neferu. A temple built by Amenemhet IV while he served as
coregent with his father, Amenemhet III, is known, but no trace
of the tombs or funerary objects of Amenemhet IV or his sister
has been found. They can be considered missing mummies.

The Middle Kingdom was followed by the Second Intermediate Period (1783–1550 B.C.), nearly 200 years of political instability, not unlike the time of turmoil following the Old
Kingdom's collapse. The period consists of dynasties Thirteen
through Seventeen, and only the tombs of a few minor kings
from the Thirteenth Dynasty have been found.

The pyramid of Ameny-Kemu was discovered at Dashur, its
upper levels gone and its lower courses covered in sand. It contained a huge sarcophagus and a set of canopic jars, so we know
that the internal organs were removed, but the body was gone
by the time the burial chamber was excavated in 1957. A pyramid at South Saqqara for the Thirteenth Dynasty pharaoh
Khendjer used an ingenious technique of removing sand to permit huge sealing blocks to fall into place. The granite plugs
rested on sand, which was removed from a hole at the bottom
so that the blocks moved slowly downward as the sand was
taken away. I.E.S. Edwards, the great authority on pyramids,
says: "By means of a hole cut immediately beneath the ceiling
and only large enough to admit a child, the robbers succeeded
in gaining possession of the entire contents of the chamber,
leaving behind nothing of any kind, not even a fragment of
wood, stone, or pottery."[3] However, even Edwards can be
wrong. Although the tomb was completed and sealed, there is
some question as to whether Khendjer was ever buried there.
The robbers' hole was so small that the thieves would have had
to break the sarcophagus, coffin, etc., into small pieces to remove them. There seems no reason to remove everything from
the tomb; broken pieces of wood or stone are not so valuable.
If the tomb had been robbed, some pieces should remain. This

would not be the only pyramid to have served as a false tomb, perhaps intended to fool robbers. Khendjer's true burial site and mummy may yet be found.

The only Second Intermediate Period pharaoh found was in the pyramid of Hor, opened by Jacques de Morgan in the latter part of the nineteenth century. The burial chamber had been disturbed, but not stripped completely. It still contained the famous wooden *ka* statue now displayed in the Egyptian Museum in Cairo. The pharaoh is shown striding forward; on his head is the hieroglyph ⊔, *ka*, or "soul." There was also a sealed canopic chest holding four canopic jars, each with an inscription to one of the four sons of Horus. De Morgan described the state of the king's mummy: "The mummy of King Hor had been broken, its jewels removed, but still remaining, very much in disorder, it is true, were many interesting objects."[4] The interesting objects included Hor's flails, scepters, and staffs of authority, which were left by the robbers because they were made of wood.

Inscriptions on the sarcophagus show the continuation of a tradition begun in the pyramid texts of the Old Kingdom. Hieroglyphs that show animals have all been rendered incompletely: the bee lacks a head, the snake lacks a tail, the birds don't have feet, etc. This was done perhaps out of fear that the animals in the magical text might come to life and either harm the mummy or run from the spell and spoil its effectiveness.

At the beginning of the Fourteenth Dynasty, as we have seen, a group of people known as the "Hyksos" or "foreign rulers" invaded Egypt. No royal Hyksos tomb has been discovered, so the Hyksos rulers are truly missing mummies. It would not be surprising, however, if they are never found. The political instability of the period would have made protection of any tombs difficult, and it is unlikely that the tombs of foreign invaders would be allowed to remain undisturbed. In any case, the Hyksos ruled from the Delta, where the moist terrain would not preserve mummies. This is unfortunate because we know little about Hyksos burial customs, and it would be interesting to learn if they practiced mummification.

While the Hyksos ruled in the north, a simultaneous dynasty,

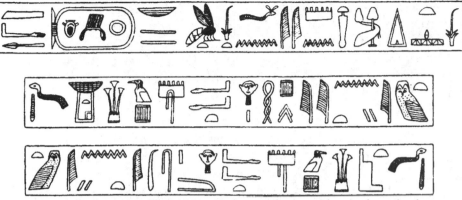

FIG. 96. *Magical spell from King Hor's sarcophagus, with animals rendered incompletely so that they could not run away from the text.* DRAWING AFTER DE MORGAN

called the Seventeenth by most Egyptologists, ruled from Thebes in the south. Thanks to a wonderful bit of detective work by Herbert Winlock,[5] we know where many of the tombs of these kings are located. An inspection undertaken during the reign of Ramses IX of the tombs of Seventeenth Dynasty kings is described in detail in the Abbott Papyrus in the British Museum. The inspection was initiated by an accusation of tomb robbing lodged by the mayor of Thebes against the governor of the necropolis, who was responsible for the security of the cemetery. The document describes the tour of inspection, mentioning the occupant of each tomb and its location. Winlock deduced that the tombs were visited in the order in which they were listed, and using such descriptions as "the high ascent north of the Temple of Amenhotep of the Garden," or "north of the Temple of Amenhotep of the Forecourt," he drew his own map of where each tomb should be. The general location was not in doubt. It was surely Dra Abu el Naga, not far from Deir el Bahri on the west bank of Thebes, and just a short walk from the Valley of the Kings. Fifty years earlier, Auguste Mariette had found the tomb of Neb-Kheper-Re Intef, one of the kings mentioned in the papyrus. Unfortunately, Mariette was too late.

Local tomb robbers found the tomb intact in 1827, just as it was when last inspected in the Twentieth Dynasty. Their find is mentioned by Giovanni D'Athanasi, Henry Salt's agent in Thebes. The British consul to Egypt, Salt was building a collection of antiquities with the help of D'Athanasi and others. Athanasi's account of the tomb explains why there are more royal tombs than royal mummies.

> *I have now much pleasure in being able to state in confirmation of this discovery, that during the researches made by the Arabs in the year 1827, at Gourna, they discovered in the mountain, now called by the Arabs, Il-Dra-Abool-Naggia, a small and separate tomb, containing only one chamber, in the centre of which was placed a sarcophagus, hewn out of the same rock, and formed evidently at the same time as the chamber itself; its base not having been detached. In this sarcophagus was found the above-mentioned case, with the body as originally deposited. The moment the Arabs saw that the case was highly ornamented and gilt, they immediately, from their experience in such matters, knew that it belonged to a person of rank. They forthwith proceeded to satisfy their curiosity by opening it, when they discovered, placed around the head of the mummy, but over the linen, a diadem, composed of silver and beautiful mosaic work, its centre being formed of gold, representing an asp, the emblem of royalty. Inside the case alongside the body, were deposited two bows, with six arrows, the heads of which were tipped with flint.*
>
> *The Arabs on discovering their rich prize, immediately proceeded to break up the mummy, as was their usual custom, for the treasures it might contain. . . .* [6]

This is one mummy that is not merely missing, but might be better classified as "missing in action." After Salt's death the coffin was purchased by the British Museum, where it remains today.

The Intef whose body was destroyed in 1827 was not the only Seventeenth Dynasty pharaoh of that name. There were two more Intefs, brothers, one of whom was known as "Intef the Elder." Their coffins were found by local tomb robbers in the same area. Heinrich Brugsch barely saved one coffin from being used for lumber! Writing in 1879, he says:

> *Here it was where, more than twenty years ago, Arabs seeking for treasure brought to light two very simple coffins of these pharaohs, not knowing what a treasure they had found. In that part of the necropolis which by the inhabitants is now called Assaseef, these coffins were discovered lightly hidden under loose heaps of stones and sand. The cover was richly gilt, and the band of hieroglyphics which occupied the middle of it contained the name of Anentef. During my stay in Egypt in 1854, when I first visited the banks of the Nile, I had the good luck to discover, in the lumber-room of the residence of the Greek consul, the coffin of a second Anentef, which was distinguished by the surname of "the Great."*[7]

Purchased for the museum by Mariette, the coffins of both Intef brothers are now in the Louvre. An inscription on the coffin of the elder states that it is a gift from his younger brother. No jewels from these Intefs ever appeared on the antiquities market, so it is likely that the bodies had been destroyed by the time the locals discovered the coffins in the 1850s.

The Rise of the New Kingdom

The New Kingdom (1550–1070 B.C.) begins after the expulsion of the Hyksos. It is perhaps from this battle for freedom that we get one of the most interesting of the royal mummies. The Sallier Papyrus tells of the situation at the end of the Hyksos domination of Egypt. The Hyksos ruler, Apophis, had his capital in the Delta, at Avaris; Seqenenre Tao II, a Theban prince, ruled in the south. According to the papyrus, Apophis sent Seqenenre an inflammatory letter stating that the hippopotami in Thebes (500 miles away) were keeping him awake and had to be silenced. The papyrus breaks off before we hear the result of the letter, but we do have the mummy of Seqenenre from

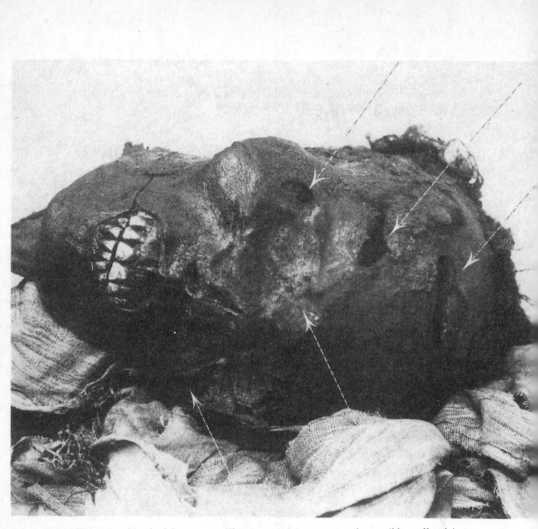

FIG. 97. *Head of Seqenenre. The arrows point to wounds possibly suffered in battle.* EGYPTIAN MUSEUM, CAIRO

the Deir el Bahri cache and its condition suggests an end to the story.

Seqenenre was unwrapped by Maspero on June 9, 1886, and everyone present was so shocked by what they found that Maspero did not complete the unwrapping. Seqenenre had died violently. There are five serious wounds in his head. The upper left two arrows and the one on the lower right of Figure 97 indicate probable ax wounds. An arrow in the upper right of the photo shows where a blunt instrument delivered a blow that broke both nasal bones and also broke and dislocated facial

FIG. 98. *The distorted hands of Seqenenre indicate that he died in agony.* EGYPTIAN MUSEUM, CAIRO

bones, causing the break in the skin indicated by the arrow on the bottom left. In addition to these four injuries, a fifth injury was sustained when a sharp weapon, perhaps a spear, was thrust into the skull below the left ear. With the exception of the blow to the nose, any one of the injuries could have killed Seqenenre.

Based on the Sallier Papyrus story, there is a tradition that Seqenenre went north to fight Apophis, where he died in battle. In support of this theory, there is evidence that Seqenenre was embalmed far from the professional embalmers' workshops of Thebes. Although the viscera were removed through the traditional incision on the left side, little else was done to preserve the body. Some aromatic sawdust was sprinkled on it and some linen placed in the abdominal cavity, but there is no evidence of traditional drying with natron. No attempt was made to straighten the legs or place the hands along the sides, as was the custom in the Seventeenth Dynasty, and the hands remain in what seems to be a final gesture of agony. Seqenenre may well have been embalmed near or even on the battlefield, wrapped, and then brought back to Thebes for burial.

However, it should be pointed out that the wounds, while suggesting that Seqenenre died violently, do not prove that he died in battle. In fact, the wounds are more consistent with his having been murdered in his sleep. The gashes on the face are horizontal, an unusual position for wounds if someone were fighting upright; if an ax strikes someone who is standing, the gash would be oblique or vertical. Also, in ancient combat the bones of one's arms are were often broken in an attempt to fend off blows. There is no such damage to Seqenenre's arms.

Another possibility is that Seqenenre received the spear wound beneath his left ear during battle and that it either killed him or knocked him unconscious. Then the four blows to the head were delivered while he was on the ground. Given the fact that three different weapons were used to bring about the king's demise, it appears that at least two, and probably three, enemies cooperated in dispatching him to the netherworld. Seqenenre's son and successor, Kamose, continued the battle against the Hyksos, and all indications are that he was more successful.

The first text to tell of Kamose's exploits was found by Howard Carter when he was excavating for Lord Carnarvon in 1908: two writing boards unearthed in the vicinity of a Seventeenth Dynasty tomb near Deir el Bahri. On one, a text in hieratic tells of Kamose's military exploits against Apophis at Avaris.[8] Here the end of the story is clear:

> When the sun shone forth on the land I was upon him like a falcon. When the time for perfuming the mouth [lunch] came, I defeated him, I destroyed his wall, I killed his people. I caused that his wife go down to the river bank. My soldiers were like lions upon their prey, carrying off slaves, cattle, fat and honey, and dividing their possessions.

When the text was first discovered, some believed it to be a literary text rather than a historical document. The question was settled in 1954 when a large stela was found at Karnak recounting the exploit of Kamose's victory over Apophis. The stela includes the detail that when Apophis was surrounded in his walled city by Egyptian troops, he sent a messenger south with a letter to the Cushite king, asking him to come with troops so that they could defeat Kamose and divide Egypt between them. Kamose gleefully relates how he intercepted the messenger.

Kamose seems to have died peacefully at Thebes. We *had* his mummy, but unhappily it is now long gone. In some ways, the finding of Kamose's mummy was instrumental in the establishment of the Egyptian Antiquities Service.

In the spring of 1857, Prince Napoleon, the cousin of Emperor Napoleon III, was planning a trip to Egypt; the emperor, happy to be rid of his troublesome relative, wanted to make sure that he had a pleasant—and long—trip. Eager to please the emperor, and knowing that Prince Napoleon wished to amass a collection of Egyptian antiquities, the Khedive of Egypt decided to salt the prince's itinerary with antiquities so that he would find treasure on every step of the way. To provide these treasures, Mariette was sent for from France, and he commandeered Heinrich Brugsch to assist him. For a frantic eight months the two excavated up and down Egypt, finding antiquities and then burying them along the prince's planned route.

Knowing the approximate spot where the Intef coffins had been found, Mariette and Brugsch decided to excavate at Dra Abu el Naga. In a pile of debris they found the unopened coffin of Kamose. According the Abbott Papyrus, when Kamose's tomb was inspected in Ramesside times, it was found to be undisturbed. At some later date, perhaps for fear of the tomb's security, the coffin was removed and buried in a pile of debris, where it remained till Mariette uncovered it.

Kamose had been buried as a warrior. Tied to his left arm was a magnificent gold and silver dagger. According to Mariette, the mummy crumbled to dust when the coffin lid was removed, and Brugsch told the same story. But mummies simply do not crumble to dust. They may indeed be fragile, and when probed their bones may break and their soft tissue pulverize, but one is never left with a pile of dust. Even Mariette said the body had enough structural strength to hold the dagger tied to its arm. The truth is that neither Mariette nor Brugsch was interested in mummies, so they left the remains of the liberator of Egypt, the first pharaoh's mummy ever discovered intact by archaeologists, on the pile of debris where they were found.

Mariette and Brugsch also found a scarab, "some amulets," and a pectoral in the shape of a cartouche with the name of Ahmose, Kamose's brother and successor. A bronze mirror was also discovered. When Prince Napoleon canceled his tour, the Khedive sent the dagger and pectoral cartouche to him as a souvenir of a trip never taken. The dagger now resides in Brussels, the coffin in the Egyptian Museum, and the cartouche, pectoral, and mirror in the Louvre. The present locations of the scarabs and amulets are unknown, and the mummy of Kamose is undoubtedly lost forever. A few months after the prince received his gifts, he used his influence to have Mariette appointed as Chief of Antiquities, and thus the Service des Antiquités came into being—in part because of Kamose.

One additional mummy of the late Seventeenth Dynasty is worth mentioning, that of Seqenenre's wife, Ahhotep I, who was also found in the debris at Dra Abu el Naga. It too illustrates why royal mummies are so rare. Ahhotep was discovered in 1858 by a gang of twenty unsupervised workmen who Mariette had set to work at Dra Abu el Naga. When the workmen discovered the intact coffin of Ahhotep, Mariette was in Boulaq, so the French consul in Luxor, across the Nile from the discovery, was notified. He sent a copy of the inscription on the coffin to Mariette. Theodule Deveria of the Louvre was with Mariette when he received the letter, and later accompanied Mariette to inspect the finds. Deveria described the incredible set of events that followed the discovery of the coffin:

> M. Maunier, the French consular agent, notified of this discovery, sent to Mariette a copy of the inscription from the coffin, sufficiently legible for me to realize that this was the mummy of a Queen Ahhotp. Mariette wrote to send it immediately to Bulak by special steamer, but unfortunately before the letter arrived the governor of the province had the coffin opened—whether from curiosity or animosity, no one knows. Whatever

it was, I should not like to find myself in that functionary's shoes the first time Mariette sees him. As usual they threw away the bandages and bones, saving only the objects buried with the mummy. Mariette got an inventory of them from one of his Arab employees. The governor, on his side, sent a list to the Viceroy, notifying him that he was sending the objects direct to the Khedival Court. To let them arrive at such a destination was to risk their partial or complete loss. The two lists were in good enough agreement, but they seemed to us remarkably exaggerated both in the number of things described and in their weights of gold. Supplied with a ministerial order giving the right to stop all boats loaded with curiosities, and to transship them on board our own boat, we set sail yesterday morning, March 21st, to cruise the Nile as far up as low water would take us. We had just about gone as far as the Samannoud would make it, when we saw the boat carrying the treasure taken from the pharonic mummy coming toward us. At the end of half an hour the two boats were alongside each other. After some stormy words, accompanied by rather lively gestures, Mariette promised to one to toss him overboard, to another to roast his brains, to a third to send him to the galleys, and to a fourth to have him hanged. At last they decided to place the box containing the antiquities on board our boat, against a receipt. To our great surprise we found in it a quantity of jewels and royal insignia, almost all bearing the name of Ahmose, a king of the Eighteenth Dynasty, while the Queen Ahhotp was not mentioned once. Their fineness of execution is more remarkable than that of the little so far known, and if I am not mistaken, there are nearly two kilograms' weight of gold, marvelously fashioned, with incrustations of hard stone and coloured enamel.[9]

It is sad to think that the mummy of Queen Ahhotep suffered more at the hands of her excavators than her husband, Seqenenre, did at the hands of his enemies.

The New Kingdom

King Ahmose is traditionally listed as the founder of the Eighteenth Dynasty, the first king of the New Kingdom, because he is the first of his family to rule Egypt unopposed. The cartouche of Ahmose on Kahmose's chest suggests that he was buried by his brother and successor. Historical texts indicate that Kamose did not complete the expulsion of the Hyksos but died before the job was done; it fell to Ahmose to complete the task. The body of Ahmose was found in the Deir el Bahri cache, and its identity is not in doubt.

Ahmose's mummy was found in its original coffin. On its inner wrappings, written in hieratic on one of the bandages, is a note stating that he was embalmed and wrapped by order of his son and successor, Amenhotep I. Ahmose's mummy is the first one known to have its brain removed. This was not done through the nasal passage—that technique would be developed later—but rather by means of a different operation. The uppermost vertebra on the spinal column is called the Atlas vertebra because it supports the head. It is missing in the mummy of Ahmose and seems to have been removed via a post-mortem incision in the left side of the neck. This procedure exposed the foramen magnum "large hole" at the base of the cranium, through which the brain was then removed. The skull was then packed with linen. This early Eighteenth Dynasty attempt at removing the brain would be refined and perfected later in the dynasty.

The Eighteenth Dynasty

Most of the pharaohs of the Eighteenth Dynasty have been recovered from the Deir el Bahri cache and the find in the tomb of Amenhotep II. Ahmose was succeeded by his son, Amenhotep I, whose mummy is the only king's mummy from the two caches that Mariette did not unwrap—because of the beauty of the wrappings. There is a question, however, about the body of his successor, Tuthmose I.

The tomb of Tuthmose I was the first constructed in the Valley of the Kings. Tuthmose's Overseer of the Works, Ineni, recorded on the walls of his own tomb some remarkable details about that tomb:

> *I inspected the excavation of the cliff-tomb of his majesty,*
> *alone, no one seeing, no one hearing. . . . I was vigilant in*
> *seeking that which is excellent. . . . It was a work of my heart,*
> *my virtue was wisdom; there was not given to me a command*
> *by an elder. I shall be praised because of my wisdom after*
> *years, by those who shall imitate that which I have done. . . .* [10]

Thus the tomb was constructed in secret, but not sufficiently to protect it. When the tomb was found by Victor Loret in 1899 it had already been thoroughly looted and contained only an empty sarcophagus and canopic chest of Tuthmose I. However, the mummy of Tuthmose I may have already been found.

When the Deir el Bahri cache was examined, it was learned that the coffin of Tuthmose I had been usurped by Pinedjem I of the Twenty-first Dynasty. Maspero believed, however, that an unlabeled male mummy in the cache was probably Tuthmose I. This mummy, No. 61065 in the Egyptian Museum's listing, was identified as Tuthmose I on the basis of a facial resemblance to the mummies of Tuthmose II and III, the son and grandson of Tuthmose I, also in the Deir el Bahri cache.[11] Clearly one can't identify a mummy on the basis of a family resemblance, but when Elliot Smith examined the unwrapped mummy, other factors confirmed, though not conclusively, that it was indeed Tuthmose I.

During the reign of Tuthmose II, the arms of mummies were folded across the breast. Prior to that they were placed along the sides, as were the arms of the mummy in question, with the hands over the genital area. The one mummy prior to Tuthmose II who *may* have had his arms crossed on his breast is Amenhotep I, the mummy Maspero never unwrapped. However, he knew the mummy was not intact because inscriptions on the bandages indicated it had been rewrapped during the Twenty-first Dynasty.

The University of Michigan expedition that X-rayed the royal mummies included that of Amenhotep I, but because of the poor condition of the body, the original position of the hands is uncertain. The right hand had been torn off and the wrist bones were missing. The right arm was bent at the elbow and was across the abdomen. The left arm was straight down by the side with the forearm detached from the upper arm. We will probably never know with certainty the original position of the arms of Amenhotep I.

The incision through which the viscera were removed is also in the correct position for the era of Tuthmose I, and thus Maspero's identification seemed correct. The problem with this identification is that X-rays clearly show that the body is that of a young man twenty-two years old at most.[12] From historical records we know that Tuthmose I ruled for at least fourteen years, which would mean he took the throne at the age of six. There is no evidence to suggest that he was a boy king. So— Tuthmose I may or may not have been found.

Tuthmose II was succeeded by his wife and half-sister, the famous Hatshepsut. She is one of the few queens to have ruled as king and was often referred to as "His Majesty" in texts. According to the standard interpretation of the historical records, Hatshepsut pushed her stepson and nephew, Tuthmose III, into the background, though he would normally have succeeded his father. After Hatshepsut's death, Tuthmose III methodically erased Hatshepsut's name from all of her monuments. According to this interpretation, which is accepted by most Egyptologists, it is unlikely that Hatshepsut's tomb and body would have remained unscathed by Tuthmose III's anger. There are, however, indications that the standard story may be wrong.

Hatshepsut's tomb was discovered by Theodore Davis and Howard Carter in 1903. The tomb had long been open, perhaps since antiquity, and certainly since members of Napoleon's expedition to Egypt visited it in 1799. They did not penetrate very far into the tomb because it was blocked with rubble and stones that had washed into the tomb and solidified to the hardness of cement (the great German Egyptologist Richard Lepsius gave up clearing the tomb in 1844 because of this difficulty). Carter and Davis agreed to clear the tomb to the burial chamber, no matter how difficult the task. Unlike Napoleon's scholars and Lepsius, they had an idea of whose tomb this was. Carter had found a foundation deposit in the area with Hatshepsut's cartouches on miniature objects.

Clearing the tomb proved even more difficult than expected. It is one of the largest ever built—more than 200 yards long and nearly a hundred yards deep—and every foot of it had to be broken through with pickaxes. The heat became so intense that the workmen's unlit candles melted, the air so bad that the lit candles gave off little light in the oxygen-deficient atmosphere. Centuries of bat dung had accumulated, so that when the workmen moved around they stirred up black clouds of it, making breathing difficult. Eventually electric lights had to be brought into the tomb, and an air pump had to clear the bat dung from the foul air. It was months before Carter and Davis reached the burial chamber.

The roof of the burial chamber had collapsed in some places, but the room could still be entered. It contained a red quartzite sarcophagus inscribed for Hatshepsut. The lid lay on the floor. Nearby was her red quartzite canopic chest, but no trace of the queen's body was found. One surprise for the excavators was that there was a second, almost identical, red quartzite sarcophagus inscribed for Hatshepsut's father, Tuthmose I. One sarcophagus for Tuthmose I had already been found in his own tomb, so this raised a puzzle. In his book about the excavation, Howard Carter notes that the inscription on the Tuthmose I sarcophagus in Hatshepsut's tomb is unusual, but makes no other comment.[13] In fact, what is unusual is that its words, which should have had masculine endings since this was supposedly Tuthmose I's sarcophagus, had feminine endings. Carter did not realize that the sarcophagus had been made for Hatshepsut but later altered for her father. One possible scenario is that Hatshepsut, when she became "king," moved the body of her father to her tomb. She left his sarcophagus in his tomb, recarved hers, which was already there, for him, and then had a new one made for herself.

When a tomb is raided by a successor, the sarcophagus and other funerary items usually are smashed and the offending name erased wherever it appears. An example of this is the tomb of Senenmut, Hatshepsut's right-hand man. When his tomb was discovered, his sarcophagus was found smashed to bits. The heavily restored sarcophagus is now in the Metropolitan Museum of Art in New York. The fact that Hatshepsut's sarcophagus and canopic chest are undamaged and that her names remain lead one to wonder if perhaps her body survived.

Elizabeth Thomas, a great authority on the Valley of the Kings, made the suggestion twenty-five years ago that the body of Hatshepsut may be in Tomb 60 of the Valley of the Kings. KV 60 was opened by Howard Carter in 1903 but only briefly mentioned in his report on the year's activities. He says that there were two female mummies inside, one of them in a coffin inscribed for Sitre, Hatshepsut's nurse. That mummy was taken to the Egyptian Museum, but Elizabeth Thomas has suggested that the mummy left behind might be Hatshepsut's.[14] The left arm of this mummy crosses the breast and the right lies along the side, which some consider to be the "royal position" for females of this period. While this is a possibility, there is an even better candidate for Hatshepsut's mummy, first suggested by Theodore Davis in his book on Hatshepsut's tomb:

> *The great find made by the Museum authorities in 1881 of the Royal Mummies which had been deposited in the "cachette," included the body of Thoutmosis I, an ornamented box bearing the names and titles of Hatshopsitu, and containing a mummified liver, and also two female bodies stripped of all covering and without coffins or inscriptions.*
>
> *Therefore, with some timidity, I trespass in the field of Egyptology to the extent of expressing my conviction that Hatshopsitu's body was moved with that of Thoutmosis from her tomb to the "cachette," and that the logic of the situation justifies the conclusion that one of the two unidentified female bodies is that of the great Queen Hatshopsitu.*
>
> *"Sic transit gloria mundi"*[15]

Davis is probably correct. Tuthmose I was found in the Deir el Bahri cache despite the fact that a sarcophagus prepared for him remained in Hatshepsut's tomb. One suspects that she was removed along with her father. Further, Hatshepsut's canopic chest in the cache contained her liver, while that in her tomb was empty. Most likely the chest with its contents would be the later, final resting place for her organs. If this is correct, the matter could be settled by a genetic comparison of this liver with the two unidentified female mummies in the cache, and with the remaining female in KV 60. The body of Hatshepsut may soon be identified.

The mummies of Tuthmose II and III have been identified. In the mummy of Tuthmose III a new position for the embalmer's incision occurs. It is more oblique than vertical and moves down a bit toward the hips. This practice continued through the Twentieth Dynasty and is quite useful for dating unidentified mummies.

Loret found the son of Tuthmose III, Amenhotep II, in his own tomb; in a side room also lay Amenhotep's his son, Tuthmose IV. With the possible exception of Hatshepsut, we thus have a complete set of Eighteenth Dynasty pharaohs up to this point. In that same side room another body was found, labeled Amenhotep III, the successor of Tuthmose IV. However, questions have been raised about this identification.

This mummy had been badly damaged by ancient tomb robbers, and embalmers of the Twenty-first Dynasty did some restoration on the disarticulated body. The mummy was reburied in a coffin whose bottom was made for Ramses III and whose lid was redone crudely for Seti I, but a small inscription to the left of the vertical Seti I inscription indicates that it is "Neb-Maat-Re" (Amenhotep III) who is inside. An inscription in hieratic on the bandages of the mummy states that: "Year twelve, sixth day of the third month of winter. On this day there was a renewed burial of the King Neb-Maat-Re, may he be given life, health, prosperity, by the high priest of Amun-Re, king of the gods, Pinedjem, son of the high priest of Amun-Re, king of the gods, Piankh. . . . " Thus both an inscription on the coffin and on the bandages attest that this is Amenhotep III. The reason for doubting the identity of the mummy is that certain as-

FIG. 99.
The bottom part of the coffin
containing the mummy of
Amenhotep III was originally
made for Ramses III and bears
his cartouches.   EGYPTIAN
MUSEUM, CAIRO

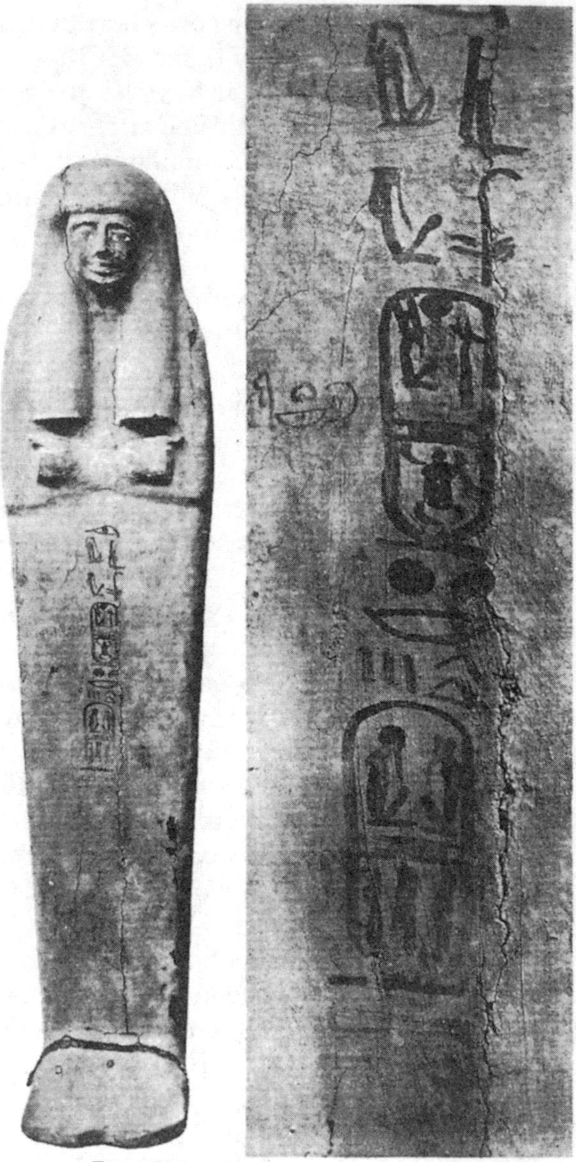

FIG. 100.
Lid of the coffin in which the mummy of
Amenhotep III was found. The large vertical
inscription shows that the coffin was reinscribed
for Seti I, but the smaller horizontal inscription
on the left shows that it was last used for
Amenhotep III.   EGYPTIAN MUSEUM, CAIRO

pects of the mummification technique had never been seen prior to the Twenty-first Dynasty.

A resinous material was inserted under the skin of the legs, arms, and neck, so that the body would have a more lifelike appearance. This practice of packing areas under the skin is not known in the Eighteenth Dynasty. Some Egyptologists believe that the inscriptions stating that this is the mummy of Amen-hotep III are wrong, and that instead it is really a mislabeled Twenty-first Dynasty mummy. This is unlikely.

When the embalmers of the Twenty-first Dynasty were called upon to restore and rewrap their "august ancestors," the term referred to bodies of the Eighteenth, Nineteenth, and Twentieth dynasties, not of their own. Also, when the process of repacking began, it relied not on resin but on what is always referred to as "a cheeselike substance" (fat and soda). The only repacked mummy in which resin has ever been used is the one in question. Thus it is not quite accurate to say that the technique belongs solely to the Twenty-first Dynasty. Given these facts, it seems probable that the embalmers and priests knew what they were doing when they rewrapped the body and labeled it "Neb-Maat-Re." The body of Amenhotep III almost certainly resides in the Egyptian Museum. The mummy of his successor, Amenhotep IV/Akhenaten, remains controversial. From our discussion of Tomb 55 in the chapter "Royal Mummies," it seems that it contains either the body of Akhenaten or of Se-menkare, his coregent. Whoever it was in tomb 55, the other member of the pair is missing. The succeeding pharaoh, Tut-ankhamen, is certain, which leaves only the last two kings of the Eighteenth Dynasty, Aye and Horemheb.

The tomb of Aye, Tutankhamen's successor, was discovered by Belzoni, who reported that it had been thoroughly looted. A later clearing confirmed this; only a few unidentifiable bones were found. In 1909 E. Howard Jones, who was working near the tomb, found a pit containing gold foil and a few objects with Aye's name on them. This was either the location of Aye's reburial or the place where tomb robbers brought their loot for inspection. In either case, it is unlikely that we will ever find Aye's mummy.

Aye's successor, Horemheb, was not related to him—he was

a military figure who seized control of Egypt. His tomb, thoroughly plundered, was discovered in 1908 by Theodore Davis. There were a few bones in the sarcophagus and some others scattered throughout the tomb, but they come from several individuals and have never been studied adequately. Faint graffiti on the walls indicate that there was an inspection of the tomb in ancient times by necropolis officials, and seem to say that the king's body was removed to another tomb. If so, there may be some hope of finding Horemheb's mummy.

The Nineteenth Dynasty

The founder of the Nineteenth Dynasty, Ramses I, reigned for less than two years, and consequently his tomb in the Valley of the Kings is both small and unfinished. Belzoni entered the tomb in October of 1817 and found it plundered, though it contained the scattered remains of two mummies of a period later than the Nineteenth Dynasty. Ramses I must be classified as missing with some hope that his body will be identified, because there are priests' inscriptions on the walls of his tomb and elsewhere that state that the king's body was removed from the tomb by his son, Seti I, and later transferred to the Deir el Bahri cache. His broken replacement coffin was found in the cache, though Ramses' body was not in it. It may be that one of the unidentified male bodies in the cache is actually Ramses I. Because we have the mummy of his son, Seti I, it should be possible through genetic testing to see which of the unidentified mummies, if any, is the father of Seti I.

The mummy of Seti I is the most beautiful of those from the Deir el Bahri cache. His entire body and face were blackened by an application of resin, but the features are clear and strikingly handsome. The head had been separated from the body by ancient tomb robbers, but the priests of the Twenty-first Dynasty restored it, placing a collar around the neck to mask the repair.

The mummy of Seti's son, Ramses II, "Ramses the Great," was also found in the Deir el Bahri cache and its identification

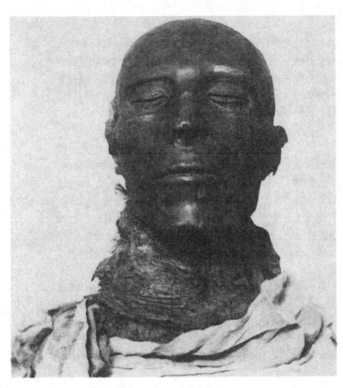

FIG. 101.
Mummy of Seti I.   EGYPTIAN MUSEUM,
CAIRO

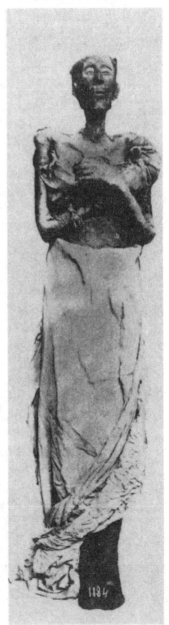

FIG. 102.
*Mummy of Ramses II as unwrapped by
Maspero in 1886.*

is reasonably certain. His name is clearly written on the coffin and a hieratic note proclaims that in year ten of the reign of the high priest Pinedjem, the body of Ramses II and his father, Seti I, were moved for safety. From the beginning, the mummy of Ramses the Great received special treatment.

In his book, *Les Momies Royales*, Maspero says that on June 1, 1886, by order of the Khedive Tewfik the mummy of Ramses II was "solemnly unwrapped."[16] In his report, Maspero noted that the genitals had been removed by the embalmers and must have been buried in the interior of a wooden Osiris statue. This is pure fantasy. No such Osiris statue containing genitals has ever been found. It is more likely that the genitals were destroyed by the rough handling the body received when it was first plundered.

Because Ramses ruled so long and died at such an advanced age, he outlived many of his sons, and so it was his thirteenth, Merneptah, who succeeded him. Merneptah was found in the cache in the side room of the tomb of Amenhotep II. An inscription on his shroud clearly indicates that he is indeed Merneptah.

The body was packed with what Elliot Smith calls "white cheesy material." Here, then, is a body predating the Twenty-first Dynasty in which this material was used. Another unique feature of this mummy is that it lacks a scrotum, a deficiency that was not the result of tomb robbers. The penis is present, but there is a clear incision visible where the scrotal sac was removed. Because it had been covered with balsam, it can't be determined whether the pharaoh was castrated before or after death. Another curious feature is a large post-mortem hole in the back of the head that seems too deliberate for plunderers' work. Merneptah died at an advanced age, and a surprising confirmation of this comes from the January 30, 1909, issue of the British medical journal, *The Lancet*.[17] At the January 19 meeting of the Royal Society of Medicine, its president, S. G. Shattock, produced microscope slides of Merneptah's aorta that showed that the artery was clogged and exhibited typical senile calcification.

In the side room beside Merneptah were his two successors, Seti II and Siptah. Seti II's wrappings were rather unusual. He

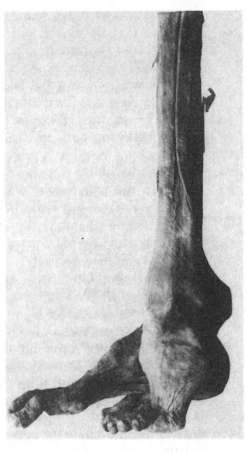

Fig. 103.
Left foot of the pharaoh Siptah, deformed perhaps by polio. EGYPTIAN MUSEUM, CAIRO

was dressed in two complete shirts, each with the cartouche of his father, Merneptah, embroidered in red and blue thread. When the mummy was unwrapped in 1905 these early examples of monogramming were handed to one of the Egyptian Museum's conservators, but have not been seen since. Another unusual feature of the wrappings is that long strings of blue faience *udjat*-eyes (amulets of the falcon god Horus' eye) and sphinx amulets were twisted around his legs.

The mummy of Siptah raises a medical question. He is often claimed be to the earliest example of polio. When Siptah was unwrapped by Elliot Smith he turned out to have a deformed left foot, exhibiting what Smith called *"talipes equino-varus,"* a deformity produced by polio. It is unlikely, however, that Siptah actually had polio, since where there is one case of polio there are usually many, and if Siptah had suffered from the disease other mummies with similar deformities would have been discovered too. Siptah's body had been badly damaged by tomb robbers, and the embalmers of the Twenty-first Dynasty placed a splint on Siptah's right arm to hold it together. In spite of the poor condition of the body, two new embalming techniques could be seen. Siptah's cheeks were filled out with linen packing, perhaps a precursor to the Twenty-first Dynasty technique of filling out the entire body for cosmetic reasons. However, the body cavity was filled not with linen, as would become standard, but with dried lichen. This material was not used with later pharaohs. Siptah is the first pharaoh to have the embalmer's incision sewn together, a practice that continued into the Twentieth Dynasty.

An ephemeral king, Amenmesse, reigned either just before or just after Seti II. We know very little about this king except that he had a tomb in the Valley of the Kings, but this tomb has not yet been fully excavated. No remains of his body are identified, and so he remains a missing mummy.

The Nineteenth Dynasty ends with the wife of Seti II, Tauseret, who took the full titles of the pharaoh and ruled as king. She and Hatshepsut are the only royal females to have tombs in the Valley of the Kings. Her tomb was altered several times, once to accommodate the body of her husband, and again when her tomb was usurped by Setnakht, founder of the Twentieth Dynasty. Tauseret's body has never been identified, but there is a strong candidate for it.

Because she prepared her tomb to accommodate the body of her husband, Seti II, and because Seti's body was found in the KV 35 cache, it is reasonable to expect that Tauseret's body was moved with her husband's. We should therefore find her in the same cache in KV 35, yet there was no coffin inscribed for her. There was a mummy who was thought to be Setnakht's because it was inside a coffin lid inscribed with his name. But when this mummy was unwrapped in 1905 by Elliot Smith, he found it to be that of a woman. No cosmetic packing material was used, so she was almost certainly embalmed prior to the Twenty-first Dynasty. The embalmer's incision is in the same place as Siptah's and Seti II's, which would date it at the end of the Nineteenth Dynasty. Her light skin, unstained by resin, places this mummy later than the time of Seti I, when the application of resins darkened the skin. All indications are that this is a mummy from the very end of the Nineteenth Dynasty. Its age is also consistent with that of Tauseret, who must have been a mature woman at the time of her death. Further, it will be remembered that Tauseret's tomb was usurped by Setnakht, whose coffin was almost certainly in her tomb at one time. Given that the mummy in question was found in the lid of Setnakht's coffin, the total body of evidence suggests that the unidentified female mummy from the tomb of Amenhotep II is the Queen/Pharaoh Tauseret.

The Twentieth Dynasty

As mentioned before, the mummy of Setnakht, founder of the Twentieth Dynasty, was not where it was supposed to be, so he too is a missing mummy. The mummy of his son, Ramses III, however, did turn up, although in a surprising place. One of the coffins in the Deir el Bahri cache was huge—more than ten feet tall—and contained *two* mummies. One was Queen Ahmose-Nefertari, who gave off such a disagreeable odor that she had to be buried under the museum's storage area for months before she could be returned to her glass case. The other mummy in the coffin was Ramses III.

Ramses III was unwrapped by Maspero in the presence of the Khedive. Inscriptions found on the bandages dated them to years nine and ten of Pinedjem, High Priest of Amun, who had restored the body. Maspero's account of the unwrapping graphically captures his disappointment:

> *One last wrapper of stiffened cloth, one last winding sheet of red linen, and then the great disappointment, keenly felt by the operators, the face of the king was coated with a compact mass of bitumen, which completely hid the features. At 20 minutes past 11, His Highness the Khedive left the room.*[18]

The disappointment was heightened because earlier that morning the group had unwrapped the mummy of Ramses the Great and had been awed by his noble features. When they unwrapped the mummy of Ramses III, the last great pharaoh of Egypt, they were hoping for another extraordinary face.

Later, a sculptor associated with the museum was called in to chip away the resin from the face. There was one surprise. The eyes had been packed with linen to make them more lifelike—Ramses III is the first mummy to have artificial eyes. In later dynasties other materials would be used to simulate them. The position of the hands was also new. The fists were no longer clenched, as they were when they held the royal scepters or other signs of authority, but were open, with the arms crossed so the hands lay near the shoulders (this was the mummy that would inspire Hollywood horror films). Maspero mentions that they stood it up to photograph it, a common early practice that causes current museum curators to shudder. One last sheet of linen was fixed to the body by a heavy coat of resin, so no examination of the incision or internal state of the mummy was possible when it was first unwrapped.

Ramses III was the last great Egyptian pharaoh. He was followed by eight more kings, all named Ramses but none with the power originally associated with that name. Egypt had begun a long period of decline from which it would never recover.

The mummies of Ramses IV, V, and VI were found in the KV 35 cache. Ramses IV had artificial eyes made of small onions, and when the mummy was placed upright to photograph it, the onions fell to the lower lids, giving the whole a very strange appearance. The frugal embalmers had closed each nostril with paste covered by an onion skin, probably from the onions used for the eyes. The hands are positioned similarly to those of Ramses III. Like Siptah, the abdomen of Ramses IV was packed with dry lichen.

The abdomen of Ramses V was packed with sawdust, with the viscera placed inside. Linen was used for his eye-packing. Small marks on his body may indicate that this pharaoh had smallpox, but there has been no microscopic confirmation of this, so it is far from an established fact.

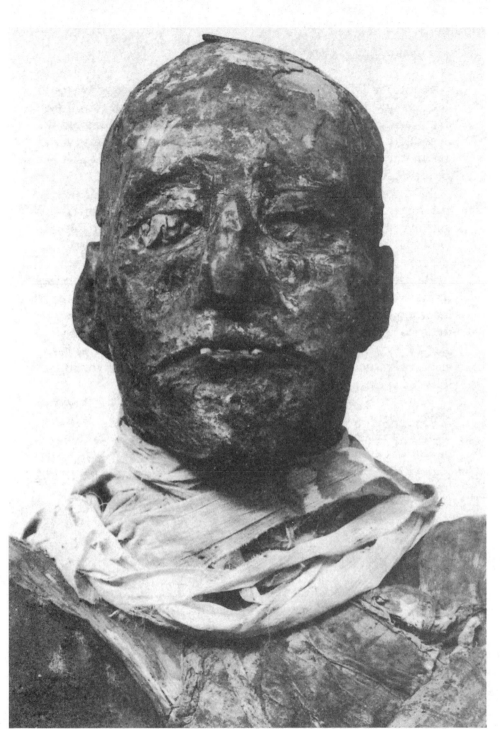

FIG. 104. *Head of Ramses III, with resin chipped away to reveal the features.* EGYPTIAN MUSEUM, CAIRO

Ramses VI's mummy was literally hacked to pieces by tomb robbers and is in the worst condition of all the royal mummies. He was crudely rewrapped, so much so that the embalmers inserted a woman's right hand and the right forearm and hand of another man. These extra right hands may have been included because Ramses' own hands had disappeared.

Ramses VII and VIII each ruled for less than one year. While a tomb has been found for Ramses VII, no trace of his mummy has ever turned up. Neither a tomb nor a mummy for Ramses VIII has ever been located, so these two Ramses are also considered missing mummies.

Ramses IX enjoyed a considerable reign, at least seventeen years. Several papyri dealing with tomb robberies in the royal necropolis survive from his reign. It is fitting that this pharaoh who so vigorously prosecuted tomb robbing was himself preserved by a later pharaoh, who moved him to the Deir el Bahri cache. His successor, Ramses X, may not have been so fortunate. His tomb has been found, but not his mummy.

The last Ramesside king, Ramses XI, reigned for twenty-seven years, during which he saw his power slide into the hands of Hri-Hor, the high priest of Amun. Ramses XI's tomb is the last constructed in the Valley of the Kings. It was never completed and probably never used, so he too is a missing mummy.

The Twenty-first Dynasty

Both high priests Pinedjem I and Pinedjem II were buried at Deir el Bahri, but there is evidence that only for Pinedjem II was this a resting place of choice. The mummy of Pinedjem I was originally placed in his family tomb rather than one constructed specifically for him. When the family tomb was plundered he was moved to the Deir el Bahri cache, where a coffin was found that was originally made for Tuthmose I but later altered for him. Pinedjem I was not found in this coffin, but in one inscribed for Queen Ahhotep, yet another indication of this mummy's travels. Pinedjem I's wrappings were disturbed and no jewelry was found on the body. For some reason Pinedjem I is not included in the *Catalogue General* listing of royal mummies in the Egyptian Museum, nor does it appear in any of the later studies done on them.

The mummy of Pinedjem II was found virtually intact, complete with jewelry and amulets that had been included in the bandages. The Deir el Bahri tomb is almost certainly his original resting place, and he is probably the last king to have been buried there. Once the tomb was sealed after his interment, it remained untouched for nearly 3,000 years. His internal organs had been removed through the usual abdominal incision, then wrapped and replaced inside the body cavity. His arms had been packed underneath the skin with mud, his cheeks filled out with linen.

The "priest kings" of Thebes were not legitimate pharaohs. Egypt was ruled by kings from Tanis, in the Delta, where Pierre Montet discovered the northern kings of the Twenty-first and Twenty-second dynasties, as discussed in the "Royal Mummies" chapter. Although Montet discovered five kings—Pseusennes I and Amenenope of the Twenty-first Dynasty and Osorkon II, Takelot II, and Sheshonq II of the Twenty-second—many more are missing from these two dynasties. Unaccounted for from the Twenty-first are Smendes, Nephercheres, Siamun, Psinaches, and Pseusennes II. Missing from the Twenty-second are Sheshonq I, Osorkon I, Takelot I, Sheshonq III, Pemay, and Sheshonq IV. As already mentioned, the Delta is not kind to human remains. If they are found, these mummies will almost certainly be in poor condition.

The Late Period

The northern rulers of the Twenty-second Dynasty had Semitic names and thus were probably not of Egyptian origin. During the Late Period, Egypt was ruled by a succession of foreigners—Libyans, Nubians, Assyrians, Persians, and, finally, Greeks and Romans. To some extent this explains why not a single mummy has been found of a ruler of Egypt after the

Twenty-second Dynasty—foreign rulers generally wished to be buried on their own soil. The few native rulers during this time were probably buried in Egypt, but it was a period of war and constant upheaval. Because few dynasties lasted very long, tomb locations would not have been forgotten and probably no burial escaped desecration. This era is so confusing that there is not even agreement as to how the dynasties should be numbered.

By 730 B.C., the Delta had degenerated into petty principalities, each with a prince who wished to be king. At this time Piankhy, a Nubian king, marched his troops as far north as Memphis and defeated Tefnakht of the Twenty-fourth Dynasty; Egypt was now under Nubian rule. The Nubian Twenty-fifth Dynasty continued under Piankhy's brother, Shabaka, who was succeeded by Shebitko, Taharqa, and finally Tannuatamun. When Tannuatamun was driven out of Egypt by the Assyrian Ashurbanipal in 663 B.C., Nubian rule ended. These Nubian kings were buried in pyramids outside the borders of Egypt.

During the Late Period mummies were intentionally destroyed by invading conquerors. When Cambyses conquered Egypt, the Twenty-sixth Dynasty ruler Amasis (570–526 B.C.) had been dead for quite a while. Herodotus tells what happened to his mummy:

> . . . *no sooner did he enter the palace of Amasis than he gave orders for his body to be taken from the tomb where it lay. This done, he proceeded to have it treated with every possible indignity, such as beating it with whips, sticking it with goads, and plucking its hairs. All this was done until the executioners were weary, and at last, as the body had been embalmed and would not fall to pieces under the blows, Cambyses had it burned.*[19]

Since Herodotus was in Egypt about a hundred years after the event, this is not so far off the mark as some other things he discusses. The story has the ring of truth. During the Late Period mummies were often covered in bitumen, which hardened to an almost glasslike texture. This would explain why the mummy did not fall apart.

The Twenty-seventh Dynasty consisted of Persian conquerors whose rulers were buried outside Egypt. Dynasties Twenty-eight and Twenty-nine were fleeting attempts at stable rule, so we know little more about them than the names of individual rulers. The Thirtieth Dynasty is the last with Egyptian rulers. The fate of the sarcophagus of Nectanebo II, the last native pharaoh, leaves little hope that we will ever find his mummy. Nectanebo's sarcophagus, now in the British Museum, is so huge and impressive that when it was found in the Mosque of St. Athanasius in Alexandria it was believed to be the tomb of Alexander the Great. Carved on the outer surface is a religious text, "The Book of What Is in the Next World," which was intended as a kind of Baedeker to help Nectanebo in his journey from this world to the next. When it was discovered by the Moslems of Alexandria, it was converted into a public bath, with twelve holes drilled in the bottom to permit the water to run out. Given the upheavals of the Late Period, there is little hope of finding any of its missing pharaohs.

10

Dead and Gone: Missing Mummies

Rummaging through mummies and papyri in an attempt to reconstruct ancient Egyptian mummification techniques can be very exciting, but, as we have seen, it can also be disappointing. Just when a mummy turns up that could provide the missing piece, as often as not it turns out to be a dud. Some mummies even have been thought discovered, only somehow to elude their excavators. Perhaps the most intriguing of the elusive mummies is that of Pharaoh Horus Sekhem-Khet of the Third Dynasty.

Horus Sekhem-Khet

Horus Sekhem-Khet succeeded King Zoser, the builder of the step pyramid at Saqqara. Little was known about Sekhem-Khet until 1951, when the Egyptian archeologist Zakaria Goneim discovered the pharaoh's unfinished pyramid a short walk from Zoser's complex. It was planned as a step pyramid, like Zoser's, but was never completed—perhaps because Sekhem-Khet ruled for the brief period of six or seven years. Originally intended to be larger than Zoser's, with seven rather than Zoser's six steps, when it was discovered it stood only twenty-three feet high and was completely covered by sand. The pyramid complex spread over acres; it was not until the 1953-4 season that the entrance finally was uncovered on the north side. Because the doorway was still sealed, despite the pyramid's unfinished state it seemed certain that the pharaoh had been buried inside. The entrance led to a descending corridor at the bottom of which huge limestone blocks stopped further penetration. When the blocks were removed, Goneim found jewelry spread along the corridor floor—21 gold bracelets, 388 hollow gold beads, 420 gold-plated faience beads, and the remains of a magic wand whose wood had decayed, leaving the gold covering behind. The fact that the gold still remained indicated that the pyramid had not been robbed. Additional confirmation lay further down the corridor: The burial chamber was sealed.

Carved out of the bedrock, the burial chamber was a large, unfinished cavern containing no funerary furniture, only a beautiful translucent alabaster sarcophagus. A burned funerary wreath lay on the lid, perhaps placed there at the time of the pharaoh's burial. The sarcophagus' sliding end panel was still sealed. As Goneim put it:

> Here we had an unfinished pyramid which, from the evidence provided by later burials, had remained untouched and probably unknown for at least three thousand years. The entrance was sealed with a massive wall of dry masonry which also had not been touched since the day it was built. Within the pyramid the entrance corridor was sealed at two other points, and these sealings also were intact. At the heart of the pyramid was an unfinished chamber, from which there was no exit save the sealed corridor, containing a sarcophagus which, from its form and design, was clearly made in the Third Dynasty, contemporary with the pyramid itself. And that sarcophagus was closed by a sliding panel which was firmly cemented into position. What more logical conclusion could one reach than that the sarcophagus contained a body, and that body was most likely to be that of the king for whom the monument was built, a king whose name we had already discovered?[1]

Preparations for opening the sarcophagus were completed on June 26, 1954. Through the two ancient holes at the top of the sliding end panel, steel hooks were inserted and from them ropes were coiled around a large pulley suspended from a scaffold. Two workmen pulled on the ropes, but nothing happened—the combination of the cement plus the panel's weight (500 pounds) made the task extremely difficult. More men pulled on the ropes until the panel finally slid upward an inch and wedges could be inserted. After two hours of work the lid was removed. To the amazement of all present, the sarcophagus was empty. Horus Sekhem-Khet's mummy had eluded the excavators.

Careful inspection of the interior of the sarcophagus indicated that it had never been used, which raised a question: What was the purpose of the pyramid? One possibility is that it was a decoy intended to misdirect robbers from Sekhem-Khet's true burial place. As mentioned before, a tomb's builders often became its robbers since they were familiar with the design. So if indeed this was a "false" tomb, the workers on the pyramid would probably have known that it contained no significant treasures. This might explain how it remained untouched for 4,000 years. The mummy of the pharaoh Horus Sekhem-Khet, therefore, may yet be found.

Queen Hetepheres

Another Old Kingdom tomb that led to disappointment was that of Queen Hetepheres, discussed in Chapter Two. There was a mystery connected with this tomb that led to both Egyptological embarrassment and to one of the all-time great remarks by an Egyptologist.

Discovered in 1926, when Tutankhamen's tomb was being cleared, Hetepheres' tomb was also considered an intact royal tomb with similarly extraordinary potential. After the tomb had been cleared enough to work on the alabaster sarcophagus, an imposing group of officials was invited to be the first people in 4,000 years to gaze on the features of the queen. One by one the august visitors were tied in an armchair and lowered into the tomb. The master of ceremonies was George Andrew Reisner, field director for the Harvard-Boston Museum excavations. In addition, Reisner had requested the presence of the expedition's artist, Joseph Lindon Smith, who has left us his wonderful account of the event:

> *Wheeler and Dunham were at either side of the sarcophagus, to operate two short projectors, which were to serve as handles for lifting the lid. Fitted under the handles was a frame of wooden beams resting on the jack screws. Reisner sat on a small box, and I was next to him, kneeling, and closest to the sarcophagus.*
>
> *In a breathless silence, the lid began to be lifted. When it was sufficiently raised for me to peer inside, I saw to my dismay that the queen was not there—the sarcophagus was empty! Turning to Reisner, I said in a voice louder than I had intended, "George, she's a dud!"*
>
> *Whereupon the minister of Public Works asked "What is a dud?"*
>
> *Reisner rose from his box and said, "Gentlemen, I regret Queen Hetepheres is not receiving," and added, "Mrs. Reisner will serve refreshments at the camp."*[2]

The absence of the queen's mummy led to speculation that Hetepheres might have owned two tombs. Reisner's theory was that the queen's original tomb was at Dashur, but was partially robbed during the reign of her son, the pharaoh Cheops. By the time officials discovered that the tomb had been plundered, the body was missing (tomb robbers frequently removed the body to unwrap it later, in safety). Rather than upset the king with news that his mother's body was missing, the officials resealed the sarcophagus and told the king that although some objects had been looted from the tomb, her body was intact. To prevent further robberies, Cheops then reburied what he thought was his mother's body along with what remained of her funerary equipment near his pyramid on the Giza plateau.

Another theory to explain the missing mummy is that the tomb was a cenotaph, or false burial site intended to mislead tomb robbers, as the Saqqara pyramid of King Horus Sekhem-Khet might have been. Perhaps here too the reason this tomb was found intact was that the robbers were the same men who had built the tomb, and would have known that it was, in the words of Joseph Lindon Smith, "a dud."

Princess Neferuptah

Princess Neferuptah is an elusive mummy quite different from those of King Sekhem-Khet and Queen Hetepheres, who were not buried where Egyptologists expected. The pyramid of Neferuptah, a daughter of Amenemhet III, was discovered in 1955 by Zaky Iskander, the great authority on mummies.[3] As with most Middle Kingdom pyramids, an outer casing of fine white limestone covered an interior of mud bricks. While the outer appearance was similar to the stone pyramids of the Old Kingdom, the Middle-Kingdom structures were not so stable; by the time it was discovered, Neferuptah's pyramid had crumbled into little more than a hill. Beneath the mud-brick rubble lay seven fifteen-foot-long limestone slabs covering an underground burial chamber.

The design of the pyramid proved to be unique, since there was no entrance to the burial chamber except through the limestone blocks covering it. The princess's mummy must have been first placed in the tomb, the tomb covered with the limestone blocks, and then the pyramid was constructed on the blocks. Therefore the pyramid was built *after* the princess's death rather than during her lifetime, as was the case with all other pyramids. Since the limestone blocks were still in place, Iskander knew he had found an undisturbed royal burial site of the Middle Kingdom. Because of his interest in mummies, this especially excited him—he would have the opportunity of examining a royal mummy undisturbed for 4,000 years.

Removal of the limestone slabs revealed a rectangular room fifteen feet long, five feet wide, and about eight feet high. Hewn out of bedrock, it had been carefully lined with fine white limestone. Unfortunately, in the 4,000 years since the princess's burial, the water table had risen considerably, filling half the tomb with water.

Funerary items could be seen below the water—an offering

table, pottery vases, and jewelry. This was not a dummy burial. A nine-foot granite sarcophagus dominated the little chamber, and with great difficulty the lid, carved from a single piece of stone, was removed. The sarcophagus was almost completely filled with water. When the water was siphoned off, all that remained at the bottom were three inches of sediment containing beads of faience and carnelian, pieces of silver, and other ornaments, undoubtedly the remains of Neferuptah's jewelry. But the princess was gone, her body completely dissolved by the water in which it had been immersed for thousands of years. There is no doubt, however, that she had been there. Analysis of the water from the sarcophagus showed traces of human protein. She was dead and gone.

Tutankhamen's Children

Even Tutankhamen's tomb involved missing mummies. The ones that almost got away were his children. When the autopsy of Tutankhamen's body had been completed and the burial chamber cleared, Carter was able to enter the small room off the burial chamber called "the Treasury." This room contained Tutankhamen's canopic chest, model boats, and numerous wooden chests. One simple box contained two miniature wood coffins, each less than two feet long. They had been coated with the black resin found on so many of Tutankhamen's other funerary objects. Across the coffins were inscribed gold bands referring to the owners of the coffins merely as "the Osiris" and "the Venerated One." Around each coffin, bands of linen were sealed with the clay insignia of the royal necropolis—a jackal above nine bound captives, symbols of Egypt's traditional enemies.

Each resin-coated coffin contained a smaller anthropoid coffin covered with gold leaf. Their inscriptions gave no indication as to their owners. Packed inside were what appeared to be small, neatly wrapped mummies, one slightly more than a foot long, the other approximately ten inches and bearing a tiny cartonage mask over the face. Carter removed the wrappings from the

FIG. 105.
External coffin (with lid removed to show internal coffin) for the smaller of the two fetuses found in Tutankhamen's tomb. PHOTOGRAPHY BY EGYPTIAN EXPEDITION, METROPOLITAN MUSEUM OF ART

FIG. 106.
Interior gilded coffin for the larger fetus, with the wrapped mummy inside. PHOTOGRAPHY BY EGYPTIAN EXPEDITION, METROPOLITAN MUSEUM OF ART

smaller of the two, revealing a five-month-old female fetus, probably a miscarriage of Ankhesenamen, Tutankhamen's young wife. When Derry examined the fetus in 1932, he found little to add to its history or condition, and never published a report on it.

The larger of the two mummies was still wrapped when Derry received it. He unwrapped it, uncovering a second female fetus, which he estimated to be seven months old. Four inches larger than its sister, who showed no signs of mummification, this one was large enough to have been embalmed. Across the left side of the abdomen ran an embalmer's incision, less than an inch long. The abdominal cavity was stuffed with linen, but Derry does not mention the internal organs, which probably were still inside.[4] Had they been removed, canopic jars would likely have been provided.

Despite the small size of the fetus, the embalmers forced linen through its nose into its cranium. Derry, never one to worry about preserving a mummy, broke through the cranium to remove the linen and found remains of the wire used to force the linen into the skull. He says little about the fetus other than estimating its age. Why young Queen Ankhesenamen was unable to carry her two daughters to term may never be known. Her body is missing and no trace of her tomb has been found.

Derry's cursory autopsy produced little information. Further studies certainly seem warranted, especially with today's more advanced techniques. However, after the 1932 investigation the mummies disappeared. In 1971 F. Filce Leek, an English dentist interested in studying the fetuses, was given permission by the Egyptian Department of Antiquities to examine and X-ray them. It was assumed that they were still in their coffins in the Tutankhamen Gallery in the Egyptian Museum, but the coffins were found to be empty. Searches through various storerooms revealed no traces, and the mummies were declared missing. But there was one clue. While the coffins were recorded in the Museum's *Journal d'Entrée*, no mention of the fetuses was made. They had never entered the museum.

Throughout his long career, Derry had been given numerous mummies and fragments of mummies to examine, but he rarely returned them. Rather, he stored them at the Kasr El-Ainy Hos-

FIG. 107. *Inner wrappings of the larger fetus.* PHOTOGRAPHY BY EGYPTIAN
EXPEDITION, METROPOLITAN MUSEUM OF ART

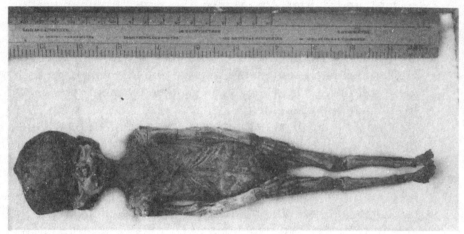

FIG. 108. *The smaller fetus.* PHOTOGRAPHY BY EGYPTIAN EXPEDITION,
METROPOLITAN MUSEUM OF ART

FIG. 109. *The larger fetus. Note the damage at top of skull where Derry opened it
to remove linen inserted by embalmers.* PHOTOGRAPHY BY EGYPTIAN
EXPEDITION, METROPOLITAN MUSEUM OF ART

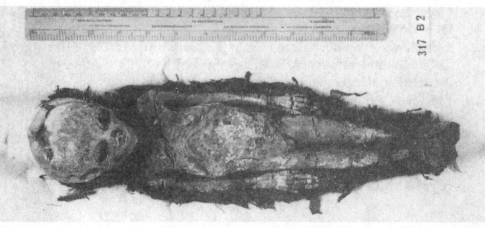

pital, where they accumulated. After his death they remained there, of no interest to anyone. In June 1992 newspapers reported the discovery of 528 mummies and portions of mummies at Kasr El-Ainy Hospital—Derry's cache. There, along with Zoser's foot and assorted other mummies, were the two fetuses. Actually, various investigators knew about the hoard. In 1978 R. G. Harrison studied one of the fetuses.[5] An X-ray of the larger of the two showed it to be deformed, with an abnormally high right clavicle, scoliosis, and spina bifida. He estimated the age as more than eight months. Had the fetus lived, Tutankhamen and Ankhesenamen would have had a deformed daughter. While there has never been conclusive proof that the royal couple were indeed the parents, such a demonstration is now possible. Genetic testing of Tutankhamen's mummy and the fetuses will probably soon establish the fact.

Tutankhamen's Grandmother

Although the two fetuses from the tomb of Tutankhamen disappeared for a while, there is another royal mummy that reappeared as a result of a find in his tomb. The reappearance involved luck, good detective work, and modern technology.

When Victor Loret discovered three unwrapped, unidentified mummies in a side chamber off Amenhotep II's tomb in 1898, no one believed they would ever be identified. The mummy that appeared on the left of the three in contemporary pictures was named "the Elder Lady," and appears in a closeup photo in G. Elliot Smith's *Royal Mummies*. The photo clearly shows the right hand extended at the side and the left across the chest, a pose we know is associated with royal women of the Eighteenth Dynasty. Edward Wente, a University of Chicago Egyptologist, suggested in the 1970s that the Elder Lady might be either Queen Hatshepsut or Queen Tiye.

Conclusive identification of the Elder Lady as either of these queens would be an important accomplishment. Hatshepsut was a major figure, actually ruling Egypt as king during one of Egypt's most powerful eras. Queen Tiye had a more traditional

FIG. 110. *"The Elder Lady," as shown in G. Elliot Smith's* Royal Mummies. EGYPTIAN MUSEUM, CAIRO

female role as the wife of Amenhotep III. There is no ancient Egyptian word for "queen," only one for "wife." Pharaohs had several wives, but only one was designated as "great wife," and this phrase is what is usually translated as "queen." Tiye, the great wife of the pharaoh, was also the mother of a pharaoh—the monotheist Akhenaten—and the grandmother of a pharaoh, Tutankhamen. With two plausible identities for the Elder Lady, the question was how either could be demonstrated. A find from Tutankhamen's tomb settled the question.

In addition to the two fetuses found in the Treasury, Carter also discovered a third miniature coffin, similar to the two that held the fetuses, but this one inscribed for Tutankhamen. Like the other two coffins, it contained a miniature gilded anthro-

FIG. 111.
External miniature coffin (with lid removed to show internal coffin) containing a lock of Queen Tiye's hair.
PHOTOGRAPHY BY EGYPTIAN EXPEDITION, METROPOLITAN MUSEUM OF ART

FIG. 112.
Internal gilded coffin with the lid removed to show the contents. The small painted coffin (B) contained an even smaller coffin. PHOTOGRAPHY BY EGYPTIAN EXPEDITION, METROPOLITAN MUSEUM OF ART

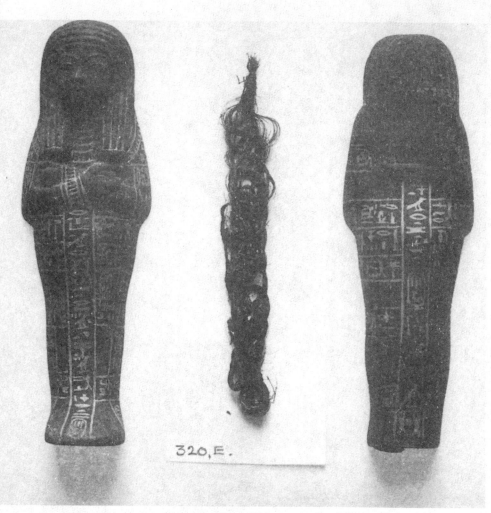

FIG. 113. *The smallest internal coffin, with its cartouche of Queen Tiye, which contained a plait of her hair.* PHOTOGRAPHY BY EGYPTIAN EXPEDITION, METROPOLITAN MUSEUM OF ART

poid coffin, again inscribed for Tutankhamen. Inside the gilded coffin Carter found a curious assortment of objects: a very small painted wood anthropoid coffin, some scraps of cloth, and a tightly bundled linen parcel containing a solid gold statuette of a kneeling king that is usually identified as Amenhotep III in his "juvenile" phase but that may be Tutankhamen. Inside the small painted coffin was an even smaller one, inscribed with the name and titles of Tutankhamen's grandmother, Queen Tiye, and containing a lock of her hair.

Often the tombs of the pharaohs included heirlooms from previous rulers or family members. Sometimes a jar used by an ancestor or a scarab inscribed with his name was placed in the tomb as a keepsake. The plait of Queen Tiye's hair may have been Tutankhamen's memento of a beloved grandmother. Like fingerprints, hair is unique. If the hair of Queen Tiye matched that of the Elder Lady, then the Elder Lady was undoubtedly Queen Tiye. The Egyptian Antiquities Organization is, however, extremely hesitant to permit samples from the royal mummies—even just a few hairs—to be removed for study. The authorities first had to be convinced that the project had a good chance of identifying the Elder Lady as the venerable Queen Tiye.

Permission was finally granted in 1975 for Dr. James Harris, the author of *X-raying the Pharaohs*, to take a cephalogram of the Elder Lady. This X-ray technique permits a precise plotting of cranial measurements. The side chamber in the tomb of Amenhotep II that held the Elder Lady was unsealed and the cephalogram taken. The computerized data from the Elder Lady were compared with those of Thuya, Queen Tiye's mother, to determine if the two women were similar enough to suggest a mother-daughter relationship. The test showed a remarkable similarity between Thuya and the Elder Lady. Permission then was granted for hair samples to be taken from the head of the Elder Lady and the plait of Queen Tiye's hair.

Both samples were scanned by electron microprobes to chart their chemical composition. Unquestionably, the hair found in Tutankhamen's tomb had come from the head of the Elder Lady. Queen Tiye was missing no longer.

Alexander the Great

When Howard Carter completed his clearing of Tutankhamen's tomb in 1930, he was asked what his next project would
be. His answer was that he intended to locate and excavate the
tomb of Alexander the Great.[6] In 1936, when Carter's health was
failing and he had abandoned all intentions of further excavation, he again mentioned the tomb. As he finished guiding the
future King Farouk and Prince Adel Sabit on a tour of the west
bank of Thebes, he told them he knew of the location of Alexander's tomb, adding "... but I shall not tell anyone about it,
least of all the Antiquities Department. The secret will die with
me."[7]

It is doubtful that Carter knew the exact location of the tomb
of Alexander the Great. However, its general location has been
known for thousands of years, and it has probably remained
undamaged since Alexander's death. This tomb would be one
of the great archaeological finds of all time, yet it remains to be
discovered. The unique circumstances of Alexander's death and
burial probably explain why his mummy is still missing.

Alexander was a Macedonian Greek, but when he conquered
Egypt, liberating it from the hated Persians, he traveled to the
remote Siwa Oasis to consult the oracle at the temple of Zeus
Amum. Alexander asked the oracle, "Who was my father?" The
oracle replied, "The sun." Alexander wanted to be an Egyptian
ruler, a god, not merely a Macedonian conqueror. Now that the
oracle had established him as an Egyptian god, he planned the
city of Alexandria with his architect Dinocrates, laying out its
streets to take advantage of the sea breezes. But Alexander
never saw the completion of his city. Soon after the planning
he left Egypt, returning only when his embalmed body was
brought back for burial.

Alexander died in the summer of 323 B.C. in Babylon. He had
been ill with fever for two weeks but ignored it, going to parties
and drinking with his generals. Finally, as he grew weaker, and
when it became obvious that he would soon die, his generals

came to see their commander for the last time and asked: "To whom do you leave your kingdom?" Arrian, Alexander's biographer, recorded his whispered answer: "To the strongest." Alexander's mystique was so great that his successor had to be someone with Alexander's blood. Alexander's wife, Roxane, was pregnant, but of course it was not known if the child would be a male, so Alexander's feeble-minded half-brother Arridaeus was named ruler, with Perdiccas as regent.

Alexander's body was embalmed in Babylon, probably in some modified Egyptian style (one tradition says in "white honey"). Here it lay in precious spices for two years while Greek craftsmen prepared a gold coffin and the catafalque to carry Alexander to Aegae, the traditional burial place of Macedonian kings. Diodorus gives us a description of the catafalque and its thousand-mile journey that he heard from an eyewitness.

The catafalque for transporting Alexander's coffin consisted of a miniature temple of gold, with a vaulted roof supported by Ionic columns. At each corner of the temple the goddess of victory held out a trophy, while all about painted friezes portrayed scenes from Alexander's campaigns. The entrance to the miniature temple was flanked by two gold lions. The wheels of the catafalque were gilded, their axles terminating in lions' heads holding spears in their mouths. The immense weight of this golden confection was pulled by sixty-four mules, each with a gold crown and a gold bell to announce Alexander's entrance to cities along the route. At each town offerings and prayers were said for the deified Alexander; it was a spectacle remembered for generations. When the procession reached Syria, Ptolemy, Alexander's faithful general who now controlled Egypt, met the entourage with his army in order to hijack the body and bring it to Egypt. The body remained in Memphis for twelve years while Alexander's tomb was being prepared at the crossroads of the two main avenues of Alexandria.

When the body was finally entombed in Alexandria, it remained undisturbed for more than a century and a half until Ptolemy IX, needing funds, exhumed the body in order to melt down the gold coffin and replace it with one of glass. The mummy of Alexander the Great was then returned to its crypt, where it was shown to Julius Caesar by Cleopatra fifty years later. As Egypt slipped from the control of the Ptolemies into the hands of the Romans, the great city of Alexandria declined. Eventually even the location of the famous library of Alexandria was lost to history. Buildings collapsed or burned; when the city was rebuilt centuries later, it had altered considerably from the original plan of Dinocrates and Alexander. Even the crossroads of the two main avenues disappeared.

The search for Alexander's tomb does not involve treasure—anything of intrinsic value would have been taken by Ptolemy IX—which is why it may have remained untouched. Many scholars believe that Alexander's body lies beneath the Nebi Daniel Mosque in Alexandria, at the intersection of Rosetta and Nebi Daniel streets. There are indeed caverns beneath the mosque, but while clandestine searches have been made, a proper excavation will be difficult because of the danger of undermining the mosque.

In 1979 an attempt was made to use psychics to locate the mummy of Alexander.[8] Their impressions led them to the Nebi Daniel Mosque, although one hardly needed psychics for that. E. M. Forster, the author of *Passage to India* and *Howard's End*, wrote a highly personal guidebook to Alexandria in 1922 that stated that Alexander lay beneath the mosque.[9] Thus it may well be that this greatest of all missing mummies indeed lies beneath the mosque, but because of the logistical and political/religious problems involved, it may be some time before anyone will again see the face of Alexander the Great.

11
The Mummy in Fiction and Film

One of the benefits of any intense research project is the serendipitous discovery of irresistible information not directly related to the topic. While looking for details of the mummification process, I came across novels and short stories dealing with fictional mummies. Soon I was relaxing in the evening by reading mummy novels. When these were exhausted, I began searching out obscure videos of old mummy movies. Although plentiful, these books and films had never been treated as a serious genre, and I began wondering if their appeal was the same as that of real mummies.

Mummies attract more visitors to Egyptian collections than do any other displays. The question of exactly what it is about mummies that fascinates has been discussed many times, and usually the same answer emerges—the humanness of mummies. Here, almost reaching out across time, is a *person*, a recognizable human being who lived and died thousands of years ago but who would still be recognized today by his friends. The same personal quality of actual mummies has also, for years, drawn people to fictional accounts of mummies, first in literature and then in films.

Of all the fictional mummies, the one that has had the greatest impact and success is Imhotep, the resurrected Egyptian priest played by Boris Karloff in the 1932 film *The Mummy*. The reason for the success of this fictional treatment above all others is the humanity of the mummy. Imhotep, or Ardath Bey, as he is called in his resurrected state, has a full range of emotions—he lives, fears, and gets angry. He is the lover desperately seeking

FIG. 114. *Lobby card for* The Mummy. *The role was created for Boris Karloff, fresh from his portrayal of the monster in Universal's* Frankenstein.

to be reunited with his love. There is a psychological completeness here that is lacking in the many fictional treatments that preceded the film. These unsuccessful portrayals, however, contained the elements that would combine to form the film classic.

The first fictional appearance of mummies took place millennia ago, for the ancient Egyptians themselves enjoyed mummy stories. One of the best is the adventures of Setne Khamwas, the magician. Khamwas was an historical figure, a high priest at Memphis who was the fourth son of Ramses II.

Three stories employing Khamwas as the central character are known from about 200 B.C. This was a thousand years after the historical Khamwas died, but by that time he had acquired a reputation as a sage and powerful magician. Only one of the three tales deals with mummies, but it is the earliest surviving version of a special plot device that would be resurrected again and again in mummy movies—the pursuit of the forbidden magical *Book of Thoth.*

The magical papyrus in the tale is hidden in the middle of the waters of Coptos inside a gold chest. In turn, the gold chest is enclosed in a chest of silver, successively enclosed in chests of ebony and ivory, then juniper wood, then copper, and finally of iron. The nested boxes are guarded by miles of serpents, lizards, and scorpions.

Naneferkaptah, a prince and magician, uses his occult powers to overcome these obstacles to retrieve the book from the waters of Coptos. The cost, however, is high. Thoth, the god of writing, hears of the theft of his papyrus and drowns Naneferkaptah's son, then his wife, and finally Naneferkaptah himself. The papyrus for which Naneferkaptah paid so dearly is then buried with him. Khamwas, also desirous of the papyrus, breaks into the tomb, but the mummy of Naneferkaptah rises up to protect it. Khamwas and Naneferkaptah play the ancient Egyptian game of *senet,* a board game something like chess, to determine who will retain possession of the papyrus. Naneferkaptah wins, but Khamwas resorts to magical amulets to steal it anyway. As a result of his theft, such incredible misfortunes befall Khamwas that he returns the magical scroll and reseals the tomb. The Khamwas story is retold in a 1990 novel by Pauline Gedge, *The Scroll of Saqqara.*[1]

The First Romantic Mummy

Théophile Gautier's 1857 *Romance of a Mummy* presages Howard Carter's discovery of Tutankhamen's tomb by more than half a century: " 'I have a presentiment that we shall find a tomb intact in the valley of Biban-el-Molook,' said a young Englishman of haughty mein to an individual of much more humble appearance. . . ."[2] The humble individual was a hired archaeologist, and, just like Carter and Carnarvon, the duo in fact discovers an intact tomb.

Romance of a Mummy is remarkable for several reasons. Displaying an impressive knowledge of ancient Egypt and providing numerous details of the customs, clothing, furniture, flowers, food, etc., of pharonic times, it is the first of several historically accurate novels set in Egypt. It is also the first to touch on the theme of the living falling in love with a mummy.

In the prologue to the novel, Lord Evandale, a wealthy Englishman, discovers the intact tomb of an Egyptian queen, Tahoser. When unwrapped, the mummy appears remarkably well-preserved.

> *As he stood beside the dead beauty, the young lord experienced that retrospective longing often inspired by the sight of a marble or painting representing a woman of past time celebrated for charms: it seemed to him that he might have loved her if he had lived three thousand five hundred years ago, this fair being that the grave had left untouched . . .* [3]

The mummy and the rest of the tomb's contents are transported to England, where the excavators find a papyrus in the sarcophagus that tells the story of the beautiful Tahoser; this is the romance of the mummy.

The daughter of a high priest during the time of the Exodus, Tahoser adored an Israelite who did not return her love. However, she is loved by Egypt's pharaoh. When the Israelite's true love, Rachel, learns of Tahoser's love for her fiancé, she suggests, in true Biblical style, that he marry both of them! This cozy arrangement was not to be, however, for the Exodus, complete with plagues and curses, intervenes, and Tahoser is left behind. Of course, the pharaoh never returns from the parted Red Sea, so Tahoser becomes the ruler of Egypt. She soon dies and is entombed, only to be found 3,000 years later by Lord Evandale. At the end of the *Romance of a Mummy* we are told:

> *As for Lord Evandale, he has never cared to marry, although he is lord of his race. The young ladies cannot understand his coldness towards the fair sex, but would they in all likelihood ever imagine that Lord Evandale is in love retrospectively with Tahoser, daughter of the high-priest Pelamounoph, who died three thousand five hundred years ago?* [4]

The Ring of Thoth

While the love in *Romance of a Mummy* is never consummated, Arthur Conan Doyle's "The Ring of Thoth" involves the reuniting of two lovers after millennia, but in a way that would be altered by the time the theme was interpreted in the film classic.

The story concerns an attendant in the Louvre's Egyptian department—actually, an ancient Egyptian who discovered a potion for immortality through medical researches as a priest at the Temple of Osiris at Avaris. He drinks the potion, but the girl whom he loves is hesitant to meddle with such mysteries. Before she decides whether or not to drink it, she dies of the plague. Only Sosra, the priest, and one of his close colleagues, Parmes, knew the secret and had taken the potion. Parmes loved the girl as well; now both men are doomed to mourn her death for eternity. Parmes devotes all his life to discovering an antidote to the potion so that he can die and join his beloved in her tomb.

Eventually he discovers the antidote and takes it. He tells Sosra about the antidote, but not its secret, so only he will join the girl in death. He does tell Sosra that one portion of the antidote remains hidden inside the ring of Thoth. For centuries Sosra, cursed with immortality, occupies his time learning the languages of the world and reading Egyptological reports in the hope of finding his beloved and the ring.

One day Sosra reads about a tomb discovered near Avaris that contained the intact mummy of a young girl on whose breast lay the ring of Thoth. He sails for Cairo to see if this mummy is his beloved, but at the Boulaq Museum, Mariette Bey tells him that everything has been shipped to the Louvre. To be reunited with the girl, Sosra takes the job of a lowly attendant in the Louvre's Egyptian department.

At the first opportunity he opens the mummy case and recognizes his long-lost love. The ring still contains the potion, which he takes, and he expires in the arms of the mummy.

The First Murdering Mummy

The first story with a thoroughly sinister mummy is "Lot 249," also by Sir Arthur Conan Doyle. The title refers to an auction lot consisting of a mummy in its case, purchased by Edward Bellingham, an Oxford student and expert in Eastern languages. When Bellingham reanimates the mummy, he sends it to murder his enemies. When caught, Bellingham is forced at gunpoint to cut the mummy's body into pieces and burn them. The secret about how Bellingham brought the mummy back to life is never revealed, but a reference is made to certain old plant leaves that he is forced to burn with the mummy. These leaves may be the prototype of the tana leaves used later in mummy films to bring mummies back to life.[5] For example, in *The Mummy's Hand* (1940) three tana leaves are required to keep Kharis's heart beating; nine give "life and motion, but never give more than nine."

While "Lot 249" contains a murdering mummy—something that the film would use—the mummy has no personality; it is merely a prop around which the mystery revolves. It is interesting that in two separate stories Conan Doyle had two essential elements of *The Mummy*: the murdering mummy and love between the living and the mummified. Had he put them together, he might have had a classic.

The Eye of Osiris

The Eye of Osiris, first published in 1911 under the title of *The Vanishing Man* by R. Austin Freeman, is the first detective story to use a mummy as a feature, but it is merely a hook to draw the reader in. Like other Freeman novels, it features Dr. Thorndyke, a brilliant sleuth and lecturer in forensic medicine at St. Margaret's Hospital, London.

In the novel, John Bellingham, an Egyptologist and collector of antiquities, disappears mysteriously, leaving behind an Eighteenth Dynasty lapis lazuli scarab of Amenhotep that he wore on his watch chain. Foul play is suspected, but the body cannot be found. Two years later, parts of a body that could be Bellingham's are discovered in a series of ponds all around London.

One of the body parts—the ring finger of the left hand—is recovered in a well near the Egyptologist's brother's house. On it is Bellingham's gold ring with the "Eye of Osiris." Because the brother and his niece are the beneficiaries of the will, they become prime suspects of the murder. The winding trail of the complex plot includes the deceased's niece doing research on the recently discovered Amarna letters at the British Museum.

After a while, Dr. Thorndyke is able to prove that the body parts do not belong to the deceased Egyptologist, but rather to a mummy Bellingham intended to donate to the British Museum. The climax of the book takes place in the British Museum, when Dr. Thorndyke produces Bellingham's missing body. The murderer had mummified Bellingham, wrapped him up, and placed him in the coffin that was sent to the museum. To establish that the body in the anthropoid coffin is indeed that of the murdered Egyptologist, Thorndyke X-rays the mummy. The description of the process provides fascinating details of early X-raying of mummies.

The Palgrave Mummy

Shortly after the discovery of Tutankhamen's tomb, novels with mummy themes appeared in quantity. Most were hastily written, and the most contrived of the sorry lot was *The Palgrave Mummy* by F. M. Pettee. The plot centers around a mummy and its anthropoid case, which has a curse in hieroglyphs running down its front. It is shipped from Egypt for study by the wealthy Paris Palgrave, but two members of his household die mysteriously before a proper examination can be made.

The curse warns that ". . . living blood shall flow, without the hint of wound. . . ." Blood does mysteriously appear on the mummy's throat, but the explanation is so far-fetched that it is less believable than the ancient Egyptian curse. Paris Palgrave explains how he did it:

> *I had just bought, a couple of days before, from a Hindoo importer, a certain little-known microbe, common to certain Hindoo provinces.... When a culture of this germ has been kept at a certain warm temperature for a period of ten days, it produces drops that resemble blood so closely that even men like you might consider it genuine.*[6]

Although here too we do not yet have a true mummy character, *The Palgrave Mummy* may well have provided the inspiration for the famous Boris Karloff portrayal of Ardath Bey. The novel's heroine, Olive Palgrave, turns into a mummy, and the description of the event is very much like Ardath Bey's death at the end of the film:

> *But as Olive Palgrave stood there, the normal, extraordinary pallor of her skin began to change, surely—uncannily. Its blond whiteness faded, or seemed to be touched by some impossible, shadowy ray. Slowly, the white of her skin blurred to amber, like her eyes; from amber to a coffee hue; from a coffee to a sepia; and from a sepia to a dun, leathery brown. As the transformation took place, the fair, healthy, girlish skin appeared to shrivel, to cling to the bones. And her eyes seemed to sink in the sockets like yellow glass.*[7]

The explanation for the transformation is that Olive, for her own amusement, had designed a vaudeville act in which she turns into a mummy. This was made possible by using a new makeup she discovered that turned brown when lit by bright light!

The Palgrave Mummy was published in 1929, and the script for *The Mummy* was submitted to Universal Studios on September 12, 1932. Thus, John Balderston, the screenwriter, might have read the awful novel and incorporated this single worthwhile aspect of it in his brilliant script. But it is more probable that all the plot devices and themes of the film—reincarnation, a love lasting through centuries, reanimation of the dead, forbidden arcane knowledge, vengeful Egyptian gods—were drawn from a body of mummy fiction that is now largely forgotten.

The Mummy Moves

The 1925 *The Mummy Moves* by Mary Gaunt is another novel that shares something with the film. Here, as in the film, the mummy turns killer, or at least that is how it appears at first. Several victims have had their throats ripped out, and a mummy in a curio cabinet is found with blood on *her* hands. The plot includes the obligatory "Hindoo" character and an exotic dark-skinned villain, but is most memorable for its Detective Dodson, who compulsively quotes Latin mottoes and is repeatedly mistaken about the identity of the murderer.

The Jewel of Seven Stars

The main precursor of *The Mummy* was *The Jewel of the Seven Stars* by Bram Stoker, author of *Dracula*. Published in 1912, the year Stoker died, it is the first story to connect the reanimation of an ancient Egyptian queen with a living, contemporary heroine. The story doesn't read nearly as well today as it did when written, but it manages to combine all the basics of the mummy horror genre.

A hidden queen's tomb is discovered in Egypt and its contents transported to England. Although the queen had made plans to resurrect, her *ka* in the meantime dwells in the body of the Egyptologist/adventurer's beautiful daughter. The key to the queen's reanimation is the jewel of seven stars—a ruby containing seven seven-pointed stars inside. Not coincidentally, the queen's severed hand has seven fingers.

The reanimation scene is much like that in *Frankenstein*, with electric lights, an operating table, and a doctor presiding. Today the scene reads more like camp art than high drama, but it does have a surprise at the end. For the true mummy enthusiast, a mummified cat also comes to life. Stoker has done his Egyptological homework, employing the then-recent researches of Budge, Petrie, *et al*. The novel itself resurrected on the screen in the 1980s in the form of *The Awakening*, starring Charlton Heston. The poorly scripted film lasted one week in the theaters, then became part of mummy history.

The Mummy Really Moves: Films

The first two decades of the twentieth century that produced the mass of mummy literature also witnessed the birth and growth of motion pictures. The few mummy movies made during these early years of cinema have been lost, but they were probably not horror films as we know them today. *Mummy of the King Ramses* was the awkward American title of a 1909 French film. In 1911, three separate mummy films appeared—one French, one British, and one American—all titled *The Mummy*. From Germany came *Eyes of the Mummy* (1918) and *Mummy Love* (1926).

The earliest horror films generally have roots in literature. *Dracula* (1930), *Frankenstein* (1931), and *Dr. Jekyll & Mr. Hyde* (1932) were all based on popular classics. No single work of mummy fiction achieved the stature of these works, but, collectively, mummy fiction provided all the themes and plot elements necessary to weave a horror legend comparable to *Dracula* or *Frankenstein*. From the 1909 *Mummy of the King Ramses* to the 1992 *I Was a Teenage Mummy*, about two dozen mummy movies have been produced. They include one undisputed classic, several routine horror films, a few comedies, and a batch of very bad films. The stars of the genre are five movies produced by Universal Studios between 1932 and 1944.

The classic monsters of the 1930s—Dracula, Frankenstein, the Wolf Man, the Invisible Man, and the Mummy—all appeared in films produced by Universal Pictures, which in turn all employed the same artists in front of and behind the camera. The director of *The Mummy*, Karl Freund, served as the cinematographer for *Dracula*. The script was written by John Balderston, who wrote scripts for the movie *Frankenstein* and the play *Dracula* as well. John Fulton (special effects) and Jack Pierce (makeup) worked on all the Universal horror films.

The Classic Mummy

Universal's *The Mummy* clearly is the best of the mummy films, and by far the most famous image of a mummy is Boris Karloff's eerie portrayal. The role was specifically created for Karloff, who was fresh from a successful appearance as the monster in *Frankenstein*. Originally the screenplay was called *Cagliostro*; it was later rewritten and retitled *Im-Ho-Tep*, and only became *The Mummy* just before release. As filmed, *The Mummy* is actually a veiled adaptation of *Dracula*, which had been filmed two years earlier. Large segments of both films are scene-by-scene parallels.

The movie rode the crest of the tremendous interest in ancient Egypt created by the discovery of Tutankhamen's tomb. Tutankhamen's actual wife's name, Ankhesenamen, was used for the Egyptian princess in the movie, although the mummy itself supposedly was patterned after that of Seti II, on exhibit at the time in the Egyptian Museum in Cairo.

According to the movie, Princess Ankhesenamen died and was buried by her father, the pharaoh. Her lover, the high priest Imhotep, risked his life to steal the *Scroll of Thoth*, which could bring her back to life, but was caught and buried alive in an unmarked grave. This grave is found by a museum expedition and Imhotep is reanimated when the *Scroll of Thoth* is read in his presence.

What is never fully made clear in the film, because the explanatory scenes were dropped from the final cut, is that Helen Grosvenor, the heroine, is the reincarnation of Ankhesenamen and recognized as such by Imhotep, now in the resurrected guise of Ardath Bey. When Helen is magically called to the Cairo Museum by Ardath Bey, she willingly goes, happy to be reunited with her lost lover, but balks when he explains that she must die first so she can resurrect and join him for eternity.

The January 1933 issue of *Mystery* magazine contains the original story of *The Mummy*. Last-minute changes in the film become evident when it is compared to the original version. In the magazine version, Helen is shown to have had many lives, starting as an Egyptian princess, Ankhesenamen, then passing to a first-century Christian martyr, to an eighth-century barbarian queen, a medieval lady, and a French aristocrat. But as the film neared completion, it became clear that more focus should be on the mummy, so these scenes were cut. They may still exist somewhere in the vaults of Universal Studios, but one vestige of them appears in the dramatis personae at the beginning of the movie, where "the Saxon Warrior" is played by Henry Victor. The scene was cut, but not the credit.

The filming of *The Mummy* is a story in itself, since it pioneered new techniques for movie production. The shooting schedule was only twenty-three days, and much of the filming was done in Red Rock Canyon, a hundred miles north of Los Angeles, because it closely resembled the Valley of the Kings in both color and topography. Little film was shot in Egypt because of the expense involved in transporting highly paid actors. Rather, a small crew was sent to Egypt to shoot background scenes, which were projected on a "process screen." The actors performed in front of this screen while the process camera synchronized with the shoot camera so the final composite product gave the viewer the illusion that the actors actually were in Egypt.

Eight hours of makeup preparation were required to transform Karloff into the mummy. At 11:00 A.M. all of his facial skin was covered with cotton strips. When this had dried, it was covered with beauty mud, into which, when it hardened, wrinkles were carved to produce the aged look. Finally, Karloff's body was wrapped with acid-dyed linen. When he stepped on the stage at 7:00 P.M. for shooting, the entire crew gasped. By 2:00 A.M. the resurrection scene was in the can, ready for posterity.

Several of the actors and production people involved in the making of *The Mummy* are still alive, but none tells a funnier

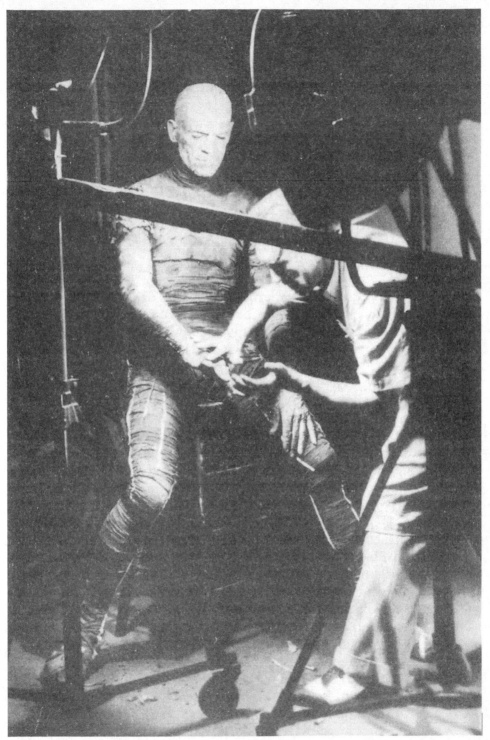

FIG. 115. *Karloff during the eight-hour makeup process on the set of* The
Mummy.

story than one of the extras, Arthur Tovey. Wearing black body makeup, he played one of the Nubian slaves who buried Imhotep. After the burial, the pharaoh's guards hurled spears at the Nubians, killing them to assure secrecy for the resting place. To keep production costs down and the number of extras at a minimum, the two halves of the scene were shot on successive days, with the same extras playing the Nubians and pharaoh's guards. Arthur Tovey played both, and thus killed himself!

The Mummy's Hand

The Mummy was a great financial success and generated sequels at Universal Studios, but none matched the original's popularity. From 1939 to 1946 Universal produced four mummy films, all similar and churned out quickly. *The Mummy's Hand*, released in 1940, featured a mummy clearly patterned after that of Ramses III. Not strictly a sequel to *The Mummy*, this film has significant differences in characters and plot from its predecessor. Here the mummy lacks personality, and an attempt is made to create fast-paced action rather than dark, brooding, psychological moodiness. The mummy is played by Tom Tyler, who had starred in Westerns and also played Captain Marvel. When Tyler played the mummy he was suffering from degenerative arthritis, so the mummy's twisted limbs were a necessity in his case. It is in *The Mummy's Hand* that "tana leaves" first appear. The high priest uses three of them to keep Kharis's heart beating and nine to give him life, although the distinction between a heart beating and life is very subtle.

This film contains several archaeological howlers, including the use of dynamite to uncover the tomb. Professor Petrie stares at the seal on the tomb, explains that he has waited a lifetime for this, then smashes through the seal and door with a pickaxe, destroying both. The best is yet to come. When Professor Petrie (sadly, the real Sir Flinders Petrie was alive when the movie was first shown) is examining the mummy, he explains that the lines in the mummy's face indicate that he was buried alive. A moment later he comments that its skin is soft and lifelike, "The

FIG. 116.
In sequels to The Mummy, *the mummy—no longer played by Karloff—was patterned after the real mummy of Ramses III, shown here.*   EGYPTIAN MUSEUM, CAIRO

FIG. 117.
The mummy wears a collar in this still from The Mummy's Tomb *because ancient embalmers added a collar to its model, the mummy of Ramses III, in order to conceal their repair to his detached head.*

most amazing example of embalming I've ever seen." This indeed was an unusual mummy, to have been both buried alive *and* embalmed.

The Mummy's Tomb, Ghost, Curse

After *The Mummy's Hand*, the sequels continued with *The Mummy's Tomb* (1942), *The Mummy's Ghost* (1944), and *The Mummy's Curse* (1945). All were unintentionally horrible, but the mummy was still modeled on Ramses III's. Tyler was completely crippled by the time *The Mummy's Tomb* was filmed, so Lon Chaney, Jr., was called upon to play the part, although much of the time it was stuntman Eddie Parker beneath the wrappings.

The mummy in all these sequels is little more than a robot, and the true protagonists are the high priests of Karnak (or sometimes Arkam) who thwart modern attempts to violate ancient tombs. In effect, the dual nature of Karloff's 1932 role—the revived mummy and Ardath Bey—has been split into two characters. Just as the Frankenstein films played off the monster against the doctor, mummy films now had a mummy and a high priest. Perhaps the most interesting element of these films is the idea of a secret cult enduring through the millennia, protecting the secrets of its gods. This device was revived by Steven Spielberg in *Indiana Jones and the Last Crusade*, in which the ancient knight still guards the Holy Grail. In *The Mummy's Hand*, the very ancient high priest, played by Eduardo Cianelli, passes his mantle to George Zucco. In the sequel, *The Mummy's Tomb*, which takes place thirty years later, the wizened Zucco nominates the much younger Turhan Bey. In the next sequel, *The Mummy's Ghost*, a rejuvenated Zucco calls on John Carradine. At the end of this film, Carradine and the mummy wind up fighting over the girl (who is the reincarnation of Kharis' forbidden love, Princess Ananka). The mummy wins, and he and his old flame sink happily into a swamp in Massachusetts.

Mercifully, *The Mummy's Curse* ended the series, though it contains flashes of imagination. Peter Coe and Martin Kosleck

Fig. 118.   *In* The Mummy's Tomb, *the mummy was played by Lon Chaney, Jr. A young Turhan Bey was his devoted high priest.*

Fig. 119.   *In* The Mummy's Ghost, *John Carradine and Kharis the mummy end up fighting over the heroine, who is the reincarnation of Princess Ananka.*

FIG. 120.   Abbott and Costello Meet the Mummy *presented a mummy named Klaris, but the terror and high priests were omitted.*

are now the guardians of the ancient cult. The swamp (now in Louisiana) is drained, Kharis recovered, and Princess Ananka revives. This time their end comes when an abandoned monastery collapses on them. Finally Universal Studios decided that enough was enough, so its last tango with a mummy came in the different form of *Abbott and Costello Meet the Mummy* (1955). Klaris (no typo) is still played by stuntman Eddie Parker, but has become a mummy the audience can root for.

Like mummies, mummy movies do not die easily. Hammer Films in England produced its own mummy series—*The*

Mummy (1959), *Curse of the Mummy's Tomb* (1964), *The Mummy's Shroud* (1967), and finally *Blood from the Mummy's Tomb* (1971). By the time these films were produced, however, the ground had been covered too well and these productions offered little that was new.

The Mummy or Ramses the Damned

One recent treatment of the mummy theme that has clear roots in *The Mummy* is Anne Rice's *The Mummy or Ramses the Damned*. In both the 1932 film and the 1989 novel, lovers are united through the millennia. As in the film, a museum expedition early this century discovers an intact tomb, this time containing the body of Ramses the Great. The archaeologists are puzzled when they find anachronisms, such as Greek and Latin inscriptions and references to Ramses knowing Cleopatra. The explanation is that Ramses, who indeed was born more than a thousand years before Cleopatra, discovered an elixir of immortality that kept him alive from the Nineteenth Dynasty until the beginning of the Roman period, when he met and fell in love with the last queen of Egypt. (The mummy in the Egyptian Museum that tourists believe to be that of Ramses II was a commoner substituted by Ramses, according to the story.)

When Marc Antony killed himself, Cleopatra asked Ramses to give Antony some elixir to save him, but Ramses refused. Then the queen killed herself, and Ramses, grieving for his lost lover, had himself entombed far away from the sun, which was necessary to revive him. There he remained in a state of suspended animation until the museum expedition opened his tomb and the sun's rays struck him. He moved, just as the mummy had in the movie.

Unlike the film mummy, Rice's mummy is a benevolent, handsome devil who adapts to modern times as Reginald Ramsey. One day, while visiting the Egyptian Museum's mummy room to see his ancestors, Ramses recognizes an unidentified female mummy as that of Cleopatra. He pours the elixir on the decrepit mummy and brings it back to life, restored to its former beauty. As in the film, the lovers are reunited after thousands of years of separation.

There are some remarkable plot twists in *The Mummy or Ramses the Damned*—but, unlike the movie, there is no resolution at the end. We are told that the adventures will continue in a sequel. While the film obviously used Tutankhamen's discovery as a model, the novel stays even closer to Carter and Carnarvon's discovery by including the mysterious death of a wealthy English lord/archeologist soon after the tomb's discovery. But one deviation from the Tutankhamen discovery is that when the archaeologists discover the sealed tomb of Ramses, again they blast their way into it!

She

The Mummy or Ramses the Damned is dedicated to H. Rider Haggard, the author of *She*. Although *She* is not overtly an Egyptian story, it is clearly the inspiration for Anne Rice's novel. Published in 1887, *She* introduces an immortal queen who lived during the late Egyptian period, although she herself was not an Egyptian. Again, lovers are united across centuries. At one point in the story She expresses her desire to go to London. She never does, but the reader wonders what would have happened if a royal immortal with supernatural powers had lived in London. Anne Rice's novel answers that question.

Throughout *She*, mummies, while not coming to life, act as props to set a bizarre mood. Drawing on the fact that mummies are highly combustible, Rider Haggard has the mysterious inhabitants of Kor use mummies as torches:

> *I stared and stared again—he was perfectly right—the torches that were to light our entertainment were human mummies from the caves!*
>
> *On rushed the bearers of the flaming corpses, and, meeting at a spot about twenty paces in front of us, built their ghastly burdens crossways into a huge bonfire. Heavens! how they roared and flared! No tar barrel could have burnt as those*

mummies did. Nor was this all. Suddenly I saw one great fellow seize a flaming human arm that had fallen from its parent frame, and rush off into the darkness. Presently he stopped, and a tall streak of fire shot up into the air, illuminating the gloom, and also the lamp from which it sprang. That lamp was the mummy of a woman tied to a stout stake let into the rock, and he had fired her hair. On he went a few paces and touched a second, then a third, and a fourth, till at last we were surrounded on all three sides by a great ring of bodies flaring furiously, the material with which they were preserved having rendered them so inflammable that the flames would literally spout out of the ears and mouth in tongues of fire a foot or more in length.[8]

⨼SU⨼M VII

Some mummy-story themes seem to be essential; one is the mysterious Egyptian figure who knows everything. Almost all of these characters are derivatives of the tall Ardath Bey from *The Mummy*, and one of these clones appears in the novel *Sum VII*.[9] Abdul has no last name, but worked in the Egyptian Museum for thirty years, is a giant, and seems to know everything about Egypt.

Abdul assists Professor Reilly, a paleopathologist whose research involves autopsies on mummies. One mummy, "SUM VII"—the seventh mummy autopsied at the State University Museum—shows early in its autopsy that it is not an ordinary mummy. His organs are intact, the fingers pliable, and cell samples revitalize when placed in nutrients. The decision is made to attempt to reanimate the mummy, and the clinical details of the procedure are the best part of the novel. The author, T. W. Hard, is a physician whose description of the open-heart procedure performed on SUM VII rings true. The book even includes arteriograms of the cerebral vessels of SUM VII and charts of his initial EKGs.

After the reanimation, an attempt is made to communicate with SUM VII, but before significant progress can be made, the

FIG. 121.
In the comic book series "The Mummy," much of the movie plot is followed, including burial alive in an unmarked grave. Here the mummy has taken the name of the actor—Carloph. COURTESY SCOTT BEADERSTADT

mummy escapes. After a series of adventures, SUM VII succumbs to the effects of the same aneurism from which he originally died. Rather than attempt to revitalize him again, the medical team (and Abdul) decide to let sleeping mummies rest, and SUM VII is reburied in his tomb, whose location is concealed, which leaves options open for a possible sequel.

The Mummy in Comics

A modern outgrowth of mummy literature are those comic books featuring a mummy as a central character. One series, called "The Mummy," is a direct takeoff of the film. It begins with a 1919 museum expedition that, as in the film, comes up fruitless until the last day, when an undisturbed tomb is found. The four-part comic series is full of inside jokes ("I understand Howard Carter is planning an expedition to start sometime next year ... Perhaps he'll have better luck."); the mummy is even named "Carloph," after the film's star. The series contains many idiosyncratic details that appear in the film—for instance, the Ardath Bey character, now called "Annubis-Rus," does not like to be touched ("An Egyptian prejudice"), and a pool of water is featured into which the characters can look to see the past. As in the film, the plot revolves around other characters defeating the mummy and freeing the heroine from his evil grasp.

Sometimes the series blends the film with Anne Rice's novel: the 3,700-year-old Carloph, for instance, is referred to as "Carloph the Damned."

The most interesting of the various mummy comic-book series is "The Living Mummy." The mummy here has a fully developed character and lives his adventures in modern times, against Egyptian backdrops. He originally died not unlike the mummy portrayed by Boris Karloff, for N'Kantu was, according to the series' first installment, a

> ... *warrior-king who freed his people from the yoke of the Pharaoh—Arem-Set ... for which "crime" he was Buried*

> *Alive. Today N'Kantu walks again, a bandage-wrapped,*
> *centuries-hardened caricature of a man in search of his lost*
> *humanity!*[10]

The series tells the tragic story of this former king, who is controlled by "[f]our Elemental Beings who held sway over Earth in Ancient Times." N'Kantu dislikes the evil things these beings force him to do, and struggles against their malevolent commands. Like many Marvel Comics characters, the hero experiences internal conflicts (as do we all). The Living Mummy has only one ambition: "The power to live, once again as a man—or to die—So that his grotesque mockery of life can finally—and forever—end!"

As "The Living Mummy" illustrates, the modern comic-book trend seems to be toward a sympathetic treatment of mummies. Anne Rice's novel served as the basis of another successful comic-book series, this one in twelve parts. The artist, Mark Menendez, used color pencils for the first four issues to create a pastel feeling in keeping with Egypt's subtle colors. The paintings for the later issues were done in acrylics, browns and antique colors that heighten the Edwardian period theme. The cartouches of Ramses II are accurate, the artifacts based on existing ones, and the mummy is a character the reader can pull for.

Along with these satisfying treatments of mummies are quite a few superficial comic-book characters who don't really provide what the true mummy enthusiast wants. One four-part series, "The Mummy's Curse," has appealing Egyptological covers, but inside waits a cloth-swathed fiend performing various violent acts. One can't always judge a mummy by its wrappings.

Epilogue

The research in this book was all in preparation for the mummification of a human body. From ancient records and the examination of mummies, we have been able to piece together the basics of the mummification process. The single most important step was the dehydration of the body through natron. To assist this process, the internal organs and brain were removed from the body by methods we have discussed in some detail. Yet with all the research completed, many questions remain. How much natron was needed? What was done with the blood? In what order were the internal organs removed? What was done with the never-mentioned gall bladder and spleen? With these and other questions unanswered, it seemed especially important to try to answer them empirically and proceed with the human mummification project.

The two memoranda reproduced in the preface of this book clearly indicate that the procedure was not to be carried out on the campus of my university—but the project didn't end because of that. I was invited to perform the mummification at the University of Maryland's School of Medicine. In January 1994 I traveled to Egypt to gather some of the materials I would need. At the same Wadi Natrun quarries used by ancient embalmers I gathered and shipped home 350 pounds of natron. In the spice bazaars of Cairo I bought the frankincense and myrrh I would need. Michael Silva, an expert in ancient metallurgy, cast the bronze knives needed for removing the internal organs. They have been made of the same alloy as used during the

Eighteenth Dynasty—88 percent copper and 12 percent tin. Also prepared was an obsidian knife for the initial incision, so I would have a "sharp Ethiopian stone" as described by Herodotus.

The mummification took place during the summer of 1994 and was done in relative seclusion; I am seeking answers, not publicity, and preferred to work without distractions. National Geographic filmed the procedure so we will have a complete record of the event. If the findings warrant it, our results will be published in appropriate scientific journals, and a few more pieces will have been added to the picture of mummification in ancient Egypt.

Notes

1. Introduction: Egypt, Land of the Mummies

[1]Budge, E. A. Wallis. *Osiris and the Egyptian Resurrection.* (University Books: Hyde Park) 1961, pp. 167–176.
[2]Petrie, W. M. Flinders. *Naqada and Ballas.* (Aris & Phillips: Warminster) 1974, p. 32.
[3]*Ibid.*, p. ix.

2. How to. Part I: What the Ancients Say

[1]Reymond, E. A. E. *Catalogue of Demotic Papyri in the Ashmolean Museum.* (Griffith Institute: Oxford) 1973, p. 37.
[2]*Ibid.*, p. 129.
[3]Birch, Samuel. *Facsimilies of Two Papyri Found in a Tomb at Thebes.* (Longmans *et al.*: London) 1863.
[4]Sauneron, Serge. *Rituel de l'embaumement: Pap. Boulaq III, Pap. Louvre 5, 158.* (Imprimerie Nationale Cairo) 1952.
[5]Blackman, Aylward M. *The Rock Tombs of Meir, Vol. V.* (Egypt Exploration Society: London) 1953.
[6]Dunham, Dows and William Kelly Simpson. *The Mastaba of Queen Mersyankh III.* (Department of Egyptian and Ancient Near Eastern Art: Boston) 1974, p. 8.
[7]*Ibid.*
[8]Herodotus of Halicarnassus. *The Histories.* (Penguin: New York) 1972.

⁹Herodotus. *The Histories*, Book II, 85–87.

¹⁰Leek, F. Filce. "The Problem of Brain Removal During Embalming by the Ancient Egyptians," *Journal of Egyptian Archaeology*, Vol. 52, 1966, pp. 112–116.

¹¹Breasted, James Henry. *The Edwin Smith Surgical Papyrus.* (University of Chicago Press: Chicago) 1930, p. 12.

¹²Smith, G. Elliot and Warren R. Dawson. *Egyptian Mummies.* (George Allen & Unwin: London) 1924, p. 61.

¹³Iskander, Zaky, and Abd el Moeiz Shaheen. "Temporary Stuffing Materials Used in the Process of Mummification in Ancient Egypt," *Annales du Service des Antiquités de l'Égypte*, Vol. 58, 1964, pp. 197–208.

¹⁴Dawson, Warren R. "Making a Mummy," *Journal of Egyptian Archaeology*, Vol. 13, 1927, pp. 40–47.

¹⁵British Museum No. 50945.

¹⁶Lucas, A. *Ancient Egyptian Materials and Industries.* (Edward Arnold: London) 1945, p. 320.

¹⁷——. "The Use of Natron in Mummification," *Journal of Egyptian Archaeology*, Vol. 18, 1932, pp. 125–140.

¹⁸Pääbo, Svante. "Molecular Cloning of Ancient Egyptian Mummy DNA," *Nature*, Vol. 314, April 18, 1985, pp. 644–646.

¹⁹Winlock, H. E. *Bulletin of the Metropolitan Museum of Art.* 1921–2, p. 34 and Fig. 33.

²⁰Rosellini, Niccoló. *I Monumenti dell'Egitto e della Nubia ....* (Pisa) 1832–44, Plate CXXVII.

²¹Winlock, H. E. *Op. cit.*, 1923–4, pp. 22–33.

²²Winlock, H. E. *Materials Used at the Embalming of King Tut-'Ankh-Amun.* (Metropolitan Museum of Art: New York) 1941.

²³Diodorus Siculus. *Library of History.* (Harvard University Press: Cambridge, Mass.) 1968.

²⁴Diodorus Siculus. *Op. cit.*, Book II, 15.

²⁵Diodorus Siculus. *Op. cit.*, Book I, 91

²⁶Porphyry. *De Abstinentia*, Book IV, 10.

²⁷Athanasius. *Vita S. Antoni*, 91.

3. How to, Part II: The Mummies Speak

¹Petrie, Flinders. *The Royal Tombs of the First Dynasty. Part I.* (Egypt Exploration Fund: London) 1900, pp. 1–2.

²Petrie, W. M. Flinders. *The Royal Tombs of the Earliest Dynasties, Part II.* (London: Egypt Exploration Fund) 1901, pp. 16–17.

³Petrie, W. M. Flinders. *Seventy Years in Archaeology.* (Henry Holt and Co.: New York) 1932, pp. 188–9.

[4]Petrie, W. M. Flinders. *Meydum and Memphis (III)*. (British School of Archaeology: London) 1910, pp. 18–22.

[5]Derry, D. E. "Mummification II—Methods Practiced at Different Periods," *Annales du Service des Antiquités de l'Égypte*, Vol. 41 (1942) pp. 244–5.

[6]Budge, E. A. Wallis. *The Mummy*. (Causeway Books: New York) 1974, p. 195.

[7]Smith, G. Elliot and Warren R. Dawson. *Egyptian Mummies*. (Kegan Paul: London) 1991, p. 145.

[8]Naville, Edouard. *The XIth Dynasty Temple at Deir el Bahri*. Vol. I (The Egypt Exploration Fund: London) 1907, Plate X.

[9]Peet, T. Eric. *The Great Tomb Robberies of the Twentieth Egyptian Dynasty*. (George Olms: Hildesheim) 1977, pp. 48–9.

[10]*Ibid.*, pp. 61–2.

[11]Moodie, Roy L. *Roentgenologic Studies of Egyptian and Peruvian Mummies*. (Field Museum of Natural History: Chicago) 1931, p. 23 and Plate XIV.

[12]Ruffer, Armand. "Notes on Two Egyptian Mummies Dating from the Persian Occupation of Egypt," *Studies in the Paleopathology of Egypt*. (University of Chicago Press: Chicago) 1921, pp. 127–138.

[13]Recently I performed an autopsy on a mummy of the early Christian period. The date was certain because the painted cartonage that encased the mummy was made from discarded Coptic manuscripts of the first or second century. Before X-rays were taken, and because of the size of the mummy, it was thought to be the body of a child. It was in fact the body of an elderly woman whose legs were missing (the embalmers again?) and whose arms had been placed where the legs should have been.

[14]Zaki, Ahmad and Zaky Iskander. "Materials and Method Used for Mummifying the Body of Amentefnakht, Saqqara, 1941," *Annales du Service des Antiquités de l'Égypte*, Vol. 42, 1941, pp. 223–255.

[15]Petrie, W. M. Flinders. *Roman Portraits and Memphis (IV)*. (Bernard Quarich: London) 1911, pp. 14–15.

[16]Thompson, David L. *The Artists of the Mummy Portraits*. (J. Paul Getty Museum: Malibu) 1976, p. 12.

[17]Just as this book went to press, the National Cultural History Museum kindly sent me copies of the X-rays of this mummy. The X-rays are ambiguous, and it is not certain that the mummy is a female.

[18]Gray, P. K. "Embalmers' 'Restorations.'" *Journal of Egyptian Archaeology*, Vol. 58, 1969, pp. 138–140.

4. The Royal Mummies

[1]Wilbour, Charles Edwin. *Travels in Egypt.* (Brooklyn Museum: Brooklyn) 1936, p. 54.

[2]*Ibid.,* p. 67.

[3]Rohmer, John. *Valley of the Kings.* (William Morrow: New York) 1981, p. 161.

[4]*Ibid.,* pp. 161–162.

[5]Maspero, Gaston. "The Departure of the Royal Mummies," *Egypt: Ancient Sites and Modern Scenes* (T. Fisher Unwin: London) 1910, p. 120

[6]*Ibid.,* p. 126.

[7]Smith, Joseph Linden. *Op. cit.,* pp. 60–61.

[8]Smith, Joseph Linden. *Op. cit.,* p. 64.

[9]Quoted in Aldred, Cyril and A. T. Sandison. "The Pharaoh Akhenaten: A Problem in Egyptology and Pathology," *Bulletin of the History of Medicine,* Vol. 36, No. 4, July-April, 1962, p. 301.

[10]Smith, Joseph Linden. *Op. cit.,* p. 66.

[11]Aldred, Cyril and A. T. Sandison. *Op. cit.,* p. 301.

[12]Harrison, R. G. "An Anatomical Examination of the Pharaonic Remains Purported to be Akhenaten," *Journal of Egyptian Archaeology,* Vol. 52, 1966, pp. 95–119.

[13]Davis, Theodore. *The Tombs of Harmhabi and Touatankhamanou.* (Constable and Co: London) 1912, p. 3.

[14]Carter, Howard. *The Tomb of Tut·Ankh·Amen.* (Cooper Square Publishers: New York) 1963, Vol. II, p. 45.

[15]Carter, Howard. *Ibid.,* p. 51.

[16]Carter, Howard. *Ibid.,* pp. 52–3.

[17]Carter, Howard. *Ibid.,* p. 82.

[18]Leek, F. Filce. *The Human Remains from the Tomb of Tutankhamen.* (Griffith Institute: Oxford) 1972, p. 5

[19]Derry, Douglas E. "Appendix I: Report Upon the Examination of Tut·Ankh·Amen's Mummy," in Howard Carter, *The Tomb of Tut·Ankh·Amen.* (Cooper Square Publishers: New York) 1963, Vol. II, p. 160.

[20]Derry, Douglas E. *Ibid.,* pp. 158–9.

[21]Leek, F. Filce,. *Op. cit.,* p. 8.

[22]Derry, D. E. "Note on the Remains of Shashanq," *Annales du Service des Antiquités de l'Égypte,* Vol. 39, 1939, pp. 549–51.

[23]Derry, D. E., "An Examination of the bones of King Psusennes I," *Annales du Service des Antiquités de l'Égypte,* Vol. 40, 1940, pp. 969–970.

[24]Derry, D. E. "Report on Skeleton of King Amenenopet," *Annales du Service des Antiquités de l'Égypte*, Vol. 41, 1942, pp. 149–50.

5. Holy Unrollers: The Mummy Unwrappers

[1]Hertzog, Christian. *Mummio-Graphie*. (Reyher: Gothe) 1718.

[2]Hadley, John. "An Account of a Mummy," *Philosophical Transactions of the Royal Society*, Vol. 54, 1764, pp. 1–2.

[3]Blumenbach, Johann. "Observations on Some Mummies Opened in London," *Philosophical Transactions of the Royal Society*, Vol. 84, 1794, pp. 177–178.

[4]*Ibid.*, p. 179.

[5]*Ibid.*, p. 182.

[6]*Ibid.*, p. 186.

[7]*Ibid.*, pp. 186–7.

[8]Rouyer, P. C. "Notice sur les embaumements des anciens Égyptiens," *Description de l'Égypte, Antiquités—Mémoires*, Vol. VI (Pankoucke: Paris) 1822, pp. 461–489.

[9]Caillaud, Frédéric. *Voyage à Meroe*, Vol. IV (L'Imprimerie Royale: Paris) 1823–1827, pp. 5–21.

[10]*Salem Observer*, June 19, 1824, p. 2.

[11]Dawson, Warren R. "Pettigrew's Demonstrations upon Mummies. A Chapter in the History of Egyptology," *Journal of Egyptian Archaeology*, Vol. 20, 1934, p. 172.

[12]*Ibid.*, p. 173.

[13]*Ibid.*, p. 174.

[14]*Literary Gazette*, April 15, 1837, p. 2.

[15]*British Press*, September 8, 1837, p. 3.

[16]Pettigrew, Thomas. "Account of the Examination of the Mummy of Pet-Maut-Ioh-Mes. . . ." in *Archaeologia*, Vol. XVII, 1837, pp. 262–273.

[17]Granville, A. B. "An Essay on Egyptian Mummies," *Philosophical Transactions of the Royal Society*, 1825, pp. 269–316.

[18]*Ibid.*, p. 274.

[19]Osborne, William. *An Account of an Egyptian Mummy Presented to the Museum of the Leeds Philosophical and Literary Society*. (Leeds Philosophical and Literary Society: Leeds) 1828, pp. 46–47.

[20]Birch, Samuel. "Notes Upon a Mummy of the Age of the XXVI Egyptian Dynasty," *Archaeological Journal*, Vol. 7, 1850, pp. 272–280.

[21]Birch, Samuel. "An Account of Coffins and Mummies Discovered in Egypt on the Occasion of the Visit of H.R.H. the Prince of Wales in

1868–9," *Transactions of the Royal Society of Literature*, Vol. 10, 1870, p. 210.

²²Birch, Samuel. "On a Mummy Opened at Stafford House on the 15th July, 1875," *Transactions of the Society of Biblical Archaeology*, Vol. V, 1877, pp. 122–126.

²³Maspero, M. *Les Momies Royales de Deir El-Bahri*. (Mission Archéologique Française: Paris) 1889, p. 525.

²⁴*Ibid.*, pp. 525–6.

²⁵G. Elliot Smith. *The Royal Mummies*. (Institut Français D'Archéologie Orientale: Cairo) 1912.

6. *Paleopathology: The Dead Are Our Teachers*

¹Schufeldt, R. W. "Notes on Paleopathology," *Popular Science Monthly*, Vol. 42, 1892, pp. 679–684.

²Ruffer, Marc Armand. "Note on the Histology of Egyptian Mummies," *British Medical Journal*, Vol. I, 1909, p. 11.

³Ruffer, Marc Armand. "Remarks on the Histology and Pathological Anatomy of Egyptian Mummies," *Cairo Scientific Journal*, Vol. IV, January 1910, pp. 1–5.

⁴Ruffer, Marc, Armand. "Arterial Lesions in Egyptian Mummies (1580 B.C.–525A.D.)," *Journal of Pathology and Bacteriology*, Vol. XV, 1911, pp. 461–2.

⁵Ruffer, Marc, Armand. "Note on the Presence of 'Bilharzia Haematobia' in Egyptian Mummies of the Twentieth Dynasty, 1250–1000 B.C.,"*British Medical Journal*, January 1, 1910, p. 16.

⁶Ruffer, Marc Armand. "Abnormalities of Ancient Egyptian Teeth," *American Journal of Physical Anthropology*, Vol. III, July, 1920, pp. 335–82.

⁷Cockburn, Aidan, *et al.* "Autopsy of an Egyptian Mummy," *Science*, March 28, 1975, Vol. 187, pp. 1155–1160.

⁸A much more contemporary smell can also cause chills. Sigmund Freud had been a great collector of Egyptian antiquities; and Anna Freud, his daughter, invited me to Maresfield Gardens, the house in which Freud died, to catalogue his collection. A large cupboard containing hundreds of small wood and faience figurines had to be opened to study and photograph each piece. It was an unusually constructed vitrine with locks on both sides of the glass, making it extremely difficult to open. Paula Fichtl, the housekeeper who had been

with the Freuds at their Bergasse 19 home in Vienna, found the keys and told me that the case had not been opened for "many years." The locks opened easily, but when the glass door swung open the unmistakable smell of stale cigar smoke filled the room—Freud's cigar smoke!

⁹Reyman, Theodore A. *Paleopathology Newsletter*, No. 3, September 1973, p. 3.

¹⁰Benitez, J. T. and George E. Lynn. "Temporal Bone Studies: Findings with Undecalcified Sections of a 2,600-year-old Egyptian Mummy," *Journal of Laryngology and Otology*, Vol. 89, 1975, pp. 593–599.

¹¹Nunnelley, L. L., *et al.*, "Trace Element Analysis of Tissue and Resin from the Egyptian Mummy of PUM-II," *Paleopathology Newsletter*, No. 13, March, 1976. pp. 12–14.

¹²Hart, Gerald. *Paleopathology Newsletter*, No. 4, December 1973, p. 3.

¹³Barraco, R. A. *et al.* "Paleobiochemical Analysis of an Egyptian Mummy," *Journal of Human Evolution*, Vol. 6, 1977, pp. 533–546.

¹⁴Reyman, Theodore A. *et al.*, "Histopathological Examination of an Egyptian Mummy," *Bulletin of the New York Academy of Medicine*, Vol. 52, 1976, pp. 506–516.

¹⁵Peck, William H. *et al.*, Report in *Paleopathology Newsletter*, No. 16, December 1976, pp. 3–6.

¹⁶Millet, N. B. *et al.*, "Autopsy of an Egyptian Mummy (Nakht ROM-I)," *Canadian Medical Association Journal*, Vol. 117, No. 5, September 3, 1977, pp. 2–9.

¹⁷Riddle, Jeanne. "Ultrastructural Findings on Peripheral Blood Elements from PUM-III," *Paleopathology Newsletter*, No. 15, September 1976, pp. 11–12.

¹⁸David, Rosalie. *Mysteries of the Mummies*. (Charles Scribner's Sons: New York) 1978, p. 87.

¹⁹Hodge, K. C. and G. W. A. Newton. "Radiocarbon Dating," *The Manchester Mummy Project*, A. R. David, ed. (Manchester Museum: Manchester) 1979, pp. 137–147.

²⁰Leek, F. Filce. "The Dental History of the Manchester Mummies," *The Manchester Mummy Project*. (Manchester Museum: Manchester) 1979, pp. 65–77.

²¹David, Rosalie. *Mysteries of the Mummies*. (Charles Scribner's Sons: New York) 1979, p. 151.

²²*Ibid.*, p. 153

²³Petrie, W. M. Flinders. *Dashasheh*. (Egypt Exploration Fund: London) 1898, Plate XXXVII.

²⁴Smith, G. Elliot and Warren R. Dawson. *Egyptian Mummies*. (George Allen & Unwin: London) 1924, p. 94.

[25]Pääbo, Svante. "Molecular Cloning of Ancient Egyptian Mummy DNA," *Nature*, Vol. 314, April 18, 1985, pp. 644–645.
[26]Barnhart, Marion, *et al.*, "Update on the Magadan Mammoth's Tissue Vestiges: Skeletal Muscle Identification," *Paleopathology Newsletter*, No. 29, March, 1980, pp. 9–10.
[27]Cockburn, Aidan. "Commentary," *Paleopathology Newsletter*, No. 29, March, 1980, pp. 11–12.
[28]Johnson, P. H. *et al.*,"Isolation and Characterization of Deoxyribonucleic Acid from the Tissue of a Woolly Mammoth." Paper presented at the Annual Meeting of the Paleopathology Association, April 22, 1981.

7. Special Treatment: Ramses the Great

[1]Bucaille, Maurice. *Mummies of the Pharaohs*. (St. Martin's Press: New York) 1990, pp. 184–5.
[2]Balout, Lionel, and C. Roubert, *et al. La Momie de Ramses II*. (Musée de l'Homme: Paris) 1985, p. 91.
[3]*Op. cit.*, p. 383.

8. Animal Mummies

[1]Harris, James E. and Kent R. Weeks. *X-Raying the Pharaohs*. (Charles Scribner's Sons: New York) 1973, p. 53.
[2]Herodotus. *The Histories*, Book II, Chapter 67.
[3]Belzoni, Giovanni. *Narrative of the Operations and Recent Discoveries Within the Pyramids, Temples, Tombs, and Excavations in Egypt and Nubia*. (John Murray: London) 1820, pp. 168–9.
[4]Davis, Theodore. *The Tomb of Siphtah*. (Archibald Constable: London) 1908, pp. 4–5.
[5]*Ibid.*, pp. 18–19.
[6]Brier, Bob and M. V. L. Bennett. "Autopsies on Fish Mummies," *Journal of Egyptian Archaeology*, Vol. 65, 1979, pp. 121–127.
[7]Herodotus. *Op. cit.*, Book III, Chapter 31.
[8]Chassinet, Émile. "La Mise à mort rituelle d'Apis," *Recueil de Travaux*, Vol. 38, 1916, pp. 33–60.
[9]Diodorus Siculus. Book I, Chapter 84.
[10]Mond, Robert and Oliver Myers. *The Bucheum*. (Oxford University Press: London) 1934, Vol. I, p. 19.

[11]Smith, H. S. *A Visit to Ancient Egypt.* (Aris & Phillips: Warminster) 1974, pp. 80–81.

[12]*Ibid.,* p. 57.

[13]*Ibid.,* p. 62

[14]*Ibid.,* pp. 60–61.

[15]Armitage, P. L. and J. Clutton-Brock. "An Investigation of the Mummified Cats Held by the British Museum (Natural History)," *M.A.S.C.A. Journal,* Vol. I, No. 6, 1980, pp. 185–188.

[16]Denon, Vivant. *Travels in Upper and Lower Egypt.* (Crosby & Co.: London) 1802, Vol. I, pp. 117–18.

[17]Emery, W. B. "Preliminary Report on the Excavations at North Saqqara 1968–9," *Journal of Egyptian Archaeology,* Vol. 56, 1970, pp. 8–9.

[18]———"Preliminary Report on the Excavations at North Saqqara, 1969–70," *Journal of Egyptian Archaeology,* Vol. 57, 1971, pp. 5–6.

[19]Martin, Geoffrey T. *The Sacred Animal Necropolis at North Saqqara.* (Egypt Exploration Society: London) 1981.

[20]Ray, J. D. *The Archive of Hor.* (Egypt Exploration Society: London) 1976, p. 41.

9.   *An Inventory of Kings*

[1]Derry, D. E., "Report on Human Remains from the Granite Sarcophagus Chamber in the Pyramid of Zoser," *Annales du Service des Antiquités Égyptiennes,* Vol. 35, 1935, pp. 28–30.

[2]Maspero, Gaston. "La Pyramide de Mirinri 1er," *Recueil de Travaux,* Vol. 9, 1881, p. 178.

[3]Edwards, I. E. S. *The Pyramids of Egypt.* (Viking: New York) 1986, p. 249.

[4]De Morgan, J. *Fouilles à Dahchour.* (Holzhausen: Vienna) 1895, p. 98.

[5]Winlock, H. E. "Tombs of the Kings of the Seventeenth Dynasty at Thebes" *Journal of Egyptian Archaeology,* Vol. 10, 1924, pp. 217–277.

[6]D'Athanasi, Giovanni. *A Brief Account of the Researches and Discoveries in Upper Egypt Made Under the Direction of Henry Salt, Esq.* (John Hearne: London) 1836, pp. xi–xii.

[7]Brugsch-Bey, Heinrich. *A History of Egypt Under the Pharaohs.* (John Murray: London) 1879, Vol. I, p. 111.

[8]Gardiner, Alan H. "The Defeat of the Hyksos by Kamose: The Carnarvon Tablet, No. 1," *Journal of Egyptian Archaeology,* Vol. 3, 1916, p. 95.

[9]Quoted in Winlock, H. E. *Op. cit.,* pp. 252–3.

[10]Breasted, James Henry. *Ancient Records of Egypt*. (Histories & Mysteries of Man: London) 1988, Vol. 2, p. 43.

[11]Maspero, Gaston. *The Struggle of the Nations*. (Appleton: New York) 1897, p. 242, footnote 2.

[12]James E. Harris and Edward F. Wente, eds. *An X-ray Atlas of the Royal Mummies*. (University of Chicago: Chicago) 1980, Fig. 6.1–6.3 and p. 288.

[13]Davis, Theodore. *The Tomb of Hatshopsitu*. (Arnold Constable: London) 1906, p. 11.

[14]Thomas, Elizabeth. *The Royal Necropolis of Thebes*. (Privately printed: Princeton) 1966, p. 138.

[15]Davis, Theodore. *Op. cit.*, pp. *xix–xv*.

[16]Maspero, Gaston. *Les Momies Royales*. (Mission Archéologique Française: Paris) 1889, p. 560.

[17]Shattock, S. G. "Microscopic Section of the Aorta of King Menephtah," *The Lancet*, January 30, 1909, p. 319.

[18]Smith, G. Elliot. *The Royal Mummies*. (Imprimerie de l'Institut Français: Cairo) 1912, p. 85.

[19]Herodotus. *The Histories*, Book III, Chapter 16.

10. *Dead and Gone: Missing Mummies*

[1]Goneim, M. Zakaria. *The Buried Pyramid*. (Longmans, Green and Co.: London) 1956, p. 114.

[2]Smith, Joseph Linden. *Tombs, Temples, & Ancient Art*. (University of Oklahoma Press: Norman) 1956, pp. 147–8.

[3]Farag, Naguid, and Zaky Iskander. *The Discovery of Neferuptah*. (General Organization for Government Printing Offices: Cairo) 1971.

[4]Leek, F. Filce. *The Human Remains from the Tomb of Tut'ankhamun*. (Griffith Institute: Oxford) 1972, p. 23.

[5]Harrison, R. G. *et al.*, "A Mummified Foetus from the Tomb of Tutankhamen," *Antiquity*, Vol. 53, 1979, pp. 19–21.

[6]James, T. G. H. *Howard Carter*. (Kegan Paul: London) 1992, p. 381.

[7]Reeves, Nicholas, and John H. Taylor. *Howard Carter Before Tutankhamen*. (British Museum: London) 1992, pp. 179–180.

[8]Schwartz, Stephen A. *The Alexandria Project*. (Dell: New York) 1983.

[9]Forster, E. M. *Alexandria—A History and a Guide*. (Peter Smith: Gloucester) 1968, p. 22.

11. The Mummy in Fiction and Film

[1]Gedge, Pauline. *The Scroll of Saqqara*. (Harper/Collins: Canada) 1990.

[2]Gautier, Théophile. *The Romance of a Mummy*. (J. B. Lippincott: Philadelphia) 1882, p. 3.

[3]*Ibid.*, p. 50.

[4]*Ibid.*, p. 245.

[5]Richard Fazzini, chairman of the Department of Egyptian and Ancient Near Eastern Art at the Brooklyn Museum, brought this point to my attention.

[6]Pettee, F. M., *The Palgrave Mummy*. (Payson & Clarke: New York) 1929, p. 249.

[7]*Ibid.*, p. 22.

[8]Haggard, H. Rider. *She*. (McKinley, Stone, & Mackenzie: New York) 1886, p. 208.

[9]Hard, T. W. *Sum VII*. (Harper & Row: New York) 1979.

[10]Isabella, Tony. *The Living Mummy*. (Marvel Comics: New York) Vol. 1, No. 8, August 1974, p. 1.

Selected Bibliography

The books and articles in this bibliography are those that are most central to the study of mummification and that are available to the reader who wishes to pursue the subject more deeply. In most cases I have tried to list the edition of a work in its most available form, and thus have listed reprints wherever possible. Only works in English are included here.

Budge, E. A. Wallis. *The Mummy*. (Causeway Books: New York) 1974 reprint of 1894 work.

Cockburn, Aidan, and Eve Cockburn. *Mummies, Disease, and Ancient Cultures*. (Cambridge University Press: Cambridge) 1980.

D'Auria, Sue, et al. *Mummies and Magic*. (Museum of Fine Arts, Boston: Boston) 1988.

David, Rosalie. *The Manchester Mummy Project*. (Manchester Museum: Manchester) 1979.

————. *Mysteries of the Mummies*. (Charles Scribner's Sons: New York) 1978.

Dawson, Warren R. "Making a Mummy," *Journal of Egyptian Archaeology*, Vol. 13, pp. 40–47, 1927.

————. "Pettigrew's Demonstrations upon Mummies: A Chapter in the History of Egyptology," *Journal of Egyptian Archaeology*, Vol. 20, pp. 170–182, 1934.

Dawson, Warren R., and P.H.K. Gray. *Catalogue of Egyptian Antiquities in the British Museum I. Mummies and Human Remains*. (British Museum: London) 1968.

Derry, Douglas E. "Appendix I: Report upon the Examination of Tut·Ankh·Amen's Mummy," in Howard Carter, *The Tomb of Tut·Ankh·Amen Vol. II.* (Cooper Square Publishers: New York) 1963 reprint of 1926 work.

————."Mummification II—Methods Practiced at Different Periods," *Annales du Service des Antiquités de l'Égypte,* Vol. 41, pp. 240–265, 1942.

Diodorus Siculus. *Library of History.* (Harvard University Press: Cambridge, Mass.) 1968.

Fleming, Stuart, et al. *The Egyptian Mummy: Secrets and Science.* (University Museum: Philadelphia) 1980.

Gray, P.H.K. "Embalmers' 'Restorations,' " *Journal of Egyptian Archaeology,* Vol. 58, pp. 138–140, 1969.

Hamilton-Paterson, James, and Carol Andrews. *Mummies.* (Penguin Books: London) 1978.

Harris, James E., and Kent R. Weeks. *X-raying the Pharaohs.* (Charles Scribner's Sons: New York) 1973.

Harris, James E., and Edward Wente. *An X-ray Atlas of the Royal Mummies.* (University of Chicago Press: Chicago) 1980.

Harrison, R. C. "An Anatomical Examination of the Pharonic Remains Purported to be Akhenaten," *Journal of Egyptian Archaeology,* Vol. 52, pp. 95–119, 1966.

Herodotus of Halicarnassus. *The Histories.* (Penguin: New York) 1972.

Iskander, Zaky, and Abd el Moeiz Shaheen. "Temporary Stuffing Materials Used in the Process of Mummification," *Annales du Service des Antiquités de l'Égypte,* Vol. 58, pp. 197–208, 1964.

Leek, F. Filce. *The Human Remains from the Tomb of Tutankhamen.* (Griffith Institute: Oxford) 1972.

————. "The Problems of Brain Removal During Embalming of the Ancient Egyptians," *Journal of Egyptian Archaeology,* Vol. 52, pp. 112–116, 1966.

Lucas, A. *Ancient Egyptian Materials and Industries.* (Histories and Mysteries of Man: London) 1989 reprint of 1962 work.

————. " 'Cedar'-Tree Products Employed in Mummification," *Journal of Egyptian Archaeology,* Vol. 17, pp. 13–21, 1931.

————. "The Use of Natron in Mummification," *Journal of Egyptian Archaeology*, Vol. 18, pp. 125–140, 1932.

Moodie, Roy L. *Roentgenologic Studies of Egyptian and Peruvian Mummies.* (Field Museum of Natural History: Chicago) 1931.

Pääbo, Svante. "Molecular Cloning of Ancient Egyptian Mummy DNA," *Nature*, Vol. 314, pp. 644–646, April 18, 1985.

Pettigrew, Thomas J. *A History of Egyptian Mummies.* (North American Archives: Los Angeles) 1985 reprint of 1834 work.

Ruffer, Armand. *Studies in the Paleopathology of Egypt.* (University of Chicago Press: Chicago) 1921.

Smith, E. Elliot, and Warren R. Dawson. *Egyptian Mummies.* (Kegan Paul International: London) 1991 reprint of 1924 work.

Smith, G. Elliot. *The Royal Mummies.* (Institut Français D'Archéologie Orientale: Cairo) 1912.

Winlock, H. E. *Materials Used at the Embalming of King Tut-'Ankh-Amun.* (Arno Press: New York) 1976 reprint of 1941 work.

Zaki, Ahmed, and Zaky Iskander. "Materials and Methods Used for Mummifying the Body of Amentefnakht, Saqqara 1941," *Annales du Service des Antiquités de l'Égypte*, Vol. 42, pp. 223–225, 1941.

Index